The Smart Money Guide to Bargain Homes

How to Find and Buy Foreclosures

James I. Wiedemer

Real Estate
Education Company
a division of Dearborn Financial Publishing, Inc.

While a great deal of care has been taken to provide accurate and current information, the ideas, suggestions, general principles and conclusions presented in this text are subject to local, state and federal laws and regulations, court cases and any revisions of same. The reader is thus urged to consult legal counsel regarding any points of law—this publication should not be used as a substitute for competent legal advice.

Publisher: Kathleen A. Welton
Acquisitions Editor: Patrick J. Hogan
Associate Editor: Karen A. Christensen
Senior Project Editor: Jack L. Kiburz
Interior Design: Lucy Jenkins
Cover Design: Jay Bensen Studios

Published by Real Estate Education Company,
a division of Dearborn Financial Publishing, Inc.

Printed in the United States of America

94 95 96 10 9 8 7 6 5 4 3 2 1

Library of Congress Cataloging-in-Publication Data

Wiedemer, James I. (James Ivy)
  The smart money guide to bargain homes : how to find and buy
  foreclosures / by James I. Wiedemer.
    p. cm.
  Includes index.
  ISBN 0–7931–0747–4
  1. Real estate investment. 2. House buying. Foreclosure.
I. Title.
HD1382.5.W52   1994
332.63′243—dc20
                                                    93–46036
                                                      CIP

CONTENTS

PREFACE

Foreclosure! The very word sends shivers down the spines of defaulting borrowers. But for investors, foreclosure properties inspire dreams of riches. There are many ways to buy a foreclosure property: you can buy directly from a distressed owner before foreclosure; you can buy "on the courthouse steps," that is, at the foreclosure auction itself; or you may find the best opportunities with government agencies or lenders who have taken over a foreclosed property. I cover all these deals in *The Smart Money Guide to Bargain Homes*.

I have written this book with the homebuyer or small investor in mind. The homebuyer has more flexibility in his or her purchase than the investor who must quickly resell the property for a profit. Such an investor must buy at a rock-bottom price in order to cover fix-up and selling costs and still turn a profit. The homebuyer can effectively afford to pay a higher price and take advantage of better financing terms for owner-occupants. There are also opportunities for investors wishing to hold the property. Buy at the right price and you can fix up properties, rent them out to generate a positive cash flow and sell them several years later for a profit. For many people, owning a few rental homes can be a great investment plan for retirement or other long-term financial goals.

Foreclosures occur in any real estate market. A down market—and parts of the country are experiencing this situation at the time of this writing—brings with it special concerns. In a down market, every buyer wants a bargain. Rampant foreclosures tend to have a snowball effect. This is a difficult environment for sophisticated investors in for the "quick kill." But there are terrific opportunities for those who are in a position to buy and can afford a long-term perspective, since the market will indeed come back. While it is impossible to predict the future of the market, this book will help you incorporate current conditions into your strategy.

As a real estate attorney in Houston, Texas, I have worked in every facet of the foreclosure process—from representing buyers and distressed owners to conducting foreclosures and training real estate professionals at local colleges. At the worst of times during Houston's foreclosure crisis of the 1980s, as many as 50 percent of real estate sales consisted of foreclosure properties. I have seen firsthand the techniques of sophisticated investors who converged on Houston from around the country and even from other countries. But you don't have to be a sharpshooter to find a good bargain. Like any investment, foreclosure purchases follow the universal law of risk and reward. The higher the reward you seek, the higher the risk you must be prepared to take.

In addition to riskier techniques, I have provided solid information on many types of foreclosure opportunities for the small investor or homebuyer, such as HUD homes, VA homes, auctions and lender-owned properties. These sales are not as glamorous as the cash-heavy purchases that can be made at courthouse foreclosure sales, but they are down-to-earth and highly practical for the typical buyer.

Everybody loves a bargain. With the information in this book, you will be off to a good start on the search for your bargain home.

CHAPTER 1

Foreclosures: Market Conditions and Your Strategy

When foreclosures abound, bargains can be found. But it takes more than just money to win at buying foreclosures. A strategy is needed. A prospective foreclosure buyer may want to fix up a property to improve its value to live in, to rent out or to resell. The strategy a buyer pursues will determine which foreclosure property to buy.

The word *foreclosure* has a special magic for many investors. It conjures up notions of houses that can be bought for a song. In one 1980s auction, for example, a condominium was sold for just over $3,000. At such prices, financing could be provided by credit card! However, the best foreclosure investors rely on more than just luck. They work at it. Increasingly, foreclosure buying requires an analysis of the market more than just luck. Good foreclosure buys exist in every market to some extent, but they are even more common when down market conditions occur. The type of foreclosed property an investor purchases will differ depending on whether the market is falling, bottoming out, rising or steady.

THE THREE BASIC APPROACHES

In any market investors will buy a foreclosed home with one or more of three basic aims:

1. To live in
2. To rent out
3. To resell

Depending on market conditions, an investor should try different combinations of the three basic approaches. In a falling market, rental homes must have cash flows above carrying costs, while homes for resale must be bought only at a tremendous discount or sold very fast. At the bottom of a falling market, home purchases for rent or resale can be made at or near market value with good prospective results. In a rising market, almost any purchase near market value can be made to work. In a steady market, a home must be purchased at a discount or have a strong cash flow above carrying costs.

NO ONE WANTS TO SELL AT A LOSS

Contrary to popular belief, no one who owns a house wants to sell it for less than market value. There is no reason to do so, for the most part. Anyone faced with foreclosure can sell the house and at least try to get market value. Really good foreclosure buys occur only under complicated conditions in which a person who is foreclosed on is forced to sell at less than full value. It usually happens when a property owner is careless or particularly unlucky.

Institutions are like other property owners. As we will see in Chapter 8, institutions such as lenders that acquire properties for foreclosure have no incentive to offer the properties at prices that are substantially less than fair market value. If a house can be sold for $100,000 on the open market, no bank in its right mind would sell for less. If a house that is worth $100,000 is purchased for $100,000, then the investor hasn't really made much of a killing.

The Market Price Is the Market Price

One question that homebuyers in a down market routinely, and perhaps improvidently, ask brokers is: "Can you find me a nice little foreclosure property for 25 percent below market value?" Of course, the answer to such a question has to be: "No way!" A market price is a market price; it's what people will sell property for even in a down market. If someone buys a property at market price in a down market, it cannot be resold immediately for a profit. No one wants to pay more for it than you did, if you bought at the market price.

To make matters worse, there are transaction costs (closing costs and brokerage fees) in the purchase and resale of such a house, and the market may fall even more by the time the house can be sold. In a down market, the selling process is often very slow, requiring the services of a very good, hard-selling broker. The days of putting up a sign in the front yard and finding buyers within hours are stories from a different era to those involved in a down market. Good brokerage is often critical to any sale at all.

It Takes Skill or Luck To Win at the Foreclosure Game

It takes some work and thought to get a real bargain by investing in foreclosure purchases. There are a few circumstances where such buys can be obtained, but it takes a sophisticated and lucky investor to get such a purchase. A lot of hard thought and good analysis must be done to see the potential for profit in houses that can only be purchased at or near market value. A good strategy is a must.

Market Conditions Can Make or Break a Deal

In order to better understand purchasing strategies, it is wise to consider the conditions in the marketplace and conduct a careful analysis of the market. For example, a house worth $150,000 is purchased at a small discount for $120,000 (20 percent below market), and takes four months and $15,000 to repair. The prospective gain may be largely wiped out if the market value of the house falls 5 percent to 10 percent during the four-month period, and resale costs are properly accounted for (5 percent to 7 percent brokerage commission, plus closing costs). None of this would account for the time value of the money invested.

On the other hand, if a house is bought at a 10 percent discount, and repairs run 5 percent but add 10 percent to 15 percent to the value, and the home is sold after six months in a market that has risen 5 percent or more in the meantime, then a profit has been made even after deducting resale costs. It makes a difference whether a home is purchased in a rising or falling market, at any price level.

It is critical to analyze the market in which a foreclosure purchase is made. Is the market steady, rising or falling? Unless this question can be answered, it is hard to make the correct foreclosure investment decision. Consider the types of markets that exist, what causes them and then try to analyze when and what types of purchases should be made.

FALLING OR DOWN MARKETS— URBAN ECONOMICS

In a down market, prices are falling or have fallen to the bottom. Down market conditions are typically generated by a variety of circumstances, but they tend to center on one basic problem: a lack of jobs. Job loss in a given city can involve a variety of fields, but the first and most important type of contraction an investor should watch for is a loss of "primary" or "export" jobs.

Economists divide jobs into two classifications: primary jobs (also called export jobs) and service sector jobs. If a very small town has one giant steel plant, then jobs at the steel plant itself are the primary jobs. Secondary or service sector jobs typically run in about a two or three to one ratio against primary jobs. For every job at the steel plant, there will be at least two jobs created in the service sector. The service category includes jobs in grocery stores, home construction, automobile sales and servicing, retail stores, medical care, local government and all other areas that essentially serve others in the community. If a service is provided to persons outside the city, however, it too can become a primary or export job. For example, Washington, D.C., provides government services for persons outside that city, so federal government positions there are usually primary jobs.

Once a loss occurs in a primary job sector, it can ultimately cause job losses in the service or support sector as well. For example, if a small town has only one major export employer, such as a steel mill, that provides 1,500 jobs in the community and is shut down completely, then most of the other jobs in the community will be lost. Initially, the unemployment might be 1,500 jobs, but eventually another 3,000 or more jobs will be lost in the service sector when the primary jobs dry up.

Similar problems exist for larger communities as well. If a larger community loses primary or export jobs, it too must shrink, just like the small town. However, a larger city usually has a wide variety of export jobs, so a loss of one or even a few industries may not be so disastrous, particularly if new industries move into town. However, if a very large city loses too many primary jobs, it must shrink, and the service sector will also have to shrink. The service sector might preserve jobs by spreading the existing business a little thinner, but even so, there will still be a loss of income among the remaining jobholders. It also takes a little while for the job losses to come to pass in the service sector, although it may be faster in some service areas than in others. For example, restaurants may lose business fairly quickly, since eating out may be a less critical expense and easier to cut, than say, core medical care, which is hard to cut back on.

Primary job loss occurs for a variety of reasons. An old plant may be shut down because it is no longer efficient, resulting in lost jobs. If a region or city depends on a certain industry, such as automobile manufacturing for Detroit, stock brokerage for New York, oil for Houston or defense for Southern California, then a downturn in that industry will reduce the number of primary jobs in the affected cities.

Surprisingly, primary job losses can occur when an industry that has been expanding suddenly shifts to a maintenance level of activity. For example, if it takes extra primary jobs to build new factories, plant and equipment for an expanding primary industry, and that industry adds jobs as it expands, then a sudden shift to a stable state without expansion will immediately translate into a loss of primary jobs in the area. Some economists call this process a *contraction*.

An astute foreclosure investor should try to pinpoint when and why primary job losses will occur, because they will have an important impact on the foreclosure market. As more and more primary jobs are lost, it is inevitable that further job losses in the service and support sector will occur. Once jobs are lost, the real estate market will be affected.

Foreclosures Due to Job Losses—It's a Complex Process

It may take years before primary job losses translate into foreclosure sales. This is partly because it takes a while for service sector jobs to be lost after primary jobs are lost. However, the foreclosure phenomenon involves more than just the straight loss of jobs. Many people incorrectly assume that the foreclosure rate moves in exact lockstep with the loss of jobs. The assumption is that once a job is lost, the foreclosure takes place because the unemployed homeowner can't keep up the payments on the house. This situation certainly causes foreclo-sures, but there is much more to the process than that.

It takes an overall loss of jobs in a community to begin triggering foreclosures on a large scale. Someone who loses a job in a strong economic environment will simply find a new job, and continue the payments on existing mortgage loans using income from the new job and savings during the interim. Lenders have many programs to bridge the gap between an old job and a new job, such as forebearance schemes involving reduced payments for a period of time to be made up later on in the mortgage. However, when new jobs can't be found to replace old jobs, then homeowners begin to have problems.

Even so, if the real estate market is healthy, then a person who loses a job and can't find a new one could always sell a house to avoid foreclosure. If the market has fallen somewhat, but a given unemployed owner has some equity in the house, then a sale at a loss will still prevent a foreclosure. The more equity the better in such situations.

The Killing Point—Zero Equity

The critical point in a down market that will trigger foreclosures occurs when real estate prices begin to fall below what people owe on their mortgage loans. Once a house can't be sold for enough to pay off the existing loan, foreclosure becomes much more likely. For a time, a well-off homeowner may draw down cash reserves to keep up pay-ments. But this is only a temporary stopgap, and it will work only if the real estate market prices recover soon. If real estate prices don't recover quickly, foreclosure is a real possibility. Borrowers can even resort to more exotic strategies such as *short sales,* and *private mort-gage insurance assisted pre-foreclosure sales,* but nothing stops fore-closure if prices fall too far.

The Foreclosure Phenomenon Feeds on Itself

Once foreclosures begin to take place on a broad scale in a city, home prices begin to fall faster and faster. Foreclosure results in lenders acquiring title to homes, and they in turn must resell the houses. Lenders are businesspeople, and they will cut prices to move out their REO (Real Estate Owned) inventories of foreclosed homes. They will use strong brokers, clever repair strategies and sophisticated in-house financing on favorable terms to sell REO houses. This practice dumps more and more houses on the market, at lower and lower prices. Unless the job situation is favorable enough to increase the number of regular homebuyers, then the real estate market in the community may become flooded with foreclosed homes that are for sale, and the glutted market results in further price drops. Even worse, houses that sit, unsold, for extended periods may suffer from vandalism or other physical problems, which makes them saleable only at lower and lower prices, if at all. In fact, a good house in a bad area may suffer a price drop through no fault of its own. Buyers stay away from troubled areas in a down market, unless the prices are really low.

This fall in prices, more than job losses, triggers a down market that will last for awhile in a major city. The job losses are the trigger for falling prices, but it takes awhile before the real effect of the job losses translates into foreclosure sales. The peak period of layoffs does not correspond to the peak in the foreclosure rate. In Houston in the 1980s, for example, the highest number of layoffs in the primary job sector occurred in 1983, while the highest home foreclosure rate was in 1987, nearly four full years later. It took that long for the foreclosure phenomenon to crest. Foreclosure feeds on itself.

Ultimately, however, unless a city continues to lose primary sector jobs, the foreclosure rate must slow down. In time, as the community downsizes, the number of buyers will come back in line with the number of houses for sale, and the down market will bottom out.

BOTTOM FEEDERS

Once the market bottoms out, foreclosure investors need to move in. Prices are at rock bottom, and since they will rise in the near future, the best time to buy is at hand, which is just what happens in the stock market when investors buy at the bottom of the market. However, smart money moves fast. Bottom feeders circulate nationwide, and increasingly, internationally. They are skilled at recognizing down markets and at placing investments when the market hits bottom. They know the strategies and the plays that will make the most money as a down market rises. They know how to buy homes, fix them up and resell them. They know how to play the game at the auctions and in dealing with lending and governmental institutions. They know about bulk sales and how to concentrate their buying patterns and repairs. Money flows into the city and prices begin to rise, in no small part because of investors.

Predicting the low point in a down market can be tricky, just as it is in a stock market. Usually, however, more solid indicators can be watched in the real estate market than in the more speculative stock market. Two statistics to keep an eye on are the loss in primary jobs and the foreclosure rate. As long as a city or a region continues to steadily lose primary jobs, further declines in real estate prices are almost inevitable. As long as jobs are lost, more and more houses will be available to fewer and fewer buyers. The supply of houses is high, the demand is low and falling, and prices will continue to fall, which will trigger more foreclosures, and the foreclosure phenomenon continues to feed on itself.

The second statistic is the foreclosure rate. Even after the primary job losses stabilize, foreclosure activity can continue. If the foreclosure rate stays steady or increases, the bottom may still be a way off. However, once the foreclosure rate begins to fall and shows no further signs of increase, then the bottom in real estate prices is near at hand, and the market will soon begin to rise. Hopefully, the bottom point for fair market price will be reached before falling to construction cost prices.

THE LONG-AWAITED RISE IN
THE MARKET

About the time many average buyers have given up hope of ever seeing an increase in real estate prices, the market will begin to rise. Savvy investors know the factors that caused prices to fall, and they know that prices will eventually rise. Once prices begin to rise, strength can return to the market with surprising speed. People who held off purchases when the market fell now leap back in to get a bargain before all opportunities slip away. In such a market, an investor must move very quickly. Leverage becomes an important strategy once again. Almost any strategy works to some extent in a rising market, but some work better than others. In the next few chapters, we'll explain more about how to play the game to win.

STEADY MARKETS

Even in a steady market, foreclosures occur. A certain number of people will lose their jobs and fail to pay their mortgages. Straight frictional job loss will account for as many as 30 percent or more of all foreclosures, even in a healthy market. Life events such as death and divorce can also trigger the process. Divorce probably accounts for 15 percent or more of all foreclosures.

People who have problems, such as a long bout of severe illness that is not covered by insurance or business failure, can lose a home in foreclosure. Bankruptcy, an ever-present phenomenon for small businesses, even in the best of times, can also result in foreclosures. A bankruptcy will only delay a foreclosure if the homeowner cannot keep up the payments on a mortgage. A secured creditor, such as a mortgage lender, is entitled to receive either the payments on the mortgage loan or the house. If the debtor does not give the house up, a mortgage lender can usually get the bankruptcy court's permission to foreclose anyway if the bankrupt borrower is unable to keep up payments.

In a down market, any need to sell the house, even for the best of reasons, can cause a foreclosure because the house can't be sold for enough to pay off the mortgage. Usually, more options are available in a steady market, so the foreclosure rate is slower. However, equity in houses may be substantial in a steady market because it isn't the market, but rather the borrower, that is most likely to be the cause of the foreclosure. Good buys for investors can be found by careful search and careful buying strategies. The risks are more calculable in a steady market, but the deals are harder to find.

THE RIGHT STRATEGY FOR THE RIGHT MARKET

Once again, three basic strategies exist for buying any foreclosed house: (1) buy to live in the house; (2) buy to rent out the house; and (3) buy to sell the house. Different combinations of these strategies apply in different markets.

The Strongest Foreclosure Buyer—The Owner-Occupant

Surprisingly, the strongest buyer in a foreclosure situation is the person who wants to buy a house to live in at a below-market price. An investor looks for the same thing, but the buyer who buys for personal use is stronger in many important ways. An investor who plans to resell must buy the foreclosed home at a price that is sufficiently below market to pay for the costs of a resale. Most investors immediately discount a foreclosure purchase by at least 10 percent to account for the costs of resale. A brokerage commission on a resale could run 5 percent to 7 percent alone, in addition to closing costs that the seller customarily pays in most states, such as the deed preparation and title insurance costs. In contrast, a person who buys a house to live in doesn't need to discount by the resale costs and therefore can afford to pay more for the house than the investor.

Money has a time value. An investor who buys a house must consider holding costs that an owner-occupant need not worry about. Unless a house can be rented out for more than enough to cover the costs on a mortgage or pay a fair return (at least equivalent to the going mortgage interest rate) on any cash invested, then the investor is losing money. If the house cannot be resold for enough to pay back all of the holding costs that the rent didn't cover, then the investor is losing money. An investor who is buying a foreclosure home for any purpose other than absolutely immediate resale needs a deep discount to recover the holding cost losses when the house is resold (or the rent rises to the point where the net income will make good on the loss).

An investor must normally pay for repairs on an out-of-pocket basis. Contractors come in, hire laborers, pay overhead and make a profit. An investor must pay a fair amount for a repair. On the other hand, a buyer who wants a house to live in can purchase a "handyman special" that requires repairs to make it livable. By doing a lot of the manual labor on such repairs, a buyer who purchases for occupancy can keep repair costs low because he or she does not have the same overhead as a regular contractor and keeps all profits.

However, a homebuyer who buys for himself or herself must consider repairs that should be done by licensed persons, such as electrical or plumbing work. Such repairs may have to meet certain building codes or standards set by deed restrictions. Ambitious remodeling projects may require that the plans be drawn up by an architect and that building permits be purchased from the city. The more repairs that require the assistance of a licensed repair person, and the more ambitious the nature of the repair, the less suitable it is for the buyer who wants a house to live in.

The buyer who buys for himself may lack the kind of ready cash that an investor has. However, the homebuyer with cash may be able to arrange deals in a foreclosure situation that are far better than what the ordinary homebuyer can buy by ordinary means. Prices can be very nice. If financing is needed, FNMA, VA, FHA and most other government-related resellers of foreclosed homes offer more attractive terms and in general favor individual homebuyers who want to live in the house over investors who buy for resale. Lower down payments are commonly required.

In the last analysis, the buyer who buys for himself or herself at a foreclosure sale may often be willing to accept a house that is priced only a little bit below market, which no investor wants. After all, simply getting a good price on a desirable house in a neighborhood the buyer really wants to live in may be an ample reward, even if the discount is not that great.

In short, the buyer who buys for himself or herself is the strongest buyer in the foreclosure market. Such buyers can easily outbid most investors because they can make the investment pay good dividends at higher prices than an investor can.

Investment Strategies in a Down Market

An investor who wants to buy in a falling market should consider one of several strategies. The buyer should purchase the house to live in, as just discussed, or to rent out.

In a falling market, a buyer may find the home easier to rent out than to resell. In a falling market, buyers are scarce and expect a bargain. Lenders are hard to find too. Even if an S&L or a mortgage company is willing to make a loan, it may be very tough to find a private mortgage insurance company that will write insurance on such loans. Without private mortgage insurance, the lender may be unwilling or unable to make a loan. The alternative is for the buyer to make a substantial down payment—at least 20 percent or more. The buyer will also need an exceptional credit history to buy a home on credit in a down market. Investment loans may be particularly hard to get in a down market; owner-occupant loans are generally more widely available.

Cash is king in a down market. Buyers are tough to find because they can't get loans, or at least not without large down payments and exceptional credit. As a result, buying a home with the aim of reselling it quickly may not be practical in a falling market, unless the foreclosure buyer luckily buys a house far below fair market value. For the most part, homes purchased during a falling market will have to be rented out until the market improves. If a loan is used to buy the home, the payment must be less than what the home can be rented for. In a falling market, rents drop along with prices, so once a loan payment is locked in, it should be far enough below market rent to ensure that a profit margin exists. However, if the rent pays the mortgage, the buyer is buying the house with little cash out of pocket. Once prices go up again, rents will go up, and the house, if purchased at a low price and a reasonable payment, will be quite valuable in the future. Homes can be purchased at below market prices in a down market, but it usually takes patience, hard work and some cash.

Buying at the Bottom of a Market

At the bottom of a market, it is less critical to buy a home with a below-market price. Purchases can be made at or near market, or even a little above market, given that prices are stabilizing and a rising market appears to be near. A small difference between home payments and rental payments will work. Financing may be possible, and probably advisable. It's time to round up cash and investors and buy as much property as possible while prices are low.

Buying in a Rising Market

In a rising market, it becomes harder and harder to find properties that can be purchased at less than market, but even if they are purchased right at market value, they will rise in value quickly. Investors and foreclosure buyers must learn to accept fewer and fewer purchases and shallower and shallower discounts below fair market value. Eventually, the pool of really good purchases will largely dry up.

Buying in a Steady Market

In a steady market, purchases should be made at a discount. Unless a house can be bought at less than fair market value, it's hard to make money. However, other strategies involving repairs or activities that can put value back into a property and increase the market value can also be used. Careful cost estimation and value estimation (appraisal) skills are very useful in buying foreclosed homes in a steady market.

PURCHASE AND SALES ACTIVITIES IN RISING AND FALLING MARKETS

Just as a good doctor can spot the early symptoms of a dreaded disease, a good real estate investor can spot the early signs of a down market. The first chilling sign of a down market is a slowness in sales. A house that is listed for sale sits and sits and won't sell. Even more ominous is price cutting. Some sellers who line up jobs in other cities, go through a divorce or experience other financial pressure just have to sell, even at a lower price. In down markets, people are wrongly convinced that homes won't sell. This is not so. Any home will sell if it is priced to move. A house priced at a dollar will sell tomorrow. What collapses in a down market are people's unrealistic expectations about what they can get when they sell a home. High asking prices have to be cut down to a size that fits the market.

Sellers with substantial equity in their houses can afford to cut prices to sell. However, the unfortunate homeowners who lack sufficient equity to permit price cutting are likely to be foreclosure victims if prices fall too much. Once the price cutting starts, it can spread quickly and keep going once it starts. Even though commentators, newscasters and pundits all say a price drop will be short lived, it may not be. If the price fall has been caused by a drop in the number of primary jobs in the area, then real trouble is ahead. Positive attitudes can improve hard economics only a little, at best.

In a down or falling market, no one wants to buy, and everyone wants to sell. Who wants to buy a house when it could go down in value right after you buy it in a falling market? The only people who want to buy want a bargain. They know the bargains are there, if and when sellers get desperate enough. Investor purchasers who formerly bought real estate to take advantage of sharp gains from rising prices in the market back away from purchases. Financing may be trickier to obtain in a down market, due in part to problems in obtaining private mortgage insurance. Loan insurers are profit oriented and do not want to insure loans in a city with numerous foreclosures. A net loss in primary jobs in a city may be followed by a net outflow of people who need to sell when they leave town. But there aren't enough buyers left in town. Prices fall, and foreclosures continue.

More and more foreclosed homes mean more and more homes for sale when the banks and lenders that acquired the properties at foreclosure sales try to resell their foreclosure properties. As these homes are pushed into a declining market, the situation gets worse. Foreclosed homes may stay unoccupied for a long time and become run down in the process. A down market is pretty miserable for everyone.

Who Wants To Buy When Markets Fall?

Actually, many people want to buy in a down market. The most common sources of buyers are simply those with jobs who need a house. However, they will want a bargain. Persons who have been renting now want to buy when prices are low enough in a falling market. Even if the value falls a little more, it's still better than renting, particularly if the persons involved are having children and need the extra space. A surprisingly large move-up segment also exists. This consists of persons who already own a house, but who now see an opportunity to buy a much bigger house for the same or a slightly larger monthly payment. They want to buy while prices are low. People who have been foreclosed on, or even those who are about to be foreclosed on, may try to buy a house if credit terms are generous enough. Three years after a foreclosure, FHA will consider a new loan.

More devious buyers also exist. Some buyers will borrow money to buy a new house for an astonishingly low payment from a lender who is desperate to sell the house (and finance its purchase on very generous terms). The buyers will then move out of their old house and attempt to rent it out. This may be possible only by subsidizing a loss: for example, if the payment on the old house is greater than what it can be rented for, or what the lender will permit the rent to be counted for (such as only 75 percent of the rent may be applied to reduce the mortgage payment for loan qualification purposes on the new home). The buyers make the argument, which is sometimes true, that they want to pick up an extra house for investment purposes while prices are down. If the tenant walks off, and the old house is foreclosed on, the buyer is now in a new and larger house. In a falling market, the old lender can't hit the buyer because there's no equity in the new house to speak of (falling prices actually are an advantage), even if that particular state's laws allowed the old lender to force the sale of a homestead to pay the old debt. In a severe down market, some people actually increase the size of their home, while decreasing their monthly mortgage payments! Sometimes, houses can fall to such low prices that the combination of subsidizing a loss on the old home mortgage (paying the difference between rental and income and mortgage payment expense) and making the payment on a new loan is still a lower total payment than the payment on the loan for the old house. Lenders who don't want to work with borrowers may get hit with such tactics as a subtle form of retaliation.

Characteristics of Sales and Purchases in Falling or Down Markets

One of the most startling characteristics of falling or down markets is the frenzied level of sales and brokerage activity. The number of houses sold actually increases in a down market. This seems to contradict the impression the city's residents have that slow selling means fewer sales. It isn't so. What happens is that a given house takes months and months to sell, but the number of houses available for sale and the number of sales are high. In fact, cities with a down market may well see all-time high figures for number of transactions.

However, the prices are terrible in a down market. It is difficult even for a good broker to organize a sale. In a down market, of course, listings (houses listed with a broker for sale) are plentiful. Sadly, some of the sellers will be desperate to sell. If they can't get enough money to pay off existing loans, then the deal may collapse.

In a down market, smart brokers learn techniques such as compromise sales, private mortgage assisted presales, short-payoffs and so on to assist in selling homes (see James I. Wiedemer, *The Homeowner's Guide to Foreclosure* [Chicago: Dearborn Financial Publishing, 1992]). With those tools, homes can even be sold when the sale price is not sufficient to pay off all loans. However, these techniques may not be widely known, and at some low point, even these foreclosure avoidance tools will become problems. Good brokers may develop connections with private mortgage insurance companies and secondary market loan owners (not servicers, the real loan owners) who can stop or delay foreclosures if a good sale is about to go through. It can get tense at times.

If the sellers in a down market are desperate, the buyers are equally difficult to work with. They expect a bargain. Their attitude is that they want to steal a house. It's a tough world, but they've got the ways and means, and some of them want everyone to know it. If it isn't a bargain, they may refuse to buy. Because lenders don't want to make loans in such environments, only the best buyers can get them. The most attractive arrangement in town is usually to sell off REO's, and that's very good financing indeed, but it makes life tougher for the ordinary seller who must compete with the providers of such financing. Cash is king in a down market, and a good buyer often has plenty of it. Increasingly in a down market, as prices come down, cash goes further and further in helping to buy a house.

It's a difficult experience for the brokers involved in the sale to match up such buyers and sellers. The closing may be downright unpleasant, as those last closing costs are sometimes fought over dollar for dollar by penniless sellers and pennywise buyers. A lot of brokers can't take the heat and get out. Serious professional brokers do the best. FSBO (for sale by owner) sales are often disastrous in a tough market. In the future, as more and more brokers across the United States represent buyers rather than sellers (called *buyer's agency*), buyers may be well represented, which means that sales in a tough market may become even more hotly contested than ever. For brokers, sales in a down market, although plentiful in number, are hard to put together, and the commission earned per sale is terrible, particularly for the amount of work involved. In some markets, extra commission has to be offered to the salesagents who find buyers. BTSA—bonus to selling agents, or higher commission splits to cooperating brokers are common tools.

Both investors and brokers in a down market must learn about the various REO sales, such as those programs run by FHA, VA, FNMA, S&L's and the RTC/FDIC. They all have their quirks, and lots of them. The sales may be by brokers, by sealed bids or by auction. Investors who are not afraid to take risks to get returns can try purchasing directly at the foreclosure sales or using some of the techniques that foreclosure

FIGURE 1.1   Foreclosure Purchase Strategies

Purchase Strategy	Risk	Reward
1. Buying before or at the true legal foreclosure sale	High	High
2. Buying at a secondary market loan owner sale (FNMA/FHLMC)	Low	Moderate
3. Buying at a private auction	Moderate	High/Moderate
4. Buying from FHA/VA (FHA/VA sales are usually easier to work with individually than RTC/FDIC)	Moderate	Moderate
5. Buying from FDIC/RTC (Best bet may be a larger purchase)	Moderate	Moderate

seminar salespeople have been advocating for years, at no small cost to their audiences!

In chapters 5 to 13, we'll see the various types of foreclosure sales. See Figure 1.1 for a chart of the possibilities.

The chart gives some idea of the possibilities, but there may be exceptionally good buys or bad buys in any type of foreclosure sale.

The principles of investment are the same for foreclosure purchases as those for any other purchase. In general, high risk, high reward, low risk, low reward. It doesn't change. Each of these strategies will be analyzed in depth.

FINDING OUT ABOUT FORECLOSURE PROPERTIES TO PURCHASE

The skilled investor knows that the key to purchasing foreclosures is finding out about the properties as they hit the market. Let me repeat: *Smart money moves fast.* Smart investors use their networking and information-gathering skills to get current information about owners who are going through foreclosure proceedings, about foreclosure and preforeclosure auctions being conducted by local lending institutions and about government agencies that have REO holdings.

The most obvious way to gather information about foreclosure opportunities is to have a real estate agent track down any foreclosures that are listed on the local Multiple Listing Service (MLS). A second way is to contact lending institutions and government agencies and request information. A third, and perhaps best, way is to use a clearinghouse service that gathers information from a variety of sources and makes it available in one place. An excellent clearinghouse is the online service called The Federal Information Network. It allows investors to use their personal computers and modems to go online and search a nationwide database containing thousands of foreclosure properties.

The "Resources" section in the back of the book lists sources that you can use to track down opportunities. It is by no means exhaustive, but it will direct you to some of the sources and information tools used by the experts in this business.

CONCLUSION

Foreclosures can be purchased at a profit in any market, up or down. Obviously, interest in the purchase of foreclosed homes increases in a down market, because of the perception that value can be obtained by purchasing when buyers are few and sellers are forced to sell by harsh economic circumstances. Nevertheless, a strategy is necessary for the best results. An investor should buy a house to live in, to rent out or to resell. Fixing up some run-down properties may be done cost effectively, that is, the costs are more than offset by the resale price, generating a handsome profit. When interest rates are low, buying a property to rent out may make a lot of sense, given that the rent will more than pay the mortgage. All of these strategies work, whether the market is up or down, but if it's down, there's a particular potential to buy and profit when the market hits bottom or is moving up again. Even in ordinary times, buying in a market with rising property values should be based on leverage. In a falling market, purchases may have to be based more on cash, with the aim of buying at a discount from a "don't wanter" who will sell at a low price.

CHAPTER 2

Buying To
Fix Up

One strategy an investor can use to make money is to buy a rundown foreclosure property, fix it up and sell it for more than the cost of the purchase and the repairs. Many homes offered at foreclosure sales and auctions are in disrepair. The rugs and paint need replacement, but the astute buyer can spot the potential of the ramshackle-looking house. A few dollars in repairs may translate into big dollars in increased resale value, rental value or value as a home to live in. Special financing strategies exist for repairs. Special precautions apply. It's not as easy as some people imply.

Foreclosure properties are often fix-up properties. No matter what kind of foreclosure property an investor buys, there are often at least some problems that need fixing. The houses with the fewest fix-up problems are those bought from lending institutions that have acquired the homes through foreclosure and then spent money to fix them up so they can be sold in good condition. The Federal National Mortgage Association (FNMA, or Fannie Mae), for example, is well known for its tendency to hire contractors to install standardized carpet (called Fannie Mae brown by those in the business) and to make enough repairs to put the house in a very showable condition. In contrast, government institutions that acquire homes from lenders after foreclosure make relatively little effort to fix up the properties. Hard-core foreclosure purchases, in which investors buy directly at legal foreclosure sales, almost inevitably involve fix-up costs.

Foreclosed properties, from any source, almost always need at least a few repairs. Figure 2.1 lists your likely repairs.

Repairs in the first two categories often add considerable value to the house for a fairly low expenditure. However, category 4 repairs may not be worthwhile and may be hard to estimate.

A house should be carefully evaluated before purchase to see what defects and repair problems exist. Even houses that appear to be in good condition but are being sold on an as-is basis may have more serious repair problems beneath a cosmetically pleasing exterior. Repairs to foreclosure home purchases often require the assistance of someone who has expertise in estimating repair costs—a repair contractor, builder or job cost expert.

A COMMON MISTAKE

Many people are convinced that a dollar spent on repairs will automatically translate into a dollar added to the value of the property on resale. This is absolutely false, and it is particularly false in a down market. The market price of a house consists of what the house can be sold for between a knowledgeable seller and a knowledgeable buyer who are not under any particular pressure to buy or sell, and the facts about the property are fairly well known to the parties. A dollar spent on repairs may or may not add value to the house. If a house cannot be repaired in any way that adds to its value on resale, then it is best to avoid making repairs or forego buying such a property altogether. The wise foreclosure investor will look for a situation in which dollars spent on repairs will add value to the house on resale.

ADDING VALUE TO A HOUSE
THROUGH REPAIRS

Repairs can add value to a house in three possible ways:

1. Make a sale possible.   The foreclosure buyer's aim is to buy a house that is worth much more than its purchase price once a few simple repairs are done. In this scenario, the lack of repairs is blocking the buyer's ability to obtain regular financing and thus impeding the

FIGURE 2.1   Common Foreclosure Repairs

1. Repairs that are almost always required
   Carpet
   Painting

2. Commonly required repairs
   Sheetrock/molding damage
   Appliance replacement

3. Common large repairs
   New roof (often worn from postponed maintenance)
   Heating and air-conditioning units (often missing)

4. Serious repair problems
   Major foundation and structural repairs
   Flooding

sale, but once repairs are done, the house can be sold at a high price. The repairs allow a sale to take place that would not have otherwise.

2. Make ordinary repairs at a lower cost than others can make them. In this scenario, the house needs repairs, but after paying the cost of the necessary repairs, it doesn't look as if much profit can be made by the normal investor. Some investors, however, who have a better eye for repair costs than others, may come up with a clever solution or have strong skills at repairs that will allow the house to be put back in good condition at a lower cost than most potential investors anticipate. These repairs add value to the house. Former builders particularly like to try this approach.

3. Change the nature and style of the house—remodel. In this scenario, the house can be repaired in a way that changes its entire style. For example, an older neighborhood with fairly ramshackle houses may be in the process of changing into an upscale neighborhood with a different style of architecture and decoration. In this instance, a good strategy is to remodel the house to suit the current tastes of the market, thereby producing a sale at a higher price than would otherwise have been possible. The investor makes money from the resale. An innovative remodeling strategy may yield big dividends by increasing resale values considerably relative to the dollars invested. This repair scheme, however, may involve a substantial investment to get the dividend.

Repair Cost Misestimation

It's easy to misestimate repair costs. Many investors add a factor into their repair cost computations, sometimes as much as 50 percent, to account for this uncertainty. Moreover, some investors double the repair contractor's estimates to get a safer and perhaps more realistic estimate. However, some contractors can do good work on time, on spec (according to plan) and at the price agreed. Experience often helps in these areas.

Construction Cost as a Percentage of the Home's Value

The value of a home consists of construction costs, which is what it would cost to build the structure from the ground up, and the land value. The portion of a home's market price that can be accounted for by pure construction costs is a significant figure. Sometimes, in different areas of the country, the value of a house may be much higher than what it costs to build it. The ratio between the price a home can be sold for and its construction cost is an important gauge for persons who are considering buying properties to fix up. If the construction costs actually exceed the fair market value of the house, then it is difficult to make repair strategies of any kind work. It will often cost more money to do repairs than the house can be resold for, if the market prices for houses are close to or below construction costs.

Unfortunately, in truly down market conditions, property values can go quite low. Although construction costs vary somewhat around the country, certain basic costs stay at similar levels. If bricks, concrete or lumber can be purchased for less money in one part of the country than another, then such items will likely be shipped to areas of the country where they sell for more (economists call this *arbitrage*) and sold for a profit. The cost of labor can vary from one part of the country to the next, but labor is also a little bit mobile. However, due to work regulations, building codes, union activities and the cost of living in an area, labor costs for construction can vary somewhat from region to region.

The big variable in real estate is land. Land price variations are where the biggest profits are won or lost in real estate. Construction costs may stay at similar levels around the country, but the land proportion of a home's price can vary greatly. In a down market, the land portion of a home's price can take a terrible beating because of the speculative element in many cities that depends on a large number of buyers and few houses for sale (high demand, low supply, to keep prices high). In a down market, this proportion falls, and the portion of a house that is allocated to construction costs increases. This set of circumstances can have an important effect on how low prices can fall in a down market and influence when they turn around and come back up again. In fact, construction costs may actually set a bottom for a falling market.

How Low Can You Go?

In a really bad down market, a bottom may be hard to find. It's tempting to say, as in the days of Mark Twain, "no bottom!" But there's always a bottom. Part of the problem with falling prices in a down market may stem from the proportion of speculative value found in houses. When houses are bid up in price, like gold or diamonds, and few sales take place in an area (a *thin market,* in appraisal terms) then the market price can reach a high level with little real support. In some parts of the country, construction costs account for only 20 percent to 30 percent of the price of a house. Such areas have a lot of speculative value. Although location has a value, that value is very dependent on the number of buyers and the net demand in the market. If demand has fallen, then such a market can fall fast and hard if there's a net loss of primary jobs in the area.

In a severe down market, prices may not hit bottom until the market price falls below construction costs with a small value assigned to the land itself. Once prices fall below construction cost, then new construction of homes is severely crippled. Homes are depreciable, just like cars, which was well known in the United States before World War II. Prior to that time, a homeowner who got as much out of a house when it was sold as he or she had put into it was considered fortunate. The phenomenon of increases in value occurred in the 1950s, 60s, 70s and

FIGURE 2.2   Fix-Up Assessment

Construction Cost as a

Percentage of Value	*Strategy*
Low (20%–30%)	Repair dollars invested yield good returns
Moderate (40%–60%)	Repair dollars invested yield modest returns
High (90% or 100%)	Repair dollars invested yield low returns

80s, although not every city saw rising values in the 1980s. It may not be the trend of the 1990s or the early part of the 21st century. In reality, houses wear out. They have to be bulldozed. Once that happens, they will not be replaced in a severe down market. The number of houses will decrease until it comes back in line with the demand, at which point prices will stabilize and the bottom has been reached.

CONSTRUCTION COSTS

If construction costs are a heavy component of a home's price, then the best possible result from spending dollars on repairs will likely be a dollar for dollar match between repair costs and the added value such dollars put into the house. If repairs are poorly done or run over budget, then the investor will lose by making repairs. On the other hand, in a very up market, or in a stable market where the ratio between repairs and market value is constant, then a few dollars spent on repairs is likely to translate into large returns.

Figure 2.2 shows the relationship between construction cost ratios and the appropriate repair and fix-up strategy.

Stable Markets

In a stable market, good repair cost estimation is critical. Fortunately, precise estimates of repair charges and the resulting added value are possible in a stable market. Experience can be a good prediction of future performance in such a market, because the variables are constant. Elaborate spreadsheets, checklists and job estimation forms can be employed in such situations with good results.

Falling or Bottoming-Out Markets

In down markets, when the proportion of a home's value is predominantly in construction costs, then repairs should be postponed or limited. Properties that require low-cost repairs should be favored. There are lots of properties around. Unless a home has an unusually low value that a few repair dollars can correct, trying to buy a property and do extensive fix-up work is a risky strategy.

Rising Markets

In rising markets, more and more money can be spent on repairs. Properties that are in poor condition may tend to lag the market as it rises; thus, they are often good buys. Financing for repairs may begin to return. Foreclosure buyers can spend fairly large amounts of money on repairs. A mistake in repair estimation may be covered, at least in part, by the rise in values that's taking place in the market.

LOCATION, LOCATION, LOCATION— CHOOSING THE NEIGHBORHOOD

Falling real estate prices and down market conditions may have startlingly different effects in different parts of the same city. Some parts of a city will lose higher portions of value than others. Some may lose no value at all and may even rise in value despite bad real estate market conditions in the city as a whole.

The absolute price levels may not be a sure guide to which areas will hold value in a down market. Sometimes very luxurious and expensive sections of a city have very high prices in relation to construction costs. Furthermore, the high prices may be based on a very thin market with very few sales. Such neighborhoods can experience sizable price drops in a down market. The areas that are likely to survive best have desirable locations and are experiencing some refurbishing and remodeling. The areas where old houses are torn down and new ones built in their place are a good bet for holding value. Such neighborhoods have an active demand that helps hold value and a higher portion of construction costs in their market price. Inherently, neighborhoods closer to the city or job-producing area (a medical center or a downtown financial area), or closer to a desirable feature such as the ocean, will tend to hold values a little better.

Such neighborhoods are excellent areas for a repair-based strategy, particularly one based on changing the type of house that sits on the lot, such as producing a tasteful rebuilt home where a smaller, unattractive older house used to be. Remodeling older houses that are still in serviceable condition may also work, just to bring the amenities and interior up to current standards and styles. Particularly important to this strategy are bathrooms, kitchens and heating and air-conditioning equipment, or adding media or game rooms and fancying up the bedrooms.

Housing Near Specific Job Facilities

Sometimes an area of the city near a plant or factory that has been shut down will see a real drop in home prices. Interestingly, some unaffected export industries, which ship goods outside the city, may help to uphold the prices of homes in the immediate vicinity. For example, if an automobile or oil market turns sour, causing prices in a city to fall, but a computer or electronics plant within the city is actively growing and shipping goods outside the city, then houses in the area around the growing business will remain strong even if the market in the city as a whole is falling. Some industries such as medical services see only a limited impact from a downturn. People need a similar level of health care in a good or bad market. Housing near medical centers may therefore hold value a little better than other parts of the city in a down market.

Areas that hold value are good targets for repair-based strategies. Investors can buy properties in such areas that need a lot of repairs, and the numbers will often work out. This is true even if the market in a city is falling. If the market is stable, an excellent strategy is to buy homes in good areas that need a lot of repairs, then make the repairs and resell for a profit.

VANDALISM AND FORECLOSURE

Foreclosures in any type of market are often associated with vandalism and related forms of property damage. For any investor who wants to buy foreclosures, damage from vandalism constitutes both a challenge and an opportunity. Buying homes with such damage and fixing them up can be profitable.

In an area with a large number of unoccupied foreclosure houses, vandalism can be a problem. Various types of vandals will look for such homes and hit them.

Round Up the Usual Suspects

Actually, it's hard to tell who does the most vandalism, but three groups of suspects can be found. The first suspect is the person or family whose home was foreclosed on. Such persons are not often thrilled and delighted with the world, given the loss of their home. They may have tried mightily to work things out with the lender, only to be met by harsh treatment, bureaucratic indifference or outright callousness. They may fight back by making sure the house will not be very useful to anyone else. Some homeowners give the sheetrock the "tire iron treatment" or what one broker called the "karate chop stuff." More serious vandalism may involve ripping out major appliances or damaging the plumbing and electrical systems. Neglect can also be effective. Even a small unrepaired roof leak can put tons of water in the ceiling. A faucet left on or a leaking pipe can flood a house and cause five figures worth of damage in a day or two.

A second group of suspects, of a fairly friendly nature, are the neighbors in the area. They are often well aware of the comings and goings at the house. It's easy for them to get in or out undetected. Plants that might otherwise die for lack of water will disappear. Even burglar alarm systems vanish. After all, "decent" people might as well get what's in the house before someone who's not so nice gets it instead.

A third group of suspects consists of professional burglars or semiprofessionals. Copper bandits are a common variety of semiprofessional burglar. They will rip out all copper pipe and wiring in the house—free of charge. More professional vandals drive up in well-marked service trucks or vans. They look like air-conditioner repair persons, but when they're through, the air conditioner and many other items may have taken a trip to someone's shop—permanently.

True vandals also exist. Their purpose is senseless, wanton destruction. They may try to tear up the house, spray graffiti on the walls or burn it down.

Terrible Looking Houses—But Beautiful to the Fix-Up Investor

For the foreclosure investor, vandalism damage is not hard to fix. Vandalized houses often look much worse than they really are. The scene of ripped out commodes and ceilings that have dropped to the floor may look awful, but it may not be that expensive to repair. Flood damage is usually serious. Missing appliances can be replaced fairly cheaply. Sheetrock repairs are not expensive, nor is paint or new carpet, which may have been needed anyway. A bad foundation or roof, which is usually not the product of vandalism, is a major cost item.

Unfortunately, foreclosed homes cannot always be viewed in isolation. Sometimes when a tract home builder goes out of business, an entire block of houses will be foreclosed on. If these homes are poorly managed, they may become vandalized and run down. If an area experiences numerous foreclosures, it too will acquire more and more rundown properties. Any appraiser will tell you that when more and more rundown, vandalized properties accumulate in an area they tend to diminish the value of other homes in the neighborhood. Appraisers call the phenomenon *regression.* The value drops in the neighborhood may exacerbate the foreclosure problem because hard-pressed homeowners who have to get out either can't sell their homes, or they can't get enough from a sale to pay off their loans. The whole neighborhood can spiral down in a cycle of declining values and destruction. The type of rental tenant that will live in such neighborhoods further compounds the problem. Some neighborhoods may never pull out. Some houses may ultimately wind up being bulldozed.

The foreclosure investor who spots the isolated house that has suffered pre- or post-foreclosure vandalism is probably looking at a good buy, provided that most of the damage is easily repaired, and it usually is. On the other hand, a whole neighborhood of trashed homes may be complicated to deal with. Investors may have to pool their efforts or arrange some kind of financing to accumulate enough capital to buy and rehabilitate a large number of houses in a short time. The houses are cheap and ready for sale, usually from banks and lenders that may provide financing, but the key would be to pull the whole neighborhood up. A large profit can be made if such a scheme works. Houses with light damage in areas that are fundamentally sound may benefit from this approach.

REPAIR PROBLEMS CAUSING FORECLOSURE—A POTENTIAL WINDFALL

Repair problems often contributed to the foreclosure on the house. The former owner's house had problems that had to be fixed in order to make the home saleable through a regular loan. Loans that allow the purchase and repair of a house at the same time are tricky to find and may be scarce in a down market. If the seller who was missing payments also lacked the cash to make the repair, and no cash buyer could be found in time, then he or she would lose the property in a foreclosure. If this type of foreclosure takes place in a good area where homes are retaining some of their value, then it is probably an excellent buy. This is the type of house that might be bought before the foreclosure, and if so, the investor may make a good deal by buying a lot of equity at a low price. A seller may even be induced to sell by offering him or her part of the profits from the resale, preferably as little as possible, from the investor's standpoint. Once the house is bought, it can be fixed up for relatively little money compared to what it can be sold for. Such arrangements are often very attractive.

SPECIAL FINANCING FOR FIX-UP STRATEGIES

An investor who desires to fix up property should look at the possibility of financing both the purchase and the rehabilitation. Surprisingly, even in a down market, financing may be available both to purchase and rehabilitate the house. In particular, FHA 203(k) financing and home purchase plus improvement loans from REO sellers may be available.

FHA 203(k)

The FHA 203(k) loan is one of the very few types of FHA loans that are still available to investors. However, the catch is that an investor buyer must buy, repair and resell ("flip") the property within 18 months of the original purchase. The 203(k) loan is really two loans in one: a loan to purchase the property and a loan to repair the property. This type of financing has problems if the market price of housing falls to the same level as construction costs in the area, because it is hard to estimate the added value that repairs will bring about. If houses are selling for more than the construction cost, then 203(k) financing may be powerful.

Obtaining a 203(k) loan requires two appraisals, one for the value of the house "as is" upon purchase, and the other for the value of the house "as repaired." In order for the 203(k) loan strategy to work, the repairs must produce a house with a value equal to the "as repaired" appraisal figure. Otherwise, life gets interesting for the lender and the borrower.

Good repair estimates are one of the keys to success with the 203(k) loan program. The budget for repairs involves paying out money by the lender to complete repairs, stage by stage. The lender will manage the repair money from an escrow account. Once repairs are completed, the house will be resold by the investor buyer. The key is to find a house that you can buy for less than its fair market value, if possible, but that can be fully repaired for very little money, and yet the repairs made will add a lot to the fair market value of the property. That situation is best for the 203(k).

To be eligible for a FHA 203(k) loan, the property must need a minimum of $5,000 in repairs, so the loan can be used to buy a house that needs significant repairs, such as foundation or roof work. That's an advantage, because this type of financing is available for major repairs, but a disadvantage because it requires accurate estimates of repair costs, even though they are for a large sum.

FHA 203(k) financing is likely to be available to investors even in a tough down market. The FHA was created to fight the depression and unlike most lenders, it will not disappear when the market gets tough in a city. One problem in many areas is that FHA financing loan limits are too low for many transactions. However, if prices drop in a down market, this type of financing may well be available for many of the homes on the market, particularly if the FHA delays in lowering its limit when the median home prices goes down, which is often the case.

Home Improvement Loans

Home improvement loans may be available to investors who put enough cash into a house or who have exceptional credit. Regular home improvement loans can be used to repair a house the investor has already acquired. Some REO (foreclosed homes owned by lenders) resale loans include money to finance repairs. They may include both the purchase money and a repair escrow for small repairs, or a special home improvement loan for larger repairs. Either way, the foreclosure investor can often obtain financing for repairs. Some larger contractors will also extend financing if a mechanic's lien is available in the state and the home has at least some equity. They are often eager for business in a down market and may be willing to extend credit to create business.

Using Loans for Fix-Up

In a falling market, using fix-up loans can be risky. In a bottoming out market, a rising market or a steady market, these loans are quite useful. Particularly in a rising market, leverage, which is using other people's money (OPM) instead of an investor's own, is often a smart practice. Keep the cash investment low and maximize returns on invested capital. Particularly if rent payments on the house can be used to keep up the main purchase mortgage payment or the fix-up payment, fix-up loans can lead to higher profits.

Fix-up strategies work in good markets or down markets. Investors must be sure that a dollar spent on repairs will generate more than a dollar increase in value. At the bottom of a down market, this may be tougher to do than in a rising market or a steady market. It is hardest to make a fix-up strategy work in a falling market, when resales at a profit are difficult, but it can work if the investor fixes up a property just to rent it out and make a profit on the rental income. In a rising market, it may be possible to use leverage, which involves borrowing money to buy the fix-up home and pay for the repairs, in order to minimize the investor's own cash and amplify the profits that can be made. Fix-up strategies require an investor who is good at estimating repair costs and the value improvements they will bring.

CHAPTER 3

How To
Make a
Rental
Strategy
Work

Many foreclosure buyers aim to buy a house at foreclosure and rent it out. In a down market, financing may be hard to get. Buying a foreclosure resale often involves special financing. This is not always true, however, even in a down market. If lenders perceive that the market may rise soon, financing may be obtainable by regular means and at regular rates.

Assume, however, that prices are really low, as they often are in a down market, and further that loans are hard to get. Rental rates, even if they are low, may still be enough to make the payments on foreclosure sale mortgages. Sometimes an investor can even make more off the rent than is needed to pay the mortgage, providing an immediate positive cash flow. This is particularly true during periods of low interest.

Rental rates are not always low in a down market. In 1993 in California, prices are low, but rents are staying high in many areas. With interest rates at an all-time low level in 1993, buying properties to rent makes tremendous sense. Even if rents fall, many people must rent because few can buy. An alert foreclosure buyer can still find good tenants in a down market.

RENTAL PROPERTIES

Buying rental properties in a falling market raises a number of interesting problems and possibilities. Landlords can chase the pool of tenants that existed when times were good, but that pool will shrink rapidly in a falling market. Good tenants will realize that it is now possible to buy a house in a down market at a low price, particularly when interest rates are low. In addition, a certain number of good tenants will lose jobs, let the lease expire and move to another city to get a new job. It may take a while for rents to fall in a down market, but if there's a net job loss and a net out-migration from the city, then slowly the supply of rental units will increase in relation to the number of tenants, and rents will fall. However, if rental unit construction stops in anticipation of a down market, and the out-migration is slow, the number of tenants may temporarily rise relative to the number of rental units and drive rents up. This situation won't last when there's a sustained drop in demand for rental housing due to continued job losses and the increasing number of foreclosed properties that need tenants.

In a falling market, alert foreclosure buyers will recognize that tenants may have to come from several new sources:

- Persons who previously had to live at home with parents can now afford to rent an apartment at down market rental rates.
- Persons who rent smaller apartments can move up to bigger or better apartments or houses.
- Persons whose credit previously had been marginal may be in a better position to rent.
- Persons who have been foreclosed on still need a place to live, and they are often forced to rent.

Rental Rates Soften in Down Markets

In a down market, rental rates are very soft. They usually fall along with home prices in the area. The reason for this is that a loss of primary jobs in a community may result in a net population outflow. If that occurs, apartment dwellers are often among the first to feel the effects of layoffs. They move out, opening up more and more vacancies in the area. Landlords try to keep the rents high, but find that practice to be unsustainable when there aren't enough high-paying tenants. Very soon landlords start cutting rents to maintain occupancy. Tenants with short leases can migrate rapidly to lower-priced apartments.

One of the first targets foreclosure investors aim at to recruit new tenants is existing apartments, particularly large ones such as three-bedroom units. While foolish landlords attempt to hold tenants at high rental rates, the investors entice such tenants out of the apartment and into a home by pointing out that it's only a little more expensive for a lot more room! Families with lots of children often love such moves. The net result is a further softening of rents as apartment landlords are forced to fight back by lowering rents on larger apartments.

CASH FLOW STRATEGIES
FOR INVESTORS

An investor can buy property and hold it for appreciation, but actually, a cash strategy may be a wise move in a falling market. Only a bold investor wants to buy a home solely for its potential appreciation, and some investors who are foolhardy enough to buy due to overconfident predictions of an early rise in the market may live to regret such purchases. In a falling market, it's still easy for the foreclosure investor to make a sure profit by using a cash flow strategy.

Banks and other lenders that acquire homes in foreclosure are often under great pressure to unload such houses at whatever price the market will pay. It's very hard to purchase homes for less than market price, but the market price in a falling market is often quite low. Lenders are often forced to offer generous financing to sell such homes. The losses may be covered, in part, by loan insurance. Some lenders may not have much choice anyway because of regulatory demands and cash flow pressures. If the financing package the lender provides produces a lower overall monthly payment (and taxes, insurance, maintenance costs and fees, vacancy and collection losses) than what the home can be rented for, then the buyer receives a positive profit in cash flow.

Some investors buy "as is" properties in poor condition, with good seller or lender financing and low mortgage payments, fix them up a bit and then charge rents that are higher than the mortgage payments. The fix-up work, done at a low cost, may allow the higher rent to be charged. At that point, even if prices of homes continue to fall, the investor can still make money just on the cash flow. The danger is that rents will continue to fall, so an investor has to be sure there's enough of a margin between mortgage payments and rental income to make a profit.

If the market is near bottom or steady, purchasing homes to rent out works very well. The good cash flow allows the use of substantial leverage. A small amount of money invested in down payments and a little in fix-up costs can allow the purchase of either a number of homes or one very large property for minimal cash. As prices begin to rise after a bottoming of the market, the investor can make money by reselling the house for more than its purchase price.

Rental Strategy 1

One way that investors buy foreclosed homes to rent out is to concentrate purchases of homes in a specific section of town. On a small scale, some investors concentrate all their purchases in one subdivision, or on a larger scale, in one quadrant of a city. It's easier to manage several properties if they're all close to one another. It's also easier to be familiar with both the purchase market and the rental market in a smaller section of a city.

Rental Strategy 2

Some investors rent to people with the potential to re-establish good credit and go on to purchase a home. People who lost a house in a tough down market or prospective tenants who have come through a recent divorce, family death or illness may inherently be good credit risks, but with a bad temporary history for the most understandable of reasons. Such buyers not only may prove to be excellent tenants but within two or three years, the foreclosure owner can sometimes arrange for a purchase loan that enables the tenants to buy the house they've been renting. That saves the costs of marketing the home and finds good buyers and locks them in when the market is uncertain or down.

Rental Strategy 3

A foreclosure buyer can purchase properties and resell them on a seller-finance basis to persons who start out as tenants. In seller financing, the owner lets the buyer pay for the house over time, plus interest, usually using a deed to the buyer and a mortgage. The interest the seller can earn in such circumstances far exceeds what bank certificates of deposit pay, and may exceed the normal market rate of interest regular lenders charge buyers who have excellent credit. If the buyer lacks bank-quality credit, the seller can justify a higher than normal interest rate and get it. A contract for deed in which the seller owns and keeps deed until buyer finishes paying for the house under a contract and a lease with option to purchase can also be used in these situations, although any of these arrangements may trigger a lender's right to foreclose under a due-on-sale clause. It is best to check with any lender the foreclosure investor has used to help buy the house before reselling it or even renting it out for a lease term of more than three years.

Rental Strategy 4

A foreclosure buyer can buy properties, rent them and count the rent toward the purchase price, which is nicknamed rent to own, or lease option. Simply rent the property and give the tenant a written option to buy the property at a later date. In an option, the seller is committed to sell, if the buyer wants to buy, but the buyer is not committed to buy. Such arrangements violate the due-on-sale clause in most conventional loans and the newer FHA (after December 15, 1989) and VA (after March 1, 1988) loans as well. However, some states do not allow enforcement of the due-on-sale clause in such circumstances. Such states opted out of the federal laws passed in the early 1980s, which made the due-on-sale clause enforceable against (meaning the lender can immediately foreclose) leases more than three years long, rent-to-own arrangements, leases with option to purchase, contract for deed plans and assumptions.

A rent to own or lease purchase bypass conventional financing for the buyer. This is a huge advantage in a market with many buyers who lack credit, but need a house. In states that allow such arrangements, the seller will remain responsible for the loan if the buyer fails to pay. In states that prohibit a due-on-sale clause, a lease of up to three years is permitted, without an option to purchase. However, the investor may offer to sell the home to the tenant at any time, but the tenant cannot get a contractual agreement that could be used to force the investor to sell.

At the very least, the prospective tenant/purchaser's credit can be checked before signing a lease or any other document. Credit information, with the tenant's or purchaser's written authorization, can be obtained from a credit bureau, or the tenant or purchaser can obtain a credit report and other credit information and provide it to the seller/landlord. Some areas have special credit services just for tenants, typically run through apartment associations or other landlords' associations.

PROBLEM AREAS

Strategies based on renting to tenants who may have marginal creditworthiness always carry certain risks. Bad tenants will trash the house, necessitating expensive repairs before it can be relet, with several months of mortgage payments to be made in the interim by the unlucky investor. Some tenants won't pay rent and will have to be evicted, which can be time-consuming, expensive and frustrating. The worst tenants will pick on small investors who have little background in property management. They know such investors may not check credit at all, or make mistakes, such as allowing the tenant to get possession without a sufficient amount of up-front cash. Such tenants can make property renting into an experience like the one depicted in the movie *Pacific Heights.* Any individual or small investor should seriously consider consulting with knowledgeable, professional property managers to get some down to earth advice about renting in a particular area. Any prospective tenant's credit should be checked, and marginal credit risks should be accepted only after careful, thoughtful consideration. Property management is a serious business that requires time and effort to master.

RENTAL STRATEGIES IN RISING MARKETS

If a rental market has been falling in a given area, due to foreclosures and *down market* problems, then the signs of an upturn to look for are no further primary job losses and a decrease in the foreclosure rate that appears to be more than just temporary. The rental market in a typical city will be positively affected by such developments. Once the loss of primary jobs slows, then the population in a city will stabilize. Once the foreclosures stop adding more and more properties to the market, then rental rates will increase fairly quickly. Once the market turns, rents can begin to go up at a considerable pace. Anyone holding rental properties will benefit. Lease terms should be kept fairly short, in contrast to the down market situation in which longer-term leases are more advantageous. A shorter lease term will permit fairly quick increases in rent as market rental rates advance. There may also be calls for rent control or tougher rent control in such circumstances, so an investor must be careful to pace the increases to a level that tenants can reasonably afford rather than a tremendous increase if the market rent rate has gone up a lot.

Even in a rising market, a certain number of rental properties will still be lost. Depending on the property, maintenance can only be deferred so long. Once about two years of maintenance is left undone, the cost of salvaging a property may be too great to make the project worthwhile, depending on the area. If a property cannot be salvaged through repair efforts, then it must be bulldozed. Otherwise, it will be declared an unsafe structure under building codes. It may be better to turn it into a vacant property, which doesn't have so many expenses or problems, and look for a resale plan. As properties are bulldozed, the remaining rental properties are that much more valuable.

Usually, a lag exists between the time when market rents begin to go up and the point at which lenders are willing to lend money for building apartments or other rental properties. This lag time means that there will be substantial upward pressure on rents when a down market gives way to a rising market. If any type of leveraging can be found, such as private investors, pension money or even venture capital, then leverage strategies on rental properties can be made to work very well in a rising market.

In a leverage plan, money is borrowed to buy the property. This necessitates a small down payment by the investor. The regular payments on the loan must be made, but as rents rise, the property's value will climb very sharply. In addition, rental income above the mortgage payments becomes greater and greater. Negative cash flows are risky. The property should rent for enough to pay the bills and make a profit. When the process begins to slow down, the property can be resold at a hefty profit. Often, the special financing needed to undertake such strategies is available only if a percentage of the profits, such as one-third or so, is offered to the special, nonbank lender.

Here's an example:

Purchase Price	$ 90,000	Down Payment	$ 12,500
Repair Costs	+35,000	Risk Loan	$112,500
Total	$125,000		

Rental Rate: $1,100 per month initially

Once the market stabilizes and goes up, the rent may go up to $1,320 per month, a 20 percent increase. If that happens, the appraiser will say the property has gone up by more than 20 percent because further gains are anticipated, and the increased rent is over and above basic expenses, so that on an income capitalization approach appraisal, the property will really begin to skyrocket. (The income approach to appraisal values property in proportion to the income it generates.) It may well double in value, depending on the capitalization rate (yearly profit rate) investors look for in the area.

Assume investors demand an 8 percent rate of return on investment (invest $50,000 and get $5,500 per year income from it) in a tougher market, but accept a 6 percent rate in the rising market. Let's assume expenses remain relatively constant. The principal and interest payment will also stay constant. Let's assume the expenses on our property are $200 per month, and the mortgage payment runs $800 per month.

The net operating income in this scenario will rise from $900 per month to $1,450 per month. If the capitalization rate goes down from 11 percent to 8 percent, then watch what happens to the value:

$$\$900 \times 12 = \frac{\$10,800}{.08} = \$135,000$$

$$\$1,450 \times 12 = \frac{\$17,400}{.06} = \$290,000$$

Rents only rose from $1,100 to $1,320, which is not that hard to do when a down market begins to rise again. A falling rate of return on your investment is certainly possible and not at all unrealistic.

The rent is more than sufficient to pay the acquisition mortgage cost. Let's assume the investor puts in only a 10 percent down payment, given the risk nature of the financing, which will demand not only the regular market interest rate, but also one-third of the profit.

Cash into the deal	$ 13,500
Cash out of the sale	217,500
Pay-off of the loan	−125,000
	$ 92,500
1/3 to risk lender	−30,833
	$ 61,667

This investor keeps $61,667 on an investment of only $13,500. Assuming the capitalization rate stayed exactly the same, which is unlikely, then the profit could have been $22,121 on a $13,500 investment. If the property had been purchased at below fair market value (and this one was purchased at fair market value, and then heavily repaired), then the multiples are quite spectacular.

Even more impressive, some of these results can be obtained in a fairly short time. Sometimes it takes as little as two years for rents to rise 30 percent, 40 percent or more coming out of a down market. The risk lender also makes a handsome profit in the bargain, obtaining a far higher return than the market rate of interest.

Although some of these figures might be quibbled with, the basic principle remains: leverage on rental properties in a rising market can be very powerful for investors. The strategy is fundamentally strong across a broad range of numbers and holds to a profit even if many of the numbers turn out to be worse than expected or projected. Of course, many of the numbers could be better than expected. In the scenario above, the property was obtained at market value. In a down market, the property might be obtained at a below-market price. If the property had been obtained at 50 percent below market (which was regularly achieved in Texas in the 1980s in bulk sales and other transactions), then the profit potential from leverage is staggering.

Several variables can see positive improvements. A very important variable in a plan involving leveraging in a rising market is the effect of repairs. Someone with a good eye may spot the property for which a few dollars in cleverly done repairs or a shift in style may work wonders in improving rents. Improved security, attractive landscaping or paint schemes, good marketing strategies and an able leasing agent who can find excellent tenants at good rent rates, may also allow much higher returns than were shown in the above example.

Another important variable is the leverage in the financing that's available. An 80 percent loan is better than a 75 percent loan. A 90 percent loan is much better than an 80 percent loan, and a 95 percent loan is truly impressive in what it can do in a rising market. In some down markets, risk lenders even make 100 percent financing available (some pension plans have done it), but the investor must have an established track record and an exceptionally well-organized and argued business plan for a particular project.

Perhaps most important, the concept of leverage in a rising market that is emerging from down market conditions can be used by almost any investor. Although large investors and national bottom feeders know the leveraging techniques, the same strategies can be employed successfully by the small investor who buys only one house. It's just a good simple plan for making money, but it depends on

1. rising rents, which occur after a down market bottoms out;
2. the availability of risk-oriented financing;
3. the minimum cash investment; and
4. basic property acquisition, repair and management skills.

HIGH RISK AND LOW RISK INVESTOR PAIRS

Some investment plans for purchasing small numbers of houses are even set up with two types of investors, a high risk investor and a low risk investor. We'll call the high risk investor a type 1 investor, and the low risk a type 2 investor. The type 1, high risk investor will go in with the cash needed to buy the property and rehabilitate it. The high risk investor will shop for a bargain, and upon finding it, will snap it up with cash, then fix it up and rent it out (*tenantize* it, for those in the business). The low risk investor will stand ready to buy a property with a strong tenant secured by professional property managers, a mortgage payment of a known level and a rent of a known level. The low risk investor is virtually assured a set profit. The low risk investor will buy the property from the high risk investor, who takes the sale proceeds and rolls on to make another deal, while the low risk investor has accumulated and will continue to accumulate more and more properties.

A variation on the strategies described above is to be an organizer who puts such deals together. Brokers may be well suited to this role. The broker can ask for a commission, or better still, a percentage of the profits, provided that the arrangement is disclosed to all parties up front and is agreed to by everyone. In such event, the organizer can put very little cash into the deal and yet realize a substantial profit. The organizer will need to be a licensed real estate broker or be a sales agent working for a broker. In addition, the broker may also have to hold a stock broker's license to put together investment opportunities.

CONCLUSION

Investors who buy houses to rent out can make money in any market, rising or falling. In fact, when interest rates are low, rental strategies work even better than they would otherwise. The cost of buying a house, measured by the monthly mortgage payment, is low when interest rates are low, yet rents may remain strong during the same period. There is a larger profit margin between the investor's mortgage payment and the rental income.

CHAPTER 4

The Big Picture

So many houses are labeled *foreclosures* that the astute investor or homebuyer should consider the tremendous range and variety of sales that are described by this term. The most important distinctions are based on the original type of loan, such as VA, FHA and conventional loans. It makes a great difference not only who made a loan, but who buys the loan after it's made and who insures it. Institutions such as FNMA may get involved in foreclosure sales. On the other hand, S&Ls resell foreclosed homes for which the original loans came from deposits. Resale of such REOs differs from other types of foreclosure resales. Here's a review of the types of foreclosure sales.

Many people mistakenly believe that the foreclosure market consists only of courthouse auctions in which frenzied bidders buy houses for pennies on the dollar. Although true legal foreclosure sales exist, most of the so-called foreclosure home market consists of resales of houses acquired by lenders at the legal foreclosure sale. The borrower actually loses legal title to the house at a courthouse-style auction. However, almost no one wants to bid at such auctions because, contrary to popular belief, it is tricky and difficult to get a really good buy. (But it is possible: read Chapter 5 on buying direct at the foreclosure sale.) Most houses at a courthouse sale are sold to the lender, who normally bids by canceling out some or all of what the lender was owed on the loan by the defaulting borrower. In return for a debt cancellation, the lender is given a deed to the property.

LEGAL FORECLOSURE SALES

The nature of a lender's rights to foreclose when a borrower defaults depends on the documents the borrower signed and the statutory rights given to borrowers by the state in which the property is located. Most borrowers are asked by most lenders to sign some form of a mortgage, together with a promissory note. The note describes the borrower's basic obligation to repay a sum of money at a specified interest rate, in certain payments, over a stated period of time, or it at least provides a means by which these matters can be objectively calculated at a given time, such as in an adjustable rate mortgage. The mortgage gives the lender the right to foreclose. In many states, the mortgage is in the form of a *deed of trust,* which also gives the lender the right to foreclose, but which usually provides for faster foreclosure processes than those available under a regular mortgage.

Lien Theory States and Out of Court Foreclosure

The question may be asked, "Who owns the house while the borrower repays the loan—the borrower or the bank?" Most people would instinctively answer: "The bank owns it." Surprisingly, in a majority of states, this is not so. In most states, the lender holds only a *lien,* which is the right to force the sale of a house or property in order to pay off a debt, in this case, the lender's unpaid balance on the mortgage loan. In a lien theory state, the lender will get a deed from the foreclosure sale.

Title Theory States and In Court Foreclosures

In a few states, more complex procedures have to be followed. *Title theory* states believe that the lender owns the house. In those states, some type of formal proceeding, often with a limited court appearance, but something less than a full-blown lawsuit, will be necessary for the lender who owns the house to be allowed re-entry and recover possession of the house. However, in some states, very elaborate procedures, with long time delays, have to be followed.

FIGURE 4.1   Ownership Theory by State

Lien			Title	Intermediate
Alaska	Minnesota	Oklahoma	Georgia	Arkansas
Alabama	Missouri	Oregon	Maine	Connecticut
California	Montana	South	Maryland	Delaware
Colorado	Nebraska	Carolina	Mississippi	Washington
Florida	Nevada	South	Pennsylvania	D.C.
Hawaii	New	Dakota	Rhode	Illinois
Idaho	Hampshire	Texas	Island	Massachusetts
Indiana	New	Utah	Tennessee	New Jersey
Iowa	Mexico	Washington	Vermont	North Carolina
Kansas	New York	West		Virginia
Kentucky	North	Virginia		
Louisiana	Dakota	Wisconsin		
Michigan	Ohio	Wyoming		

Nonjudicial Foreclosure

In many lien theory states, the lender is also permitted to foreclose without filing a lawsuit in court or going to trial. Such states often use a deed of trust, under which the borrower pre-authorizes the private sale of the home by the lender in the event of a loan default. Quick, expedited procedures are provided to advertise, post, mail and file or record (in the deed records) a foreclosure notice at least a few weeks in advance of a foreclosure. The time varies from state to state, but usually it's about 21 to 30 days, which is three to four weeks. The notice time is only part of the foreclosure, however; it may take several months from the beginning of the borrower's default or even the commencement of the lender's foreclosure to complete the foreclosure.

Once the preliminary notices are given, interested persons are invited to attend the public sale of the property, which is at a place fixed by law or fixed in the foreclosure notice, in most states. Bidding is usually by cash to the highest bidder. Lenders, however, are usually allowed to bid some or all of the outstanding balance on the loan in place of cash. Many people who are forced into foreclosure are put in that position because the loan balance exceeded the value of the home. In most states, when this situation occurs, only the lender wants to buy. Investors are looking for those rarer situations in which somebody whose home is worth a lot, but on which only a little is owed, is nevertheless going down in a foreclosure sale. That's a bargain, but most houses go to the lender.

Judicial Foreclosure States

A significant number of states, regardless of whether they are title theory or lien theory states, will require formal court action in the form of a lawsuit to effect a foreclosure. These are called *judicial foreclosure* states. The advantage of this procedure is that it provides a means of soundly establishing the title in the name of the buyer at the court-ordered foreclosure sale; the disadvantage is that it is often time consuming and expensive. The process can destroy or at least define the exact rights that any other lienholders, tenants or title claimants may have to the property. In many states, judicial foreclosure gives a defaulting borrower considerable protection. In these states, the lender may be forced to come to some arrangement with the defaulting borrower in which the borrower simply deeds the house to the lender.

LEGAL PROBLEMS AFTER FORECLOSURE

Foreclosure can be a messy process. Some borrowers will put up a fight to save their home. Sometimes lenders make mistakes when foreclosing. It may take months after a foreclosure before the title is put into a condition in which it can be resold on a safe basis. Those who buy directly at the legal foreclosure sales can sometimes get the best deals or the worst deals, depending on what problems pop up after the foreclosure. Interestingly, even the best of the foreclosure investors who buy at the courthouse steps may lose a house or wind up in litigation through no fault of their own, and after following some of the most rigorous procedures possible. It takes time to clear up all the problems. Most buyers are much safer to buy after the foreclosure, and long enough after it or under such circumstances that few problems are likely to arise. Here are a few of the problems foreclosure sales run into after the foreclosure.

Redemption Rights

Many states provide the borrower with a *right of redemption* for a statutorily set time period after the foreclosure sale. During a redemption period of approximately two months to nearly a year in some states, the defaulting borrower who lost title to the house at foreclosure can nevertheless get the title back by the high bid price at foreclosure to whoever bought the house at foreclosure. Once the redemption price is paid, the borrower reacquires title and the lender or any other foreclosure buyer loses it.

Deficiency Judgments

Many states allow the lender the right to claim a *deficiency judgment* after a foreclosure. If the home the lender forecloses on has gone down in value, which often causes foreclosure, and the low value falls below the amount owed on the loan, then the lender may be entitled to sue the borrower to recover the lender's loss, either as part of the foreclosure process or in a separate lawsuit after the foreclosure. These suits can result in claims and counterclaims between the defaulting borrower and the lender, which could result in difficulties in clearing title to the property on a subsequent resale after the foreclosure.

Bankruptcy

Bankruptcy can often cause problems after the foreclosure. Lenders may be put on a bankruptcy payout plan (called *Chapter 13*) although the first lien lender on a residence is entitled to full monthly payments, without reduction, but most of the other payments made by the borrower (excluding child support, but including IRS taxes) can be reduced. Alternatively, if the borrower lost title during a foreclosure to a lender or a foreclosure buyer, the borrower may be able to get the house back through bankruptcy if there was any equity (the house was worth more than was owed against it) at the time of the foreclosure.

Tenants

Some landlords who are falling behind on a mortgage never tell the poor tenant that the ax is about to fall. In almost every state, once the primary lender forecloses on a lien or right that predated the lease, then the tenant can be tossed out after the foreclosure, although most states give tenants some protection by slowing down the lender's time to recover possession under such circumstances. Even if the tenant's lease has not yet expired, leases will generally not survive a foreclosure.

ONCE THE LENDER ACQUIRES THE HOUSE

The lending institution that arranges the foreclosure is the primary lender, i.e., the lender that deals directly with the borrower. Primary lenders include S&Ls, mortgage companies, banks and private investors. These primary lenders usually hire the trustee or attorney who will undertake the legal foreclosure. Once the foreclosure is complete, the house will be deeded to the lender.

Most lenders do one of several things once they acquire a property. They can

1. Sell the property directly, which is called an REO (from the term Real Estate Owned). The house may be sold through a real estate broker or a variety of other means. See Chapter 7.
2. Get rid of the property to a loan insurer or loan owner.

The Influence of Loan Insurance

A variety of entities insure the repayment of loans; such insurance is called mortgage insurance. In the event that the regular borrower fails to repay a loan, then a loan insurer will pay it off. There are many types of loan insurers.

Private mortgage insurance companies are among the most recently developed loan insurers. They've been around since the 1950s, but their great growth period was not until 1972, when the Federal National Mortgage Association (FNMA) decided to buy privately insured loans in addition to government insured loans. At that point, private mortgage insurance grew enormously, and it has been a major factor ever since.

Private mortgage insurance companies are very concerned when a foreclosure occurs. The primary lender may not be that concerned with the foreclosure if it is fully protected from any losses by a private mortgage insurance company. In fact, some lenders can be positively ugly to the borrower about the situation. The borrower who is faced with foreclosure may urge the lender not to foreclose by saying: "You don't want another foreclosed home on your hands! Work with me!" The borrower may be greeted with a rude turndown from the lender, because the lender won't be hurt. However, the private mortgage insurance company (PMI), which will have to pay a loss if a foreclosure occurs, is very concerned. The PMI company will often try to work out a deal with the borrower if there's any way the house can be saved.

If the house can't be saved from foreclosure, there may be a good investment opportunity for a foreclosure buyer in what is called a PMI-assisted presale. Foreclosure most often occurs when the house can't be sold for enough to pay off the loan balance. However, such houses have not lost all of their value. In this situation, the private mortgage insurance company, which will have to absorb a big loss if the house forecloses, will instead try to pay a smaller amount of money to help get the house sold. In these situations, a seller who still has some cash and wants to save a credit rating may be a big help. The PMI company will cover much of the loss; the seller covers the rest. The PMI company saves money, and the buyer gets the house at a below-market price, at least to the extent of the seller's contributions, and possibly to the extent that the lender or PMI company will take a small loss to prevent a bigger one.

If the house goes into foreclosure, then a PMI company may wish to pick up the house from the lender after the foreclosure sale. By this means, the PMI company can arrange the resale of the property and possibly keep losses to a minimum. The lender would normally be paid the full loan balance by the PMI company, which would then resell the house to recover as much of its money as possible. It may be better to do this for the PMI company than to let the house sit unsold for a long time after the foreclosure. The PMI company would then have that much larger a loss to cover in the end.

PMI resales are a source of foreclosed homes for ordinary buyers. The deal on the purchase may be excellent. PMI insurance may be easy to get on a loan to buy such properties, even in a down market!

HUD/FHA/VA Resales

Some lenders that acquire title to property from foreclosure may have FHA mortgage insurance (also called HUD mortgage insurance) or a "guarantee" from the Department of Veterans Affairs (VA). A VA guarantee operates almost exactly like mortgage insurance, in that the lender who acquires a home out of foreclosure can deed it to the VA, which will pay off the loan balance and take title to the house. The FHA does the same thing, in that when a lender acquires a home out of a foreclosure, the lender will deed it to HUD in exchange for which HUD will pay off the lender's loan. Currently, HUD and the VA will not always cover the full extent of the lender's loss. VA guarantees never have. However, lenders are often so eager to get rid of foreclosed homes that they will dump them on FHA/VA even if the full loss is not paid. Sometimes even HUD and VA won't accept the houses. If not, the lender has another tough-to-sell REO home. If the agency does accept the property, though, then the HUD or the VA will have acquired a house and can resell it through their special programs. (See Chapters 10 and 11 for much more extensive coverage of these programs.)

Secondary Market Loan Owners/Buyers

Certain large institutions, such as FNMA (Federal National Mortgage Association), FHLMC (Federal Home Loan Mortgage Corporation) and a wide variety of private institutions purchase loans from primary lenders. If such loans go into default, then the secondary lender who actually owns the loan will suffer much of the loss from any foreclosure, assuming, of course, that private mortgage insurance didn't cover the whole loss. That actually can happen quite easily in a down market. Private mortgage insurance only covers losses of 12 percent to about 30 percent, depending on how much coverage the primary lender purchased or the secondary loan buyer required. Any drop in value below what is covered on the unpaid balance, and the lender or loan owner will suffer the additional losses. Actually, if there is a loan owner, the loan owner will suffer it.

Loan owners can be rough on primary borrowers during hard times or down market periods. For example, the secondary loan buyer usually exacted a warranty that all of its standards were followed when the loan was created. If a loan goes into default, the secondary market loan buyer may call the primary lender, demand the full paperwork on the loan (by overnight air express to a regional headquarters) and then relive the creation of that loan through a crack underwriter who knows every standard for such loans to a very high degree. If the original lender made a mistake in creating the loan, and it didn't meet the standards, the secondary market loan buyer may even return the whole loan, and demand its money back, just as you or I return bad milk to a grocery store and get our money back. If a primary lender sells a secondary lender bad goods, in this case, a loan that did not meet the secondary lender's published standards, then the primary lender may take the full loss in the situation.

By the way, any outside foreclosure buyer who wants a good price on a home might be able to get one when the lender forecloses the bad loan and needs to resell the property in a hurry for cash to pay off the secondary loan owner who wants a refund for the bad loan.

As a result of such treatment, or the threat of it, many primary lenders have learned the wisdom of following secondary market guidelines when creating loans. When the primary lender has adhered to the guidelines, the secondary market loan owner will be stuck with the loss. In order to minimize the losses from such sources, secondary market lenders often arrange auctions or resale programs. They may take title to a house after foreclosure, fix it up at the secondary lender's expense and help resell it by auctions or special brokered sales. Such secondary lender assisted sales are covered in Chapter 9. These sales are an important source of homes for foreclosure buyers.

S&Ls

Savings and loan associations are an important primary lender in many parts of the country. Unless an S&L has sold a loan to FHLMC, which was set up to buy loans from S&Ls, then the S&L will normally provide the funds for its loans from deposits or, perhaps on a more ambitious level, by selling some type of security or mortgage-backed bond. Once the loan goes into default, the S&L will foreclose and obtain title. By such means, S&Ls can acquire a lot of properties, or to restate the situation, a substantial REO inventory. If that REO inventory gets too large, and the S&L suffers too many losses on its loans, then it will be shut down by the federal government, which will then take over the S&L's REO inventory. That's where Resolution Trust Corporation (RTC) and Federal Deposit Insurance Corporation (FDIC) properties come from. They are covered in Chapter 13.

PURCHASE FROM SECOND
LIEN FORECLOSURES

Other types of lenders exist, such as second, third or fourth lien holders. Particularly in states that have seen high equity growth in the past, such as California, second or third liens, or more, are quite common. These loans are not necessarily used to purchase the property, but rather to provide the homeowner with cash. Later on, if the house is sold, the buyer might have to assume several loan payments as a condition of the purchase. However, as long as equity grew, the buyer could get another cash loan.

Unfortunately, in a down market characterized by foreclosures, the existence of second, third or later liens can complicate matters considerably. If home values fall below what is owed on all the liens against the home, then the owners can't sell for enough to pay off the mortgage. If the borrower can't keep up the payments on all the loans, due to a job loss or income drop in a declining local economy, then the situation can get rugged.

Several alternatives exist once a borrower can no longer keep up all the payments on all the loans, and like a juggler, prepares to drop the ball on one or more loans. The later lienholders may be justifiably concerned about foreclosing in a down market. If the owner can't make any payments on any loan, then the primary or lower lienholders are likely to foreclose. If the first, or senior, or prior lienholders foreclose, then the later liens are wiped out, in every state. A junior lienholder must either foreclose quickly to get the house before a first lienholder does, or make sure the first lienholder stays paid.

In some cases, the later lienholder will advance funds to make payments on an earlier lien, which can be done if a substantial amount of equity is left in the property. If the equity left in the property will not support a loan to make payments, then the second lienholder may have to foreclose.

Most later liens provide that a default on an earlier lien gives the later lienholder the right to foreclose. This is sometimes called a *wrap* arrangement. If the borrower defaults on a first lien payment, then the second lienholder hopefully has a mechanism in place to learn when it happens. Otherwise, the earliest a second lienholder may find out of a primary lien's impending foreclosure is with the first lienholder's initial mailing, recording, posting, advertising or other action to foreclose. Once a second lienholder learns of an impending prior lien foreclosure, then the second lienholder must act. Either the missed payments on the earlier loan must be paid and the loan brought current to stop the foreclosure, or the second lienholder must foreclose due to the default, which some junior liens allow. Alternatively, the junior lienholder must advance funds to pay up on the first lien, or even pay off the balance on the first lien, and then foreclose to recover the sums advanced.

Any way you look at it, the later lienholders will acquire a lot of properties in a down market. Once they acquire a property, particularly if the first lien had to be paid down or paid off, or even it is merely assumed, the later lienholder will probably want to sell it quickly to recover its money and its credit. If any equity remains, then the price may be cut simply to move the property. These could be interesting opportunities for investors, but look out for the stack of payments on the earlier liens that may have to be kept current.

A more savage possibility is that higher priority lienholders may deliberately foreclose whenever the higher priority lien runs into default and junior lienholders or the borrower are slow to act. If a higher priority lienholder succeeds in foreclosing, then the later liens are wiped out. This can have the effect of generating a large equity in a hurry, which an investor may be able to snap up.

First lien	$100,000 (owed on loan used to buy the house)
Second lien	$100,000 (cash loan during marriage)
Third lien	$200,000 (part of a divorce settlement)
Current property value	$350,000
Equity if	$350,000
first lien	−100,000 (balance on first lien)
forecloses	$250,000

In the above situation, the foreclosure by the first lienholder would put a property on the market with $250,000 in equity. The second lienholder would be well advised to move first, and that way, the property would be on the market with $150,000 in equity. In fact, the second lienholder might make a killing just by buying the property. The second lienholder could even offer the borrower the opportunity to deed the property back to the second lienholder, who might then buy up the first lienholder's rights and foreclose.

LOANS CAN BE BOUGHT

One of the all-time favorite techniques in foreclosure purchases concerns the purchase of loans that are default. It is generally possible to buy a loan. It is particularly easy to buy one at a fair price, or even a reduced price, if it is default. Most lenders would just as soon get their money out of the situation and go. A defaulted loan can be foreclosed by the new owner. This may set up a situation where a foreclosure can generate a lot of equity.

Possibilities for Sharp Dealing

One problem in a down market might be the borrower who attempts to buy up a prior loan position with the deliberate intent of not paying it, foreclosing it and destroying second or later lienholders. Such tactics are probably illegal. A bankruptcy may not necessarily wipe out the second lienholder debts if fraud is involved in trying to destroy them. Legitimate investors should be wary of such schemes.

Divorce situations may often lead to such tactics because persons in a divorce may lack personal credit to buy up or bid for properties in foreclosure to the full amount of a lien. Also, the bitterness that accompanies a divorce may lead desperate borrowers to resort to schemes based on the plan outlined above.

Much more complex versions on the above scenarios are easy to imagine, and may very well play a role in states with complex lien structures. Variations might include funneling money in and out of overseas bank accounts, or obtaining assistance from divorce or bankruptcy attorneys who might be willing to help put together a complex scheme for a fee. However, such business plays, if done with the deliberate intent to hurt creditors, may trigger the application of *fraudulent conveyance* laws to invalidate suspicious loan or property transfers, or generate straight fraud suits for misrepresentation and dealings with lenders in bad faith.

CONCLUSION

In most states, the borrower owns the house, and the lender holds only a lien, which is the right to force the sale of the house to pay off a debt, such as a loan. The process of forcing such a sale is called *foreclosure*. In every state, procedures exist requiring the lender to notify the borrower of a foreclosure, and in most states, give the borrower an opportunity to cure the default before the property is offered for sale to the general public, which is notified by posting and/or advertisements. Most often, the lender buys the property at foreclosure. In many states, even after foreclosure, the borrower is permitted the right of redemption, which allows the borrower to recover the house by paying up the missed payments on the old loan, or paying it off altogether, which is much more common. Lenders in many states are afforded the right to sue the borrower for a deficiency judgment for the unpaid balance on the loan after crediting foreclosure sale proceeds, or the fair market value against what was owed on the loan.

Bankruptcy will usually delay, but not stop, a foreclosure. A home lender will be able to receive title to the house or continued payment in bankruptcy. Otherwise, the bankruptcy court will allow a foreclosure. A knowledgeable borrower can draw out the foreclosure proceedings in many states, making it harder for the lender to foreclose.

Investors may try to buy homes before the foreclosure, or at the foreclosure in cash, but only after careful consideration. It's important to recognize that foreclosure is never a sure thing.

CHAPTER 5

Buying at the Foreclosure Sale

Investing to make higher than normal profits may involve higher than normal risks. Buying directly at the foreclosure sale usually involves cash, an "as is," "where is" sale with little or no opportunity to look at the property before buying it and a host of potential title problems, which may be expensive to find out about before purchase and potentially more expensive if you don't. There is a risk of losing the house to the person who was foreclosed on in the event the former homeowner declares bankruptcy. It's all part of the game. Investors can become almost obsessive about chasing down a house at a really good price at the foreclosure and buying a bargain such as most people only dream about.

It is possible to buy a house directly at a foreclosure sale. Although most so-called foreclosure sales are actually resales of homes bought by lenders at the true legal foreclosure sale, the actual legal foreclosure sale is open to the public in every state. Anyone can buy, but it's a buy at your own risk affair. The sale is usually conducted by a sheriff, a constable or a lawyer acting as a trustee. They may or may not be at all helpful, and sometimes can be downright difficult to work with. Getting a good deal at such a sale is not always easy because no homeowner likes to lose a house for less than it's worth. In a down market, buyers will sometimes ask a real estate broker: "Can you find me a nice little foreclosure home at 20 percent below market?" The answer is usually "No!" Market prices are market prices. Market prices are the prices homes will sell at even in a down market. It makes little sense for any owner, whether it's an individual or a bank, to sell at below-market prices. Nevertheless, hope springs eternal among investors that somehow it's got to be easy to buy a foreclosure at less than a market price, and thereby get a "deal."

Actually, it is possible to buy foreclosed properties at less than market prices, but it is not easy. The deepest discounts below fair market value occur in purchases of properties directly at the legal foreclosure sale or just before foreclosure from the homebuyer. Under the terrible pressures of a soon-to-occur foreclosure, homeowners may have to sell a valuable property for less than its worth. For the homeowner faced with foreclosure, it may be a choice of getting something for the house, even if it's low, or losing everything when the lender forecloses. Under such circumstances, deals may be found.

Unfortunately, it's not easy for a typical homebuyer, who lacks ready cash, to get a good deal at the actual foreclosure sale or just before. People who buy homes directly at the foreclosure sale must realize that the fundamental rules of investment still apply in foreclosure: where high profits are possible, high risks exist. If you choose this route, be careful! Sometimes those high-priced foreclosure seminars make it all sound so easy, but beware. The risks are there. What follows is an analysis of purchase strategies for buying homes before foreclosure, then during foreclosure, and the downside risks after buying directly at a foreclosure sale.

THE LEGAL FORECLOSURE SALE

Buying directly at the legal foreclosure sale is a risky and dangerous business. It is strictly *caveat emptor,* let the buyer beware. The process has many disadvantages. There is no financing. Such purchases require cash, lots of it, just to bid and buy. The title needs to be checked in some manner before the purchase, or the buyer could buy seriously deficient title. The property's condition is not well known. Generally, an interior inspection of the property to be purchased is not possible before the sale. The property may prove difficult to market. Or it could be tied up in litigation after the sale, particularly in bankruptcy court, which is abysmally slow. On the other hand, the returns for those who succeed can be considerable. It may be possible to double one's investment on a single sale, a 100 percent return. No other type of foreclosure purchase has as much upside potential.

PREPARATION FOR A FORECLOSURE SALE

The common procedure for buying directly at the foreclosure sale is to

1. obtain the foreclosure list;
2. evaluate the properties; and
3. inspect and appraise the properties.

After that, the foreclosure purchaser will wait until the day of the foreclosure sale to bid. The bidding procedure almost always requires cash.

Reading the Reports

The key to success in purchasing before and at the foreclosure sales is to buy high equity cheap. In a typical foreclosure listing service report (if one is available in your area), look for a fair market value that is higher than the amount owed on the loan. Such a house has positive equity and therefore it may be a good buy. Good foreclosure reports should list the original note amount; otherwise, it will have to be researched at the office of county deed records. A financial calculator, a computer with an amortization program or an old-fashioned book of financial tables can tell the alert foreclosure investor the remaining balance, based on the original loan amount, its date and the interest rate. Add at least four to six months of missed payments, plus the interest on each (at about 18 percent) and at least $500 for trustee's attorney's fees. That will give you a good idea of what the lender's minimum bid for the house will be at the foreclosure sale. It tells the balance that must be dealt with if the home is purchased directly from the owner.

On the other hand, a house with zero or negative equity, which is the most common situation for foreclosure properties, is not a good buy. It won't sell without cash assistance from some source, so the owners are walking off because they either cannot or will not make the loan payments. Such homes are usually of no interest to an investor.

Some foreclosure reports publish information about what homes sold for at the last public foreclosure sale. These REO (Real Estate Owned) reports show homes that were bought by the same lender that undertook the foreclosure. This information can be highly useful in tracking foreclosures as they move into subsequent resale. Some services also provide trustee lists, including phone numbers, for the more common trustees. They also provide lienholder lists with the names of lenders who are foreclosing. Any serious foreclosure investor should subscribe to such reports.

Evaluating the Property and the Deal

Review the risks.   Basically, risks should be dealt with effectively by good research. The buyer should check title, inspect the property, appraise its marketability and weigh the risks involved, such as bankruptcy. The buyer should cull a list of properties and be ready to move.

Look for high returns.   Nothing produces a return quite like buying at the foreclosure sales. It is entirely possible that a house may be purchased for only half of what it is worth. I can recall a property that was listed with a $41,000 original loan figure and a $160,000 tax value. That home could be purchased at the foreclosure sale for less than $41,000 because its loan balance would have been paid down. The returns can be so high that many investors target a 100 percent return. This sharply limits the number of properties that will be evaluated, but a safety margin may be needed. Smaller returns are open to question, given the risks.

Map out a target list.   The astute investor knows he or she can't buy everything. A careful list is needed. Possibly it may consist of properties in the area the investor knows best or lives in. Remember that many, many of the properties will be taken off the market before the foreclosure.

Properties disappear before they are sold.   The market is competitive. Foreclosure investors who deal directly with owners may reach them and deal with them before anyone else can. Even properties that are not picked off by an investor before the sale can be withdrawn. Many settle or reach a workout when the borrower comes up with the back payments due. The VA often fails to turn in its bids. VA homes are often pulled from the foreclosure sale "by the handful," according to one attorney who has handled thousands of foreclosures. The trustee may discover that he or she needed to file an IRS notice. To be safe, the trustee pulls the house from foreclosure and reposts it for sale the month after next. Possibly the lender was just trying a scare tactic. A third or more of the properties posted may disappear before they are sold. Even more of the good, high-equity properties seem to disappear.

Keep track of matters.   It does no good to get one's hopes up for a house that will disappear before the sale. Persistent efforts to call the homeowner and the trustee prior to sale may help the buyer pare down a list for purchases at the last minute before foreclosure or at the foreclosure sale itself. Many houses settle the day before foreclosure; the borrower comes in with enough money to convince the lender to stop the foreclosure. The day of the foreclosure sees the filing of bankruptcies and court orders to stop foreclosure (called temporary restraining orders or TROs), which knock out a certain percentage of houses.

BUYING AT THE FORECLOSURE

Some buyers prefer to buy at the actual foreclosure sale. The investor is in no way taking advantage of the borrower's misfortune in such circumstances, because at a courthouse sale, either the lender or the investor will get the house. However, there are some disadvantages as well as advantages to this approach.

At the Foreclosure Sale, Cash Means Cash

The buyer at the foreclosure sale in most states must bring cash. Probably it is best to bring a stack of cashier's checks in varying denominations. The cashier's checks can be in denominations of $20,000, $10,000, $5,000 and $1,000 amounts. A roll of one hundred dollar bills allows the bidder to make the small change. The cost of buying so many cashier's checks is a problem. They have to be purchased each month unless their interest income is to be foregone. The investor should allow time to get them from the bank before the foreclosure sale.

Many trustees will allow the bidder to pay for the house with one large cashier's check that is well over the amount of the bid, and then they will subsequently refund the difference. This may leave one short for another purchase, however. Also, it is critical to obtain a receipt in such circumstances. Many trustees or their assistants will write out a receipt on the spot. If they don't volunteer one, the bidder should ask for one and create it if necessary. One of the best ways to do this is to have each check photocopied and have the trustee or the assistant sign each copy. Make a note of the property on the photocopy. This makes a very effective receipt. The actual cashier's check must be endorsed to the trustee on the back.

Spotting the Trustee and Bidding

Spotting the trustee is a valuable art that takes time to acquire. Some states require trustees to be visible and to identify themselves clearly, or even organize a courthouse auction so that homes are sold one at a time. In other states, chaos reigns supreme and locating the trustee is critical. Trustees tend to stand in certain spots and to sell at certain times. It may take many visits to learn who they are and how they operate. It may even be necessary to make appointments to see trustees, just to learn what they look like. Experience is about the only hope on this front. The trustee must be spotted and then the investor buyer must wait and listen carefully until the desired property is offered for sale. Then the investor must outbid anyone else who is there.

The best bet is to know what the house or property is worth so well that a maximum figure has been calculated. Do not bid above it. A trustee or the trustee's assistant who will talk to you before the foreclosure offers begin may be able to tell you whether the property is available for sale, the minimum bid that the lender will accept and the maximum bid that the lender will make. That can save some time and trouble. Listen carefully and try to look at the list. Be patient. It may take a while.

After the Bid

The successful bidder at the foreclosure sale can look forward to a trustee's deed. This is seldom delivered the day of the foreclosure; most often, it is delivered the day after. Sometimes the trustee will arrange for the buyer to pick up a key. Possession therefore may be delivered even more promptly than the trustee's deed.

Misplaced Glamour

Although buyers at the foreclosure sale appear to be making a killing, and sometimes they do, it is not a good game for most people. Many people come, buy once, discover there are more problems than they imagined and never return again. Often, they never realize the targeted profits they anticipated because the property they bought had unexpected structural problems, the resale was too slow or they wound up with a house in the bankruptcy court. Generally, it takes a lot of time, a lot of effort and a lot of skill to buy this way. By the time that kind of investment is made, the profit may be gold that no longer glitters.

THE RISKS YOU CAN CONTROL

Mountain climbers categorize the hazards they face in climbing a mountain as being objective or subjective. The objective hazards are known, and action can be taken to prevent them from causing problems. Subjective hazards exist, the nature of which may not be known, and for which effective preventive action may not be possible. Foreclosure purchases are characterized by both types of hazards. The objective risks are described in this section.

Failure to check the title before purchasing at a foreclosure imposes serious risks. Here are the three major ones:

1. The buyer could purchase unknowingly from a second or third lienholder, rather than the first lienholder, leaving the buyer stuck with paying the first lien.
2. The old owner may have IRS liens that are too large to be paid off without losing much of the profit on the purchase and may cause the loss of title.
3. The property title may have been deficient to begin with.

Purchasing from a Second, Third or Later Lien

A lien that is recorded earlier than any other lien is a first lien. However, later liens can be recorded, despite the existence of a first lien. A buyer who buys from the foreclosure sale of a second or later lien runs the risk of losing the property if any of the earlier lienholders forecloses. Often, the first lien on a house is the lien for the loan the buyer bought the house with. A second or later lien may be added for improvements, such as a pool or repairs. If the first lienholder forecloses, the later lien is destroyed. So a purchase from a first lien foreclosure is relatively safe. However, a second lien foreclosure will not destroy the existence of the first lien. This means the buyer from the foreclosure of a second lien must make the payments on the first lien loan, or else it will go into default and foreclose, which destroys any ownership rights the buyer at the second lien foreclosure had. That buyer receives no reimbursement if this happens. He or she has simply lost out.

There is the horror story told of a particular trustee who sold a property in the morning to a hapless buyer by foreclosing a second lien. That afternoon, the same trustee sold the same property again to another buyer by foreclosing on a first lien. The poor buyer at the morning sale owned the property for only hours before losing it to the afternoon buyer! The morning buyer is not entitled to a return of the money paid. The whole sale is probably legal, although it smacks of fraud.

The astute buyer at the foreclosure will try to learn the priority of the lien he or she is buying from. Some buyers, who have a strong stomach, simply eyeball the foreclosure listings and try to guess which one is a second or later lien. Certain lenders are more likely to be second lien lenders than others. This method can work, but it is hardly foolproof. One mistake could cost someone tens of thousands of dollars. The serious buyer who plays the averages may be willing to take such risks.

At one foreclosure sale, a hot tip circulated about a house that was to be foreclosed on in the afternoon. I ran an emergency title search (you need to be well-funded and know whom to call) and discovered that the lien was an incredible fifth in line. It is little wonder that the loan was so small and the tax value of the property so high! It looked good on paper, but it was a terrible buy. Later liens are often mechanic's liens for unpaid improvements to homes. This may mean the property was in bad physical condition along with having poor title!

A new problem area seems to have come up concerning civic association assessment liens. These liens are being foreclosed on frequently. Often, the managers for the civic association show none of the care that a good lender would show in talking to the owner of the house and trying to work things out before posting the house for sale. In many of these situations, improper notice is given, leaving the foreclosure buyer at risk of losing title to the house after the sale due to improper foreclosure. More important, the first lien loan is generally not destroyed by the civic association foreclosure, so a buyer must pay it, along with the back due civic assessment. These may not be good deals at all.

Even if a person is buying at a supposedly safe first lien sale, a second lienholder could show up and demand payment. Second lienholders have a right to receive payment, if they are present at the foreclosure to claim it. Otherwise they lose out if they wait. This does not always happen, but what a nasty surprise if it does! It is obviously important to know if the lien being foreclosed on is the first and if there are any second liens. However, the trustee may or may not be willing to tell a prospective buyer the priority of the lien that is being foreclosed on. Trustees have no duty to do so. Nor does the lender make any warranties at foreclosure sales. Once again, be sure you know what you are doing before you put cashier's checks into someone's hands to get a title that may be nearly worthless.

IRS Liens against the Property

The borrower who is being foreclosed on may owe the U.S. government $1 million in taxes. This may create a serious lien on a property with a value of $50,000. The IRS is the largest filer of liens in Harris County, commonly filing 800 to 1,000 liens every few weeks. They are diligent and relentless in filing liens against defaulting taxpayers. They have the computers and manpower to get it done, and they do.

Once an IRS lien is filed of record at least 30 days before a foreclosure sale, the foreclosure sale will not affect the validity of a lien. The IRS lien is therefore different from other second or later liens in that it has special rights. The IRS lien, however, converts to a right of redemption after a foreclosure sale (provided the IRS received proper notice), but the right of redemption has a time fuse. If the foreclosure trustee notified the IRS 25 days in advance of the foreclosure (that is 25, not 21, days) about the planned foreclosure, then the IRS lien is effective for only 120 days after the foreclosure sale. During that time, the IRS can foreclose its tax lien on the property. In such circumstances, the foreclosure buyer will get his or her money back, but not the profit expected on the purchase. If the house is worth $90,000 and the investor paid only $40,000 for it at the foreclosure sale, then that investor may recover the $40,000 from the IRS, but the IRS will keep any extra money it gets from its own foreclosure sale to help pay off the back taxes. Then it will discharge the tax lien on the property. The foreclosure investor may lose much if not all of the $50,000 profit.

If the IRS is not told of an impending private foreclosure sale, then the real trouble begins. If the IRS did not receive 25 days' advance notice of a foreclosure, then its tax lien is unaffected by the foreclosure. Any buyer at the private foreclosure sale would then have to live in fear of a subsequent IRS foreclosure on the property for a minimum of six years, at which time the IRS could, within 30 days, elect to renew the lien again. The IRS could move to foreclose at any time during the six years or however long it has the lien.

To be sure this won't happen, the astute foreclosure buyer may ask the trustee for an affidavit that the IRS was properly notified at least 25 days before the foreclosure. That way, the risk is limited to 120 days. Unfortunately, trustees frequently fail to give the IRS proper notice. This is often discovered right before the private foreclosure. If so, the trustee may pass the foreclosure sale, file the notice and then foreclose the next month. However, this sudden yanking of a potential jewel of a property from the foreclosure line-up is distressing in itself, particularly if one's hopes were up about buying the property at a low price.

If the IRS lien on a house is large, most investors will not buy at the loan foreclosure, assuming that they even know about the tax lien. If the IRS lien is small, then the foreclosure buyer could simply pay it off after the private foreclosure sale, but this obviously decreases the investor's profits. Unfortunately, any homeowner who has not been able to make the payments on the house loan is a very good candidate for nonpayment of IRS taxes as well. It is another serious hazard.

Title May Not Be Good To Begin With

Any time a house is sold, whether through foreclosure or by some other means, there is always a risk that the title is not good. The size and strength of the title insurance industry is a monument to our legitimate concerns about the safety of title to real estate. The normal concerns are amplified in a foreclosure sale. Many foreclosure sales take place due to divorce. The foreclosure may be improperly motivated if one spouse tries to foreclose to hurt the other spouse, when only a questionable basis for the foreclosure exists. Foreclosures may take place when a business collapses. There may be numerous abstracts of judgment against the property that is being foreclosed on. If these judgments date back far enough, before the lien that's being foreclosed was recorded, then they are a concern.

Any foreclosure buyer who asks "Isn't title on these homes pretty good?" should not be bidding at a courthouse foreclosure sale. Potential buyers must protect themselves against title problems by learning how to judge title, have it checked or research it themselves before buying. Don't find out about the problems after the fact! Even if the problems are curable, the cure could take months. It could be costly. Remember to be concerned about title enough to be a buyer, and not merely a payer.

Property Condition—A Big Risk

Brokers seem to have favorite expressions to describe foreclosed homes that are in poor condition. One says that they have received the "tire iron treatment." Another describes the wrecked house in terms of "karate chop stuff." The roof may leak, like a waterfall. The foundation may be in two—or more—pieces. The air conditioner may have "sprouted little legs" and vanished. Some subdivisions in some cities have even seen busloads of banking and mortgage insurance executives on tour, looking at foreclosure neighborhoods, making the local neighborhood into the star of a freak show. Hard core courthouse foreclosure homes are not the homes of choice for those who want to buy a neat, dainty place to live in. Homes bought at foreclosures can be some of the worst property condition risks in a down market.

Inspections—Hard To Get

If a buyer plans to buy directly at the foreclosure sale, it may be impossible to get inside the property before the purchase. It is usually possible to drive past the property and inspect it from the outside, which may be termed a *windshield appraisal.* A practiced eye can spot foundation cracks. Sometimes cracks can be seen in the street, which extend through the yard and touch the house. Cracks that appear to open outwardly are particularly dangerous. Damage to the roof is fairly self-evident. Be sure to check the roof, front and back. Loitering is not advisable.

Some investors get out of the car and walk around the house. If this takes place at night, when they know they have no business being on someone else's property (or they are told to leave and do not) then they may be charged with criminal trespass or even be shot. The foreclosure may not have put the homeowner or occupant in a good mood, and some homeowners do keep and bear arms. They may well open fire on the investor. Consider it part of the objective hazards. Nevertheless, some investors do walk around and hop the fence to get into the backyard. Do you feel lucky?

Sometimes an investor will find that the house is abandoned. Then it may be possible to get inside the house and inspect it. However, there are problems. Aside from chance meetings with assorted odd characters, there may be crowds of other investors who are trying to hustle the same deal. At least no eviction will be needed, unless someone moves in after the investor sees the house.

The condition of any property sold at foreclosure is not guaranteed in any way by the trustee. Neither the trustee nor the lender has any obligation to check into the property's condition before taking the money for the house. It is strictly a "buy at your own risk" situation.

Marketability

More than any other single risk, the risk of not being able to resell a property at a good price is regarded as the most serious by the professional foreclosure buyer. This risk is very real. When the market is falling, it may be possible to buy properties fairly easily at foreclosure sales, but it is hard to resell them, even if they are offered at good prices. However, once the market rises, foreclosed homes become harder and harder to buy, and the discounts melt away, but if you get a home, it can be resold readily and for a good profit. I have known some very capable foreclosure buyers who could solve all the other problems, but not the resale problem, so they got out of the business.

In order to know if a property is a good deal, or if it will resell, you must know its true worth. The first problem is the lack of a sound appraisal. The tax appraisal given in the foreclosure lists is suspect because it may be out of date or too high. Some professional foreclosure buyers hire appraisers to appraise the properties they are considering buying.

Recognition of value is not the only factor. One has to consider that costs will be incurred.

1. Resale costs. At least 10 percent of its value on resale will be spent on broker's fees, points and other sales expenses. These costs are frequently overlooked. The most powerful bidder at foreclosure may well be the one who buys a house to live in, because that buyer won't have to contend with this cost.
2. Fix-up costs. It costs money to repair the roof, fix the driveway, install a new air-conditioner, and all the other things needed to resell the property. Money must be allocated for this purpose. It may ruin one's profit if unexpected costs appear.
3. Holding costs. Assuming that the property can be fixed up and resold, there is no telling when this will happen. A margin may be needed so that a generous price cut can ensure a quick resale. Even then, the repairs may take an unexpectedly long time, as can sales. The property could always wind up in bankruptcy, with a long delay in recovering one's investment, minus its profit.

HAZARDS YOU CAN'T DO MUCH ABOUT

The Durrett Problem

One of the most serious risks involved in buying foreclosure properties directly at the foreclosure sale is the potential problem a future bankruptcy may cause. If the debtor who is losing a house files a bankruptcy after the foreclosure sale, then the investor buyer at the foreclosure sale may lose ownership of the house to the trustee in bankruptcy.

Imagine the following scene. The investor has just bought a house at a foreclosure sale for half of what it was worth on the open market. Subsequently, the debtor receives a knock on the door from a visitor. "Who are you?" asks the investor. "The trustee in bankruptcy" is the reply. "What do you want?" asks the investor. "The house!" is the reply. "Let me explain something to you!" the investor may say. The investor may try to explain that the house was bought and paid for in cash. The investor can even show the bankruptcy trustee a trustee's deed signed by the foreclosure trustee. The investor can show that all state law requirements for a foreclosure sale were complied with. It is all to no avail. The trustee in bankruptcy may nod "yes" to everything the investor says, but nothing will stop the trustee from taking the house. If the bankruptcy trustee wants the house, the investor will lose it.

Months later, after a battle in the bankruptcy court, the investor should be able to recover the money paid for the house, but there will be no interest paid on the money that was tied up in the meantime. Nor will there be reimbursement for the attorney's fees the investor had to pay. The house will be lost to the bankruptcy court. The investor will also lose the terrific profit that was envisioned.

The reason all this could happen is called the Durrett Rule. The Durrett Rule developed from the area of bankruptcy law known as fraudulent transfers. This may require a background explanation on how the bankruptcy process operates.

Fraudulent transfers.   Prior to a bankruptcy, many people attempt to give their assets away to friends, family members or business associates. That way, when they land in the bankruptcy court, there will be no assets to distribute among the creditors, whom the debtor may dislike anyway. A potential bankrupt may look through the records for a last time and conclude that he or she is doomed, financially. With that in mind, the potential bankrupt might give a car away to a son, a truck to a friend and office equipment to a business associate. The courts have developed rules to prevent this unfair practice from happening. A deliberate effort to transfer an asset right before bankruptcy will be held to be an invalid transfer in the bankruptcy court.

Sales are transfers.   As the rules tightened, however, potential bankrupts have become more clever. Suppose the potential bankrupt says "I'm not giving away a thing. This is a sale." But if the car is sold to the son for ten cents on the dollar ($500 for a car worth $5,000) then is this nothing more than a thinly disguised giveaway? The courts treat it so. The cutoff point is 70 percent.

The 70 percent solution.   If an asset is sold before bankruptcy for less than market value, then the transfer may be subsequently invalidated in bankruptcy court. The trustee will demand the return of the asset that was sold too cheaply. The trustee has a strong arm in bankruptcy and may rip assets out of the hands of buyers (even resale buyers) and haul them off to the bankruptcy court. There, the assets can be sold and the proceeds can be distributed among all the creditors on a fair basis. The person who bought the asset from the bankrupt and lost it to the trustee can get the purchase money back, but not the asset itself or the profit.

Unfortunately, there is no longer any safety even at the 70 percent sale level. The Durrett Rule only said that sales at less than 70 percent were presumptively invalid and subject to reversal; it never stated that sales over 70 percent, but less than fair market value were safe. In fact, the Bankruptcy Code and the fraudulent conveyance laws allow any sale at any price less than full fair market value to be invalidated through bankruptcy.

Lawful foreclosure sales may still be fraudulent transfers for bankruptcy purposes.   The rule about fraudulent sales or transfers has been extended to include foreclosure sales as well as ordinary sales. Even though a sale may take place in the context of a legal foreclosure proceeding in accordance with all applicable state laws, the sale may still be invalidated under the Durrett rule. The sale may be invalidated even though it was an arm's-length sale and there was no deliberate plan to defraud creditors.

If a foreclosure sale occurs as much as a year before the defaulting borrower declares bankruptcy, then the sale may be set aside if it was

1. for "less than reasonably equivalent value"; any sale below fair market value is subject to attack, but under the Durrett Rule, any sale at less than 70 percent is presumed to be improper;
2. the borrower "was insolvent or became insolvent as a result of such transfer." Bankruptcy Code, Section 548(a)(2)(A) and 548(a)(2)(B), respectively.

Insolvency is determined under a balance sheet test, which is met if the sum of the debtor's debts is greater than the sums of its assets, at fair valuation, exclusive of property exempted under the Bankruptcy Code or fraudulently transferred.

Hedging one's bets.   Fortunately, Durrett Rule invalidations are not common. However, they are a distinct risk for foreclosure buyers who purchase a significant number of properties for less than 70 percent of fair market value. Sooner or later they will land in the bankruptcy court on one of their purchases.

It may be worth considering factors that would decrease the risks for foreclosure buyers caused by the Durrett Rule. Obviously, any sale at market value is safe, but the investor buyer can't make a profit in such circumstances. If the debtor who is losing the house at foreclosure is highly solvent, then Durrett will not be a problem. If the debtor has declared bankruptcy within the past seven years, then he or she may not declare it again until after the seventh year; so the bankruptcy-based Durrett case would not apply, although a state's fraudulent conveyance law might. If the debtor is already highly insolvent in a very obvious way, then the Durrett Rule does not apply since the foreclosure must precede the insolvency or cause it under Section 548 of the Bankruptcy Code. More expensive homes tend to go into bankruptcy more readily than less expensive ones. Unoccupied homes are much less likely to wind up in bankruptcy than occupied homes, that is, occupied by the borrower who is losing the house.

If a foreclosure sale is undertaken as part of a deliberate effort to put the home's equity out of reach of creditors, then it may be invalidated in bankruptcy, even if it is made for an amount above 70 percent. A trustee may invalidate any sale, including a foreclosure sale, made before bankruptcy with the actual intent to hinder, delay or defraud any creditor of the debtor declaring bankruptcy as stated in Bankruptcy Code, Section 548(a)(1). An investor buyer should beware of second lien foreclosures, divorce foreclosures or any other foreclosure in which the investor might be accused of involvement in any scheme to defraud other creditors.

Redemption Rights

Many states give homeowners a right of redemption, which is the right to buy a house back for a certain time period after a foreclosure sale. This right may be cut off in some states by court action, but in others there is no way to shorten it; it's just fixed by statute.

One possible solution in such states is to negotiate directly with the homeowner and work out an arrangement in which the homeowner quitclaims any rights he or she has to a redemption, in exchange for a little cash. Some states allow this practice, some don't and in others it may depend on the circumstances. Check with a lawyer in your state.

NO DEAL IS A SURE THING

There is no way to get a sure thing in foreclosure sales. Anyone who buys homes directly from owners before foreclosure or at the legal courthouse foreclosure sales must be aware that this is a dangerous game, and the courts in many, many states have so ruled. It is the last stronghold of *caveat emptor*—let the buyer beware.

CONCLUSION

Buying before the foreclosure is probably not practical for the small investor. It takes too much cash and involves too many risks. Problems with title, property condition and, above all, resaleability plague such sales and must be resolved through substantial effort and a little bit of luck. However, for those determined to get the deepest discounts and the most incredible deals, the actual foreclosure sale probably generates the greatest potential profit. But let the buyer beware; high profits involve high risks.

CHAPTER 6

Buying Directly from the Owner before Foreclosure

In most states, the borrower owns a home up until the moment of foreclosure. The game plan for a foreclosure investor is to contact a homeowner with a suitable house just weeks or days before foreclosure, then pay a little cash to the owner, get a deed, bring the payments on the old loan current and then assume the loan, refinance the property, or resell it quickly and pay off the old loan. Any one of these strategies can net a buyer tens of thousands of dollars in equity profit for an investment of only a few thousand dollars or even less. Seminar promoters have made a lot of money advocating this type of deal. It is practical to buy houses just before foreclosure, but some dos and don'ts should be followed.

Seminar promoters offer a grab-bag of strategies for buying before foreclosure. Many of these strategies are only marginally practical, at best, for the small investor or individual buyer. Buying a house from a desperate homeowner right before foreclosure, by assuming payments on the homeowner's existing loan and making up the missed payments, may allow a cash-poor buyer to obtain a house that can be resold for twice the loan balance, sometimes for a few thousand dollars. Such deals are very unusual, and they are risky. The average small investor, however, should be prepared to act if a lucky preforeclosure opportunity comes along. Be able to recognize such a deal and how to deal with it.

When real estate markets in a city fall, foreclosure seminars increase in popularity. For a substantial enrollment fee, the foreclosure seminar experts will tell you how to steal a house. Who could quibble over the price of the seminar when, after all, you'll make far more once you close your first foreclosure purchase? Those seminars usually emphasize the same practices outlined in this chapter, plus a few extras. However, almost every popular foreclosure purchase strategy covered at those seminars is covered in this book as well, along with a realistic assessment of the downside risks and how to manage them. Yes, deals can be had and money can be made from foreclosure purchases, but you have to work at it.

THE CIRCUMSTANCES

Many people are puzzled about why anyone whose home has sufficient equity in it to be of interest to a foreclosure buyer ever got in the foreclosure position at all. If the house is worth something, why didn't the owner sell it before the foreclosure? There are a variety of reasons for this. Some are depressed about a job loss, business failure, or divorce. They are not thinking straight. Some never did. Some keep believing things will get better. It's a sad touch we can't help but be sympathetic about. They thought they would get a job; they kept looking. They didn't find it. They thought they could borrow money or make some quickly. They failed. They kept missing payments. Nothing happened. They heard stories of payments missed for a whole year without foreclosure. It wasn't true for them. They tried to work with the lender, but it didn't work. Somehow they thought things would turn out. They just couldn't bear to put the house on the market and list it with a broker. Now they are hit with the foreclosure notice. They are going to lose the house and it's just too late for a conventional sale using a broker. They'll lose the equity in the home, probably completely, at foreclosure, in addition to getting a very black mark on their credit that will haunt them for years. It all went wrong. We have to look at it from the standpoint of "there, but for the grace...go I." Sadly, it happens.

BETTER TO DEAL

The foreclosure buyer, however, is more like a hero than a villain for buying the house when a borrower is faced with foreclosure. At least once the house is going to be sold at foreclosure, the foreclosure buyer almost always proposes a deal that is better for the homeowner who's about to lose the house than what will happen otherwise: foreclosure with a total loss of all equity and credit damage. If it isn't the foreclosure investor who makes the profit, it will be the lender. Either way, the homeowner loses.

Unfortunately for homeowners who are faced with foreclosure, only a few of the many houses that will be available are good prospective purchases for foreclosure buyers. The key is equity, and the name of the game is to buy a lot of equity for a little money. If a foreclosure investor can buy a house for half its value, it's a very good deal indeed.

Generally, the homeowner whose house has equity is better off dealing with a buyer before the foreclosure sale rather than letting it go on the block at the foreclosure sale. That way the homeowner can get at least a little cash up front and a better sale price on the house, avoid the foreclosure and keep the credit rating stronger. It may be painful in the short run, but it's a big help in the long run. Remember, there is life after losing a house in a down market, and it can be harder or easier, depending on what the homeowner did at the time a foreclosure loomed ahead.

STRATEGIES FOR BUYING
BEFORE FORECLOSURE

Anyone who wants to buy a home can try a variety of strategies before the foreclosure ax falls on a hapless homeowner. It may be possible, albeit infrequently, to buy the house on an assumption arrangement for very little cash. Alternatively, it may be possible to buy the house for a little cash, hold the lender off with a little cash, refinance the house quickly and make a very attractive return. Finally, for the investor who has substantial cash assets, some very good deals may be available.

Assumptions—The Foreclosure Seminar Special

One of the most popular of all the seminar foreclosure strategies is the assumption. Although this is a very good strategy, the circumstances that allow you to pull it off don't occur very often. Even so, if you know how an assumption works, and you see the opportunity to do it, go for it! You can make a killing with a small effort in a matter of weeks, for hardly any cash.

Here's the basic assumption play. First, the homeowner faced with foreclosure must have a special type of loan, one that is assumable without the need to get the lender's permission. In an assumption, the seller will move out, the buyer will move in (or move someone else in as a tenant) and the buyer will take over the seller's old loan payments. The old loan will not be paid off when the assumption buyer buys.

A further refinement is necessary for the best assumption deals to work: the borrower faced with foreclosure should have a *no-approval* loan. Unfortunately, a very great number of mortgages in the United States today have provisions that absolutely prohibit no-approval assumptions. If the loan documents have a due-on-sale clause, then they are not assumable without the lender's permission. Generally, lenders won't give such permission, and if they do, it will only be after making sure that any assumption buyer has lots of steady income and great credit. A few states, however, force lenders to allow assumptions to take place by banning due-on-sale clauses. In most states, the Garn-St. Germain law passed by the Congress has made the due-on-sale clause enforceable. The only states left out of Garn-St. Germain are those such as California that chose to opt out of this federal law at an early stage.

All too often, the only reliable way to determine whether a no-approval assumption can be done with conventional loans is to consult an attorney. A quick call to the lender may provide the same information, but lenders are not always to be trusted in such matters. Generally, if the lender says the loan is assumable without approval, then you can do it. Otherwise, get a copy of the loan papers and check with a lawyer.

A few loans are always assumable without the lender's approval. These are older HUD and VA loans. If the VA or FHA loan originated before a specified date, then it may be assumed in 1993 without the lender's approval. Here's a quick chart:

FHA loan was created—
Pre–December 1, 1986
    no approval assumption is OK in 1993
    approval assumption is also OK
Post–December 1, 1989
    approval assumption only

VA loan was created—
Pre–March 1, 1988
    no approval assumption is OK in 1993
    approval assumption is also OK
Post–March 1, 1988
    approval assumption only

Armed with the date and the type of the loan, we know we can do a no-approval assumption with older FHA and VA loans.

A recent variation on the assumption theme involves refinancing. If the buyer takes over an FHA loan, at least six months pass after the sale and the interest rate on the loan can be reduced through refinancing, then it may be possible for the assumption buyer to obtain refinancing through the FHA's streamline refinance program. Originally targeted to help homebuyers in distress, this program could be adapted to permit lucrative refinancing for a not fully creditworthy buyer, without regular lender approval of the buyer's income and credit and with a full release of the seller from liability when the refinancing is done. See if it works for you.

Unless a state opted out of the federal Garn-St. Germain law, then the due-on-sale clause is found in most conventional mortgages and is enforceable. Only a few non-VA and non-FHA loans are assumable without the lender's approval. These include very old conventional loans, such as those before about 1973, when due-on-sale clauses first began to see widespread use. Second, sales from a divorce or other nonregular lender transactions may be missing the due-on-sale clause, thus becoming assumable by a buyer without the lender's approval. Otherwise, it helps greatly if the loan is an FHA or VA loan.

Putting the Assumption Deal Together

The first move by an investor buyer in an assumption deal is to find someone who has an older FHA or VA loan, and further, is about to lose a home in foreclosure. You can find out whether a home is in foreclosure by examining the public filings for foreclosures with the local county clerk or recorder, or by locating and subscribing to a foreclosure listing service that sells such information to investors, usually for a few hundred dollars per year. If there is no such service, then check with the county clerk or recorder, because notices of an impending foreclosure must be filed in some form of record, in virtually every state. By checking on an individual house or, for a small fee, using the assistance of a title insurance company's computers, it should be possible to locate the date and very probably the type (FHA or VA) of loan for a given homeowner.

Now, once we know that the owner has a no-approval FHA or VA loan, then we approach the homeowner who's about to be foreclosed on, very carefully. You have to talk to the homeowner, and you have to ask for the deal. Until the moment of foreclosure, the borrower is the owner in the great majority of states, and at least has a right to possession until foreclosure in the remaining states. Now, here's the pitch.

The owner is faced with a foreclosure, and you have researched the notices to know that. You can use those notices to remain in contact with a lender or a trustee, and make sure the foreclosure is going forward. All too often, a desperate homeowner finds a friend, a family member or just someone or some way to make the payments current and keep the house out of foreclosure.

You ask the owner, who is faced with foreclosure in a matter of weeks or days, to deed over the title to the house to you, the foreclosure buyer. In return, you'll pay off any outstanding, unpaid loan payments and bring the loan current, thereby stopping the foreclosure. In addition, you may need to offer the homeowner at least a little cash directly, to get the deal together. The homeowner will sign the deed (you may bring a notary public along to notarize it at the homeowner's house), and then you, the buyer, must record it.

Immediately thereafter, you make the delinquent loan payments, and begin making regular payments on your new house. However, you then advertise the house in the newspapers or bring in a broker, and sell the house to a buyer whose credit doesn't have to be approved. It's an easy sale, particularly in a down market when there are a surprisingly large number of buyers without good, loanworthy credit. But wait! The buyer needs to do much more than simply agree to take over the payments from you. You'll ask the purchaser to pay cash for as much of the equity in the house as possible. If you can, sell the house for market value, but otherwise, discount it to attract the cash buyer. Let's look at the numbers, for a possible deal (actually these numbers are based on a real deal that was executed).

Fair market value of home	$80,000
Outstanding FHA loan balance	−35,000
Equity	$45,000

The foreclosure investor took over the FHA loan balance, paid all payments current and gave a little cash to the former owner.

Cash to make up missed payments	$1,800
Cash to the old owner	+ 1,000
Cash required to make the deal	$2,800

The foreclosure investor obtained an appraisal to verify the value of the property and advertised it in the newspapers for about two weeks at 20 percent less than its fair market value, thereby receiving dozens of calls from interested buyers, who had sufficient cash to buy.

Appraised fair market value	$80,000
20% discount to cash buyer	− 16,000
Asking price	$64,000
consisting of	$34,000 in cash
	$30,000 assumption balance

The buyer was willing to pay the costs of the closing, which aren't much in a no-approval assumption. So now let's look at the profit:

$34,000	cash
− 2,800	cash invested
$31,800	
− 600	(appraisal + ads)
$31,200	net profit

The transaction took about four weeks. No wonder this strategy sells a lot of seminars!!

Caution: In some states the deal described above may be illegal. It could be considered taking unconscionable advantage of a person in foreclosure, which may not be allowed. It is highly advisable to consult an attorney in a particular state before attempting a similar deal.

All FHA and VA loans are assumable on an approval basis, even the newer ones. Better still, neither the property condition, nor the appraised value of the property has to meet with the lender's approval to do a full approval assumption. Only the assuming buyer's credit and income has to be approved, and even then, only by the regular FHA and VA loan approval criteria without any added requirements in the assumption situation. The buyer's assumption of the loan would have to be approved fairly quickly, however, to reliably stop the foreclosure. However, help may be at hand from the local FHA or VA field office in the area, either one of which may encourage the private lender to back off from a foreclosure for enough time to do a deal. You'll be off the hook on the loan as soon as a new buyer is found.

The big drawback to the assumption strategy is that it is hard to find such properties. In a very down market, opportunities arise more frequently, but they are still hard enough to find, particularly for the homes in good condition with plenty of equity. Even when they can be found, the streets may be lined with limousines disgorging potential investors who want to hustle a deal with the homeowner. They may have just finished a seminar on foreclosures. They may have more cash, and less sense, and pay a hefty price for a big risk in the hope of making a good profit. But if you ever find one of these deals, it can make you a bundle.

Buy the House First, Work with the Lender Later

Another strategy for buying homes before the foreclosure involves getting a deed from the homeowner, then making up the delinquent payments to stop the foreclosure and finally making arrangements with a new lender, or the old one, to refinance the old loan. It is best if the old lender is willing to cooperate. If not, then the transaction may well be illegal if the delivery of the deed triggers a due-on-sale clause in the mortgage, or it could fail if the lender refuses to reinstate the loan simply with a few missing payments (some lenders will accelerate the payment schedule and make the entire loan balance due before the foreclosure).

One ruthless seminar promoter even encouraged investors to get a deed from a foreclosure owner for a very few dollars, if any, then throw the deed in the trash and walk out if the lender won't deal with the investor on reinstatement or sale of the property, or wait long enough for refinancing through a new lender. In any case, the buyer in such situations must be very careful not to sign anything that could make him or her liable to repay the old owner's loan, until the transaction is completed, preferably with a new lender on a refinancing basis.

Of course, with refinancing, the house could be held for a long time, particularly if the investor lives in it. If the investor wants to rent it out, financing may be hard to arrange, especially in a down market. One extra trick might be to line up a buyer on an earnest money contract for a subsequent resale. If that can be done, the old lender may become a believer and will be more willing to work with the investor.

THE MORE CASH, THE BETTER

The deals outlined above could be put together with only a little bit of cash. However, if more cash is available, then more deals are possible, and in a down market, cash talks. For the homeowner faced with foreclosure, cash could pay bills, take care of moving expenses and put a roof over one's head for a few more months. Generally, the foreclosure investor will offer the homeowner cash to sign, cash to clean up and cash to move out. It is generally inadvisable to pay all the cash up front.

Opinions differ on how to use cash. One school of thought holds that as little cash should be used as possible—just enough to get the deal going. There are too many uncertainties already to risk significant amounts of cash. Perhaps as little as a $100 each to sign, clean and move is enough. The other school of thought holds that in a competitive market, cash talks. Use enough money to get the deal and beat the competition. Cash may keep the owner out of bankruptcy. Cash will open the door and make the deal work.

The basic strategy is to pay off the homeowner's loan balance in full. An old loan balance may be small enough that it can be paid off directly, which will stop the foreclosure either by law or in practice, because most lenders will stop a foreclosure for a full payoff of the whole loan. However, the lender may not be willing to accept the back-due payments alone. A cash-rich investor may find it more expedient to pay the loan off and worry about resale and refinancing later.

Winning Strategies for Investors with Cash

If an investor buyer has cash, the range of deals that are open is wide, but remember, cash must earn a return that equals current interest rates at a minimum, and once put at risk, a premium profit is needed to justify the investment. However, some buyers want to make deals but may not have that much cash readily available. In that case, several possibilities exist to get cash. First, the investor could get cash if a suitable deal can be located and locked in, possibly through the use of an earnest money contract with a homeowner who is about to be foreclosed on. A higher offer might get the contract and beat the pure cash operator's offer, which would be lower. Second, if you have enough cash to do a deal, but cannot hold it in the property for an extended period of time, or you need to make an existing pool of cash last longer and work harder, then consider locating a good foreclosure deal, then line up a buyer who plans to buy with a regular loan. That buyer doesn't have the cash to do the deal, but you do. Have that buyer prequalified through a lender, and get a letter pre-approving the buyer for a loan up to a certain dollar figure for a limited time. Then use your own cash to buy the property, and then lock in the buyer immediately with an earnest money contract committing your prequalified buyer to buy. Close the deal in a few weeks and your cash is back in action. However, be careful about the Durrett Rule, explained in the last chapter, which may cause a delay of up to a year before a regular resale can be completed, and also beware of any redemption laws in the state. A final thought is to use your money as risk cash, but find other investors to tie up cash for longer periods once you've found a good deal. Give them a cut of the profit, but keep plenty for yourself. Your co-investors get a good deal at a lower risk; you get a very good deal at a higher risk.

DEAL WITH THE OWNER
BEFORE FORECLOSURE

Speed is essential in this game. Sometimes the potential foreclosure investors who play this end of the business will virtually line a block with Germany's best cars. They are all out to arrange a deal with the homeowner, who may or may not be cooperative.

The Uncooperative Homeowner

Some homeowners will not do business with a foreclosure buyer. I know one broker who counted 35 doors slammed in her face before she gave up. Foreclosure investors may be greeted with obscenities and cries of "vulture" by irate residents. Some of them feel that they have better things to do than trying to sell their home to someone who wants to buy it for half of what it's worth. Most of them have taken a beating from creditors, and they are good at slamming doors. The impending foreclosure has not left them in a good mood. After all, where are they going to live next month? The foreclosure investor must take it all in stride.

Methods of Reaching the Homeowner

Some people specialize in getting through doors. One of the best I know tries to create a friendly, low-cost image. He recommends driving an inexpensive car rather than a luxury car. A Toyota or a Volkswagen may work well. A person who is about to lose his or her house may react with a "what a shark!" attitude toward an investor who drives a fancy limousine, wears a three-piece, pin-striped suit and puffs a fat cigar. On the other hand, the youthful "cute kid" with the low-cost car, the loose Izod and the track sneakers may create a better image. If the owner is going to lose the house, it might as well be to someone who is likable. My friend was in his early twenties, had a 50 ampere smile and radiated a boyish demeanor. Moreover, he showed up at the door with a thick stack of bills, which he thumbed through in front of the peephole to make the owners open the door and talk. They did. Of course, this approach is a little dangerous if there are muggers around.

Other investors try a fast push approach. They talk fast on the phone. They talk fast at the door. They virtually push the door open.

They don't even admit to the possibility that the house is not for sale. They just push until they get the papers signed. The worst method of reaching the homeowner I have ever heard of involved paying a child to take a note to Mommy or Daddy in the house. That's disgusting.

Hanging in Until the Last Minute

Sometimes an owner will talk to everyone but sign with no one, hoping for a better deal. Eventually, the investors give up and go away. A buyer who calls back shortly before the foreclosure may have some luck. Another problem is that efforts to stop the foreclosure may finally fail a day or two before the foreclosure. At that point, a favorable deal could be made by an investor who has stayed in contact with the owner. Sometimes people who plan on buying at the foreclosure sale even arrange a purchase with an owner who was called only about the status of the workout efforts, only to discover those attempts have not only failed, but the owner is now ready to deal.

CONCLUSION

Buying directly from the owner before foreclosure has many advantages. It may be possible to get the house before any competitors or at least to view the house beforehand. It may be possible to assume an existing FHA, VA or pre-1972 conventional loan, without triggering the lender's foreclosure, and if so, it drastically reduces the cash that may be required to buy such homes. Houses can be spotted by subscribing to foreclosure data services, but plenty of skilled negotiating must be done to get a house. There are also plenty of risks from the bankruptcy courts and other sources. However, a small investor who can repair a house or get it rented out may well have an advantage in price bidding and controlling fix-up costs over any other investor. This type of buyer can make some very favorable transactions.

CHAPTER 7

Buying Distressed Sale Properties

Not all foreclosures are done by lenders. Specialized foreclosures are done by the IRS and property tax officials or result from court-ordered judgments that may have nothing to do with nonpayment of a loan. Certain life events such as divorce cases, probate proceedings or bankruptcy can also create an unusual forced sale that closely resembles a foreclosure sale. These specialized sales take time to master, but for those who do learn them and learn them well, there are some nice dividends to be earned. Not everybody takes an interest in these sales, but that's why they are a good source of good deals for those who do.

Most foreclosures occur because a borrower cannot keep up the payments on a mortgage. However, other types of foreclosures can occur, but they account for only a small portion of all foreclosure sales. Unfortunately, buying distressed sale properties is better suited for an investor with a lot of cash than for a buyer who simply wants a good price on a new home. However, in some circumstances a fairly ordinary homebuyer can get a good deal through distressed sales, without having a bank vault of cash in hand.

CONSTABLE AND SHERIFF SALES

Although in some jurisdictions, the mortgage foreclosure sale is conducted by a constable or a sheriff, such official sales are usually done for other reasons, in particular, the loss of a lawsuit. The end result of a lawsuit is a judgment, that is, a document prepared by the winning side and signed by the judge that states how much money the winning side is owed. However, as one judge put it: "Winning the judgment is only half the battle; collecting it is the other half." Enforcement of a court judgment is done through a variety of writs and procedures. The easiest is to have the court clerk's office prepare an *abstract of judgment* or AJ, which is recorded in the real property records. The AJ shows an unpaid judgment. Title companies will generally not insure clear title to a buyer unless an AJ is cleared and a release is filed.

Once a judgment has been won at trial, then written up and signed by the judge, it can be enforced. Usually this is done by a separate order, such as a *writ of execution* or *order of sale*. Once these orders or writs are issued, the sheriff or constable will give notice of a sale and then conduct the sale for the public. Unfortunately, most of these sales are for cash to the highest bidder and therefore are of limited interest to a typical homebuyer. However, sometimes the properties are priced so low that they can be within reach of a homebuyer with some cash. Also, judgment sales may be for second or third liens, or mechanic's liens, and the sums may allow ownership of the property to be obtained at a small price, but then a first or prior lien (or more than one) will have to be dealt with. If prior negotiations have occurred, then it may be possible to reinstate the earlier loans and thus acquire a property at a bargain price.

PROPERTY TAX SALES

Property tax sales are usually conducted in the same manner as judgment sales. However, in some states an interested person can simply go to the tax assessor's office, pay the delinquent taxes on a property and acquire title. Most states do not allow this practice. Instead, they call for a public sale to the highest bidder, usually conducted by a sheriff or constable after notices are posted, published and mailed.

LIFE EVENT SALES

A variety of life events can trigger sales under pressure. Although these sales are not necessarily conducted under court order through law enforcement officers, they may nevertheless be forced sales for the persons involved. It may be possible for an outside buyer to get an exceptional deal on a valuable piece of property. Sales due to divorce, probate or bankruptcy deserve some consideration.

Divorce Sales

One of the most frequent causes of foreclosure and one of the most common motivators for sales in general is divorce. When a marriage breaks up in this age of two-income families, there may not be enough income for either spouse to keep up mortgage payments. In a divorce, a couple may be under heavy pressure to sell the house. The attorneys often push a sale, particularly when there's equity in the house, as a means of generating cash with which to settle the financial disputes and pay the attorney's fees. A divorce lawyer can be a real estate investor's best friend by providing useful tips about property to buy, but check the properties over first. An interested buyer may also be able to consult the local court dockets through the court clerk's office to determine who is in the midst of a divorce. The divorce paperwork may well spell out where and what the house is. A timely offer to buy the house may net a good deal. It may be possible to bypass a brokerage fee and increase the cash generated by the sale, from the divorce litigant's perspective. As a result, the divorcing parties may sell for less.

Alternatively, some brokers are good at finding divorce-motivated sellers. Unfortunately, many divorce sellers require cash. Plan ahead and be pre-approved for a loan before going after such a house. Armed with a lender's pre-approval, it may be possible to beat other bidders, even if they're higher, because they will be slower to buy than a pre-approved buyer. Pay some cash and see if you can't get an exceptional price. Remember, the parties are under pressure to sell, at any price. They'll give up some equity to a buyer in such situations.

Probate

A set of circumstances similar to those in a divorce can also apply when a person dies. Payments can no longer be made. While most state probate laws are set up to delay foreclosure, they also provide procedures by which foreclosure can be accomplished in the courts. Find a situation in which a person has died and the family needs to sell the house to pay the costs of the probate, among other expenses. However, in some states the probate court orders an *appraisement* to find the home's market value and will not permit it to be sold for less.

Purchasing through probate will probably require a great deal of patience. It can take a long time to push the necessary papers through the probate courts and their clerks. However, if a state has an *independent administration* in which direct court supervision is not needed for dealing with estates, the sale may be fairly rapid, but the executor in such situations is much better able to sell the property at close to fair market value.

Obituary pages, macabre as it may sound, provide an excellent preliminary list of possible estates. Watch the court dockets, and offer to buy at an appropriate time. Like divorces, probate situations can offer attractive opportunities to buy property.

Bankruptcy

Bankruptcy may cause property held by the debtor to be sold to pay off debts. However, this is mostly controlled by the bankruptcy court and bankruptcy trustees. Get to know bankruptcy attorneys; they know of cases where real property must be sold. However, sales at substantially below fair market value should be few and far between if the persons involved in the bankruptcy are at all astute.

However, bankruptcy information is readily available. It is possible to get a complete listing of a bankrupt debtor's assets, including real estate, and the values assigned to each property, along with any outstanding balances and the names of creditors who hold liens. Just go down to the federal bankruptcy courts for the area, and there will normally be an office with bankruptcy files that any interested member of the public can inspect. It's easy to scout out good properties this way.

OTHER TROUBLE

Homebuilder Sales

When homebuilders start to go bust, they may be very eager to sell off existing housing inventories. Sometimes homebuilders help arrange financing for the homes they sell. If down market conditions develop in the area, then homebuilders may get some of the homes they sold back, particularly if they're involved in the financing through in-house mortgage companies or company resources. If so, then the homebuilder who reacquires the property must sell it again, usually soon, and often at a discount.

Distressed homebuilder sales can be very good deals, partly because of the possible seller financing. Better still, if the property needs work, the homebuilder is normally in a very good position to get good repairs done at a low price on houses the builder constructed to begin with. Often, foreclosure resale efforts by homebuilders are directed at ordinary homebuyers, rather than cash-heavy investors who won't pay quite as much. Even so, the ordinary homebuyer can often get a property for a very good price from the distressed homebuilder, who may almost be desperate for cash.

Environmental Clean-up Projects

Another strange distressed property deal involves buying a home with an environmental problem. Sometimes lenders are in no hurry to acquire such properties, even if the borrower is in default. If the environmental problem can be cured, then a foreclosure investor may see an opportunity to make some money.

The game plan would be to buy a house that has been priced artificially low due to the environmental problems it suffers from, such as asbestos, lead paint, radon or formaldehyde odor. Asbestos is now less costly to remove than it used to be. The problem is that asbestos removal workers must comply with NESHAP (National Emission Standards for Hazardous Air Pollutants) removal regulations, which includes wearing paper suits and glass bubble helmets, so they look just like astronauts. Some removal contractors will even remove the asbestos for a set price and take a percentage on any profit of resale.

Here's the plan. Once the investor spots a house that is selling for too little because of an environmental problem, then he or she lines up contractors and cash to buy the property. If the property can be obtained through purchase at a foreclosure sale, then it may be possible to remove the asbestos for a nominal cost and retenantize the property, causing its value to shoot up.

Buying from Troubled Companies

Another possibility is to buy company stock as a means of controlling land, rather than the land or house itself. Such entities may be set up as limited partnerships, limited liability partnerships (in some states), or corporations. Such business organizations have ownership interests that can be bought and sold.

If the homebuilder goes through a troubled period economically, then it may be possible to purchase not so much the land itself but the company's stock or ownership interests. Once a buyer controls a corporation, particularly a small individual corporation that just holds legal title to one property for the benefit of an investor, then an outsider who can acquire stock in that company can gain effective control of an asset.

The game plan is buy stock or bonds with the intent of becoming the legal owner or the holder of valuable lien rights. The market value of a stock in a corporation that is known to be in trouble may be very low. If the corporation owns valuable land, then it may be possible to buy effective control of that land for a fraction of the price that it would be available at otherwise.

Even an ordinary homebuyer could purchase a house by buying up limited partnership rights or corporate rights. Some of the owners of real estate limited partnerships or corporations in a down market are very hard pressed to keep up mortgage payments on all properties held. If an individual property has its own corporation or limited partnership, the owners might be willing to sell at a very reduced price. Such assets could also be purchased in a bankruptcy, probate or divorce sale. This option may be too problematical for the ordinary homebuyer, but it might provide a vehicle to buy effective control of real estate for a fraction of its true value.

IRS TAX SALES

The Internal Revenue Service can obtain real estate and resell it in at least two ways. First, it can simply seize property for nonpayment of taxes and sell it. This practice is termed *seizure and sale*. The second way occurs when the IRS redeems property after a lender or other lienholder has foreclosed on it. If the IRS held a lien on the property, then it may take title to the property sold at a non-IRS foreclosure from whoever bought it, at the foreclosure sale price. If the IRS was properly notified, then it has only 120 days to take title; otherwise, it has six years and 30 days!

The IRS handles the sales of property it seizes. It uses revenue agents rather than real estate brokers to market its properties. The manner of sale is prescribed by law. First, notice must be given, then a sale must be conducted, by either sealed bid or public auction.

Notice of the Sale

As soon as practical after the seizure of property, the IRS shall cause a notice of sale to be published in "some newspaper" that is generally circulated within the county where the seizure was made. The notice must specify the time, place, manner and circumstances of the sale. It must also specify that the sale is only of the "right, title and interest" the taxpayer had in the property. By law, these notices must appear 10 to 40 days prior to the actual sale. Look in the legal notices section of your local newspaper: they are not carried in the commercial foreclosure listing services. They must be researched from the local newspapers. There are other ways of finding out about IRS sales, however.

The IRS usually assigns a property to a revenue agent who takes charge of the sale. To help market properties, the IRS keeps lists of frequent bidders or likely bidders and an alert revenue agent will call people on the list. It is a startling experience to see a phone message from an IRS revenue agent who works in the collections department! Actually, these agents are quite friendly and will make a brief sales pitch about the house they are trying to sell. They may give the price any broker has listed the property for before the IRS seizure. They may have a comparable property sale in the area to talk about. They often have the property tax value for the real estate. They can also tell a prospective bidder whether the home is occupied or not. Upon request, they may try to arrange a tour of the house for one or more prospective bidders, although if the house is occupied, they need the permission of the owner. The key to being on the IRS phone list is to be a regular bidder or look like one.

It is possible to go to the IRS office and take a look at a list of properties that will be sold in the near future. Anyone who wants to buy regularly should ask to be put on the IRS list of prospective bidders. It would be invaluable to find out the name of the revenue agent for the property and give him or her a call before the sale. If you call early, the IRS may be able to arrange a visit, particularly if the property is vacant. At the very least, it is highly advisable for any prospective buyer to at least drive by the property before bidding on it.

Sealed Bid

If the IRS sells by a sealed bid, it will normally set a minimum bid, but keep that figure secret until all the bids are turned in. The IRS will mail a bid form to anyone who requests one. The bidder must remit the greater of $200 or 20 percent of the highest bid figure submitted. Bidders may bid on more than one house. The bids must be turned in by means of a securely sealed envelope. They will be opened publicly at the time, place and manner set by the public notice of the sale. The winner will be announced by the revenue officer who conducts the sale. The officer may then demand full payment of the purchase price by cash or cashier's check. However, the IRS may defer full payment of the purchase price to a later time. If it is not paid, the IRS can institute a suit to recover the price or declare the sale to be null and void and any monies already paid will be forfeited.

Public Auction

The revenue agent handling the sale may decide to hold the public auction either at the IRS office or on the site of the house. All the bidders can come and "hold up their popsicle sticks" to identify one bidder from the next, as one revenue officer put it. If the IRS sells by auction, then the minimum bid will usually be announced in advance of the sale. There are several possible outcomes:

1. The property will sell at or above the minimum bid to the highest bidder.
2. The sale will be adjourned to a later date, but not later than one month after the date set in the original notice.
3. The property will be "declared purchased at such price for the United States," which is the minimum bid.

If there are no offers at or above the minimum bid, and the United States does not want it, then the property may be released to the taxpayer, but the costs of the attempted sale will be added to the unpaid taxes.

The minimum bid.   By law, the IRS must set a minimum bid for property. Actually, the first and most important determination the IRS makes is whether to seize the property at all. If the IRS is seizing the property, it has probably determined a minimum bid already. The revenue officer who has been assigned to sell a particular property will usually help develop the minimum price for the property, which will be based on a variety of factors. First, the IRS will look for any existing liens on the property that are older than the IRS lien. Second, the minimum bid must cover the costs of sale. Third, the minimum bid should be high enough to pay some of the taxes the taxpayer owes. Anything over that is gravy to the seizure buyer. However, unless seizure buyers can make a significant profit, the IRS knows they won't buy. Therefore, the minimum bid will probably be significantly below the market value.

However, there are some limitations on how low the IRS sales price will go. A sale for only 5 percent of the market value on a home was ruled to be an invalid sale in the case of *Ringer v. Basile.*

High bid.   The high bid wins the house. The IRS has the right to payment on the spot, by cash, cashier's check or treasurer's check.

Sale Documents

The IRS uses two documents in its sales of real estate:

1. Certificate of sale—issued upon full payment
2. Deed to real property—issued 180 days after sale

The winning bidder will be issued a *certificate of sale* when the full bid amount is received by the IRS. The certificate is good evidence for the IRS's right to make the sale and conclusive evidence of the regularity of the sales procedures. For the first six months after the sale, the high bid winner does not really own the house. During that time, the defaulting taxpayer still has the right to redeem the house. However, 180 days after the sale, the IRS will issue a deed to the high bidder and promptly record it. Once the deed is issued, prior liens are cut off. Whatever rights, title and interest the taxpayer had now pass to the winning bidder.

The Condition of Title and of the Property

The IRS regulations say it best. When the IRS sells real estate, it sells only the right, title and interest of the delinquent taxpayer in and to the property seized. There may be prior outstanding mortgages, encumbrances or other liens. If these existed before the tax lien, then they are valid after the IRS seizes and sells the property. All seized property is offered by the IRS on as as is and where is basis and without any recourse against the United States. Once the hammer falls at the auction, the high bidder is responsible for the real estate, even though he or she does not yet have possession! According to IRS regulations: "No guaranty or warranty, express or implied, shall be made by an internal revenue officer offering the property for sale" as to the validity of title, size, condition or fitness of the property for any particular use. The high bidder may not rescind the sale or reduce the bid price once problems with the property are discovered after the sale. It is extremely difficult to sue the government. They are immune from suits under state law theories. It is one of the last strongholds of the old maxim: "Let the buyer beware."

Right of Redemption

For 180 days after the sale of real estate seized by the IRS, the defaulting taxpayer (or other people having an interest in the property) can recover full ownership of the property by paying the high bidder the amount of the high bid, plus 20 percent per year interest.

The right of redemption generates some potential problems for high bidders. A high bidder who pays off an expensive lien runs the risk that the original defaulting taxpayer may redeem the property, for which the lien is now paid off.

Please note the broad range of potential claimants under the right of redemption statute. It includes more than just the owner. In fact, a lienholder would have the right to redeem the property by repaying the high bidder plus 20 percent interest. This has led to an occasional horror story. What happens if a person, perhaps even one's own neighboring bidder at the seizure sale, buys up a junior lien, and waits until after the sale to redeem? Or alternatively, suppose the interloper buys up the rights to a pre-existing lien and forecloses it after the IRS seizure sale. Notice would go to the "last known address of the debtor as reflected in the records of the lender." A seizure buyer might not get any notice of the foreclosure, which could take place at a very reduced price. Nothing really prevents this. As a result, a wise high bidder at an IRS seizure sale may try to contact the defaulting taxpayers and arrange to have them quitclaim their interest in the property after the sale. Likewise, the high bidder will have to pay off existing lienholders or otherwise neutralize them. A title check is highly advisable.

As a strict matter, the IRS lien cannot be assigned; therefore, it may be difficult to assign a right of redemption. Investors who buy property at an IRS foreclosure sale are always at risk of losing it if the original taxpayer redeems it.

CONCLUSION

A variety of methods are available for buying properties that are about to be foreclosed on due to legal troubles from divorce, probate or bankruptcy. Unfortunate life events are a good source of sales to investors, who may find that one person's loss is another's gain. However, such an environment places a premium on the ability of the buyer to learn quickly and master complex procedures.

Property tax and IRS sales are another source of distressed property sales outside the normal foreclosure channels. Property tax sales are often slow in coming, but a buyer must be quick to profit from an IRS foreclosure sale. Buying foreclosures that occur due to unusual events is one way to distance yourself from other buyers of foreclosed homes. It requires time, patience and effort to learn how to buy at distressed property sales, but once learned, the benefits are considerable.

CHAPTER 8

Buying from
Lenders

Most foreclosure sales are made to lenders. However, upon obtaining a house from a foreclosure, the lender normally turns around and offers the property for sale to interested buyers. Sometimes the houses are sold directly by bank, S&L or mortgage company personnel. At other times, they are sold by outside brokers. Any way you look at it, these are the most common of all foreclosure sales and the easiest at which to buy. With enough looking and a little bit of luck, it's possible to buy a house at a very good price.

REO DEFINED

Of all the foreclosed properties that any investor can buy in a down market, and even more so in a normal market, the most common is the REO, which stands for *Real Estate Owned*. A similar term is OREO, or *Other Real Estate Owned*. Either way, REO properties have been acquired by a lender from foreclosure. They are the repossessions or repos of the real estate world. Most often, REOs are owned by savings and loan associations. In the past, S&Ls were the largest lenders in the residential field. The term REO probably comes from the way real estate appears on the balance sheet for an S&L, under the category of "real estate owned." Since assets on a balance sheet are ranked in order of liquidity, REOs generally come in toward the bottom of the list, meaning that they are hard to get rid of. During the S&L crisis, many financial institutions throughout the country acquired title to foreclosure REOs.

Types of REO Properties

Typically, an S&L holds several varieties of REO properties. The first group would be residential properties, including single-family homes. Of all the REO properties, these are among the most valuable because they will sell faster than other properties. Next in the residential category come condominiums, which may be financed in an REO sale when few, if any, lenders would make a loan on such a property. S&Ls often own whole blocks of condominiums because they financed many sales in one complex, only to lose them all when the condominium complex suffered repeated foreclosures and serious value drops.

There are also commercial REO properties, such as apartment complexes, office buildings, shopping centers and vacant land. Income properties, particularly apartments, sell quickly. Vacant land does not sell well at all. Some institutions may be stuck with vacant land for years to come.

MARKETING RESIDENTIAL REOs

Banks, S&Ls and other REO owners generally set up departments to manage and sell their REO properties. The REO owner can elect to market in one of several ways. It can use an in-house approach in which the S&L hires its own staff to market the REOs with little or no outside assistance. Alternatively, it can retain outside property managers and brokers to market its properties. The latter approach is more common. However, a well-organized REO department should have an in-house manager or small staff that knows the business, even though outside brokers do most of the actual selling. The in-house staff can either control each sale or simply give the broker a set range within which to negotiate; any price within the range is acceptable to the S&L. When selling residential properties, REO departments generally have at least three levels of operation.

Level 1—the overall managers for the REO department. The senior personnel in an REO department supervise REO managers and usually have the authority to accept or reject specific purchase offers made on REO properties. Sometimes there are no more levels than an immediate supervisor for REO managers, but in larger lending institutions, more levels are possible. The worst situation is when the bank or S&L has been invaded by government personnel (this procedure is not voluntary—it is done as a precursor or as an alternative to simply shutting an insolvent S&L down) who have the right to approve or disapprove the specific sale of any house or other REO property. Another possibility is that the bank or S&L became insolvent and was purchased by a better-managed solvent S&L. In that case, approvals for specific sales may have to go to personnel at the outside bank. The more levels that approvals for sales have to go through, the longer it takes, and the more uncertain the process becomes. It is best if the decision-making authority for the sale of houses is placed low in the chain of command, only one level up from REO managers.

Level 2—the REO manager. REO managers are generally assigned a specific inventory of houses to market and sell. The inventory may be selected geographically or by type of house (large, small or condominium). The REO manager generally deals directly with brokers. Investor buyers will deal with the broker, who deals with the REO manager. Investor buyers may be stuck with the broker an REO manager assigns to a specific property. Unfortunately for investors, the REO manager controlling sales negotiations may or may not have much experience with selling real estate. Such managers should have a real estate license in most states, but they do not always have it. REO managers usually have a background in banking. Quite possibly they are MBAs fresh out of business school or very close to it.

REO managers may have a lot of properties to work with or a few. (I can recall at least one instance in which the REO manager had 400 properties to manage.) The more properties the REO manager has to manage, the tougher it is for the investor to work with him or her. However, high inventories often mean lower prices. As REO managers become more experienced, investor buyers will be able to deal with them on a more businesslike basis, but it's harder to get a good price. The more properties the REO manager has to deal with, the more dependent they are on their brokers.

Level 3—the independent real estate broker. Most S&Ls and other institutions that market REOs have found it advantageous to market their properties through outside brokerage firms. Although brokers are easy for investor buyers to talk to, their job is usually to drive the hardest bargain they can for the selling institution, and some are very good at it. Brokerage firms have the experienced professionals needed to move houses in a tough market. Anyone buying REOs will usually end up dealing with the broker, not with the bank itself.

REO brokerage operations may be either large or small. When the REO market first opened up, it tended to be dominated by large brokerage firms that took on almost the whole REO inventory for a bank or an S&L. Smaller companies have managed to obtain more and more listings, as S&Ls found that they got better results with smaller, more aggressive brokerage firms. REO managers also liked working with the smaller firms because the REO manager had more control and was very important to the smaller broker, while the larger firm might try to outmaneuver the REO manager at a higher level in the S&L's management. Such maneuverings complicate life for investor buyers.

REO LISTINGS

REO listings are almost always short, relative to the market period. REO listings are usually exclusive-right-to-sell listings, giving the broker the exclusive right to sell the property and earn a commission. If the property sells during the list period, the listing broker for that property gets a commission. Commission structures have been some-what unusual in the REO field. Some S&Ls have structured their commissions based on the volume of properties that particular broker sells for the S&L. The more properties sold for that particular S&L, the higher the commission. This is probably a poor way to structure commissions because it ignores the relative difficulty involved in selling any particular property. The properties the broker gets to list are usually chosen by the REO manager. If the broker proves to be a performer, he or she will probably get more listings.

Otherwise, REO listings are usually done on standard Multiple Listing Service (MLS) type of forms. However, some S&Ls have been known to allow brokers a few days before putting the house into the MLS computer. The MLS rules usually require the listing to be entered within four days. However, a hot property can be sold in four days. Some brokers advertise their REOs and attempt to keep both sides of the commission by finding a buyer before anyone else gets a chance to do so. REO brokers may be expected to indemnify or reimburse the bank or S&L for any problems that arise in the course of the listing.

REO EARNEST MONEY CONTRACTS

REO earnest money contracts are usually standard form contracts, but with addenda that are unique to a particular selling institution. A "property condition" addendum is commonly added to make the sale into an "as is, where is, with all faults" type of sale, which means the investor buyer must check the property out before buying it. The institution makes few guarantees in such sales, nor can it be relied on to keep promises made if it is in a state of bankruptcy. Some banks make no repairs at all before attempting to sell on an "as is" basis, but others can and do make many repairs. Even so, they will still often add an addendum to make it an "as is" sale, after performing a negotiated set of repairs. Investor buyers should expect to get more repairs from institutions that have been bought out by solvent banks or S&Ls and fewer repairs from those that are about to be taken over or are being managed with active government supervision. Such institutions lack funds and REO investor buyers should not expect to negotiate for the seller to pay much on repairs.

Investor buyers should expect to get a special warranty deed under most REO earnest money contracts. This type of deed does not provide the buyer with good protection against title problems in a foreclosure resale situation. In any event, not every state uses warranty deeds. However, the S&L or bank usually provides title insurance when selling REO properties. REO titles are usually fairly reliable; the bank or S&L acquired it from foreclosure. However, a Durrett Rule exclusion may exist on the title policy. This means the house could be lost due to subsequent bankruptcy on the part of the former owner who was foreclosed on. This is a danger if the S&L or bank has held the REO property for less than a year.

ADVANTAGES OF REO HOME PURCHASES

In general, REO properties have a number of advantages relative to auction or bid foreclosure resales. Figure 8.1 is a list of some of the advantages.

FIGURE 8.1   REO Properties

	REO Property	Auction/Bid Property
Maintenance program	Ongoing up to closing Reasonable quality	Minimal (Except FNMA)
Condition of the home	Usually repaired and restored to marketable level (varies)	Minimal
Owner's title policy	Almost always provided	May be provided
"Low" move in	Often provided	Usually not
Repair allowances	Commonly provided	Usually not
Warranty	Commonly provided	Usually not
Free appliances	Commonly provided	Usually not
Low earnest money	Common (sometimes zero)	Usually $1,000+
Personal checks	Usually accepted	Good funds usually required (cashier's check)
Inspections	Commonly provided	Usually not
Hours available to show property	Usually at buyer's convenience	Limited times and circumstances (except VA/FHA)
Professional broker	Almost always	Maybe
Broker bonuses	Common	Uncommon
Price ranges	Usually a wide range $30,000–$500,000	Limited range on any government connected home (FHA/VA and FNMA) (most less than $100,000)

Financing—The Key Advantage

REO properties have some of the best loan arrangements of any of the foreclosure resale properties. Because S&Ls and banks are eager to get rid of their inventory of REOs, they offer loan programs that are designed to promote sales. Among the areas where REO financing is better than other types of financing are the following:

- Low or no down payment
- Easy assumability
- Competitive interest rates
- Less severe credit standards than other loans
- Financing on properties that can't be financed otherwise

Although down payments of 10 percent are about the minimum that is practical for any conventional (nongovernmental) loan that involves mortgage insurance, REO sales are often different. (In California, regular down payments are still being charged in the early 1990s, despite some down market conditions.) REOs may offer loan plans with 5 percent, 3 percent or even zero down payments. Many REO loans are assumable without a requirement for the lender's approval of the buyer's credit during the first five years or so of the loan. Loans for REO properties generally offer excellent interest rates. They may even pay points to make sure the interest is in a good low range.

Perhaps one of the most important ingredients of REO financing is the easier credit checking. To obtain a loan with private mortgage insurance, a borrower must meet fairly stringent credit standards. A loan may be denied for as little as two or three 30-day "slow pays" on a credit bureau report, that is, the borrower paid a bill late by over 30 days. An REO loan, by contrast, might easily overlook such problems. However, even REO loans have their limits. A recent foreclosure or bankruptcy, such as one within the last two years, will generally be fatal to an REO loan.

Sometimes it is possible to obtain financing to buy an REO property that few other lenders would lend on. A good example would be the sale of condominiums. As related earlier, S&Ls may own whole blocks of condominium units in one complex. If the unit is located in a condominium complex that has suffered from numerous foreclosures, then it is very difficult to get a loan to buy one through a regular lender. Most lenders demand at least 80 percent owner occupancy before they will consider lending money to help someone buy a condominium. Even an 80 percent occupancy may not be sufficient, if the occupants are mere tenants. In contrast, if the condominium unit is purchased as an REO from a bank or an S&L, then the institution will provide financing, often on very advantageous terms.

DISADVANTAGES OF BUYING REO HOMES

S&Ls and banks may be bureaucratic and hard to work with. A number of problems seem to come up in REO sales. Here is a short list:

Price problems—Part I. All too often, it is hard to get a good price on an REO. The bank or S&L simply wants more money than the property is worth. The institution's staff may not have a good sense of value administratively, or they may be too optimistic or just desperate to avoid writing up a big loss that the regulators will note. For a variety of reasons, S&Ls may not accept an offer at a reasonable price. For example, one broker submitted a bid at a certain price figure, which was about $5,000 to $10,000 below what the S&L wanted, so it was rejected. The market at that time was falling, so a few months later, the bank priced the house nearly $20,000 below what it had been (and well below the offer that had been rejected). The broker found another buyer and submitted another offer on the house, which again was about $5,000 too low from the S&L's standpoint. Again the offer was rejected. The price continued to fall, but by that time the infuriated broker refused to submit any further bids. Getting the bank to approve a fair price is a problem.

Price problems—Part II. One of the trickier problems involved with REO sales concerns the market value of the home relative to the sales price: the price may be high. Since the bank is often providing the financing, the appraisal would be interesting to look at from the buyer's perspective. The sales price could easily be above the appraised value of the home, if its condition were fully considered. The REO property may be in a neighborhood of REOs or distressed real estate, in which case obtaining a reliable appraisal may be difficult to begin with. The brokers, including a cooperating broker who shows the buyer the house, all work for the seller, to whom they owe their fiduciary loyalty. If they can sell the house for more than it's worth, it is arguably their fiduciary duty to do so, without telling the buyer what's happening. By law, a broker cannot treat the buyer unfairly, but if the buyer pays a few thousand dollars above the market value for the house under circumstances where it is tricky to estimate market value, this is not unfair to the point of being illegal. The buyer may never be shown the bank's or the S&L's appraisal. As a result, particularly in a rising market, it is entirely possible that a buyer will pay too much for an REO property without really knowing it. It would not be a bad idea for an REO buyer to obtain a Broker's Price Opinion (a broker's estimate of price; less formal than an appraisal), or ask to see the bank's or S&L's appraisal before committing to a particular purchase price. (Good luck getting the appraisal!)

Time problems.   Another problem with REO sales concerns dealing with a multilayered bureaucracy. This is particularly a problem if the S&L has federal regulatory personnel in its offices who insist on reviewing specific transactions. It is also a problem when the S&L has been taken over by another S&L, in which case approval might have to come from out of the state from a different office in a different S&L. The potential for trouble is considerable. One only wonders if a buyer will become discouraged and wander off.

Sophistication problems.   Sometimes the REO department at an S&L is seriously deficient in its real estate skills. Its personnel may be very inexperienced in real estate sales. They may have little idea about what goes on in the real estate world. They may not know how an MLS works, or the problems with appraisals, or the details of contracts. As a result, many things can and do go wrong.

Regulatory problems.   S&Ls and banks are all increasingly controlled or operated by agencies of the federal government. As a result, buying REOs can mean a host of problems. One of the nastiest comes when the bank or S&L promises many things, but then is taken over by the government. If this happens, a countersuit against the bank for deceptive trade practices, failure to honor commitments or problems with the loan may be removed to federal court where the claims will be dismissed. Government agencies have the "D'oench Duhme doctrine," which effectively makes it all but impossible to sue a bank or an S&L that has been taken over, even if they are clearly in the wrong.

It's no fun when the toilet in your rented house explodes and no one cares! If you move out, they'll sue and then smash your legal defense (nonworking plumbing) to nonpayment of rent with the D'oench Duhme doctrine.

Crookedness problems.   Once in a while, the S&L one is dealing with may have crooked owners or employees. There's no telling what mischief they've been up to or plan on being up to. To avoid detection or keep things going, they may do almost anything. They may cause the house to be misrepresented or convert checks or even use fake papers. They are not safe to deal with.

SPECIALIZED REO MARKETING TECHNIQUES

REO houses and condominiums can be sold outright on a house-by-house basis to buyers who can arrange a loan, either through the REO owner (often an S&L) or by outside financing. However, there are at least three commonly used techniques that do not follow the rules. These are:

1. Tenant sales
2. Bulk sales
3. Retail project sales

Also, private mortgage insurers are involved in some sales.

Tenant Sales

In the tenant sales option, the REO homes are rented to a person who is a likely buyer. The prospective buyer does not currently have sufficient income or credit to qualify for a regular loan, but there is a good possibility that he or she will have the necessary qualifications before long. Such a prospective tenant should be carefully prequalified, with the ultimate purchase in mind. In the meantime, the property can be leased to the prospective buyer. The lease payments may be counted toward the purchase. The tenant has the option to back out of the purchase.

The tenant sales approach affords the buyer the opportunity to look over the house and become familiar with it. It allows the bank or REO owner to bring in cash immediately through the rents paid, rather than wait month after month for a creditworthy buyer to appear in a tough market. If the property were to stay vacant, it runs a much greater risk of being vandalized or damaged; it probably runs down the property values in the area, where the REO owner may have other properties; and it would generate no income to pay taxes and insurance. If the property were rented to a tenant who has no chance to qualify for a regular loan, then the REO owner probably has an inferior tenant who might be unreliable in paying rent; who would be a hindrance when the property is shown to prospective buyers; and who might tear up the property because he or she won't be staying long.

Bulk Sales

Smaller investor buyers can still participate as one member of a much larger deal such as a bulk sales arrangement. In a bulk sale, a prospective buyer (or organizer for smaller buyers) purchases dozens or even hundreds of houses from the REO owner in one pass. The REO seller's objective is to sell the good houses with the bad houses. This saves the costs of selling each individual house, such as brokerage fees and advertising. Because it saves the REO manager time and money to sell houses as a block, bulk purchasers should expect to pay a much lower price per house than they would have paid for each house individually. REO owners should take care to force the REO purchaser to buy good houses and bad houses, rather than just pick a few of the best and buy those at a discount.

Once the sale takes place, the bulk purchaser is in a position to sell houses one by one over time as values increase. Their rehabilitation costs can be paid for by ongoing sales. Because bulk purchasers can buy carpet, paint and drywall in large quantities, perhaps even directly from the factory, repair costs can be lowered. Continuing rehabilitation contracts can be let, or a person or persons can be hired to do the rehabilitation, which further lowers costs and increases the quality of the rehabilitation. The bulk purchaser can expect to realize a handsome profit on the resale. The bank or REO owner gets a quick sale and a lot of cash up front.

The individual investor benefits by participating in a bulk sale because a small investment can be spread over many properties, which is safer than putting all your money in one house. You can play a better set of averages, while at the same time use the bargaining power of large money to procure a good deal. All it takes is a little organization. Real estate brokers have been organizing such projects for years. Group investments in real estate are often referred to as *syndications*. They have many advantages for small investors who are limited in time and funds.

Retail Project Management

Another potential syndication project would be a retail project management deal. In this type of arrangement, a block of condominiums in one complex or perhaps a block of houses in one subdivision, is sold by the REO manager as part of an integrated, coherent sales project designed for that one complex or subdivision. The complex or subdivision can be marketed, rather than each individual condominium or house. These projects require careful planning, but they can be highly successful in reducing marketing and other selling costs. One salesagent or brokerage firm could be hired to sell a whole series of properties in one area. This may be more efficient than selling off each property through separate listings with different brokerage firms.

PMI Sales

Private mortgage insurance companies frequently acquire a large number of properties during down market periods. They can offer to insure loans on their REO homes, which makes it much easier for buyers to get loans. PMI companies frequently organize auctions and bulk sales. They often provide the money needed to fix up properties, so they can sell a high quality product, relatively speaking, with good financing. Smaller investor buyers may find such deals very attractive, but it's trickier to beat the market price when purchasing these homes. Nevertheless, you may get very good value for an invested dollar.

CONCLUSION

REOs are the most common of all foreclosed properties. They are usually sold by professional brokers, have good financing and may be fixed up. They can be purchased by submitting a contract offer much like that used for regular real estate listings. Although the profit an investor can make in REO sales is not as great as that for other sales, these deals are far more realistic, and good opportunities abound in a down market.

CHAPTER 9

Showtime— Private Auctions

Many foreclosure homes are being sold at public auctions that are organized and run by professionals. Some people think that auction marketing may be the way of the future, particularly for foreclosed home resales. Interested buyers can sometimes get an excellent deal, but there are tricks to buying at an auction, any auction, and some tricks that are unique to real estate auctions. Houses need to be previewed, a bid must be developed that will not be exceeded, no matter what, and auctioneering tactics, such as planted shills, faulty bidding and bad paperwork must be dealt with by an investor to succeed in getting that very special deal.

Many people assume that all auctions of foreclosure properties constitute the actual, legal foreclosure. In fact, many, if not most, auctions of foreclosures really are private commercial operations. Private auctions are not the actual legal foreclosure sale, but rather the subsequent resale of properties purchased by lenders (or investors) at the true legal foreclosure sale at the courthouse.

Each auction is different, which makes it hard to find common characteristics to describe. When the market is falling, auctions are common. When the market is rising, many government agencies such as the FHA and the VA have enough luck with their sealed bidding programs that they can discontinue auctions. FNMA auctions are usually conducted only when the market is pretty down. The details of those auctions are covered in Chapter 10. Also, conventional sellers have been using auctioneers to sell houses with considerable success. Nothing seems to fire the homebuying public's imagination quite the way an auction does. They are probably here to stay, at least in a limited form, for some time to come. This section of the book will describe private auctions in general terms.

AUCTION MARKETING

Auction marketing of real estate may have potential nationwide. It has been proposed for use on a larger scale in conjunction with the sale of homes and other properties held in inventory by the RTC and the FDIC. Auctions can often result in a sale when few other means can. Auctions can be held in at least one of two ways:

1. A minimum bid is set, which may be announced at the outset of the bidding.
2. A "sale absolute" is held.

Sale Absolute

In a *sale absolute,* there is no minimum. Whatever is bid, no matter how small, is what the property will be sold for. At one VA auction in Houston, a condominium once sold for $3,000. Obviously, the sale absolute procedure gets houses sold, but potentially at fire sale prices. In order to avoid auction sales at prices that are too low, an astute auctioneer will keep a count of the crowd as it comes in. From past experience, the auctioneer or auctioneering company will know that it must have a minimum number of bidders, including bidders who are known to be substantial, in order to generate a sufficient number of bids on a property to keep it from becoming a fire sale. If the attendance count is high enough, the auctioneer may announce to the crowd at the beginning of the bidding that a sale for a house is to be a sale absolute. At that point, the frenzied crowd often roars with anticipation. They may go a little bit crazy in hopes that they will be the lucky bidders who obtain a valuable property at a very low price. Only an owner who is truly desperate to sell, or exceedingly canny in crowd counting, should ever attempt this procedure.

One other method is to throw a few homes up for sale on a sale absolute basis as a marketing device. Advertising for the auction may specify that a certain number of homes are to be sold on a sale absolute basis in order to increase attendance. It's a risky procedure, but it may work.

Auctions with a Minimum Bid

The most common way to operate an auction is to assign properties a minimum bid. Even if the RTC and the FSLIC Resolution Fund choose to use auctions to market their properties, they are required by law (FIRREA) to sell distressed properties in distressed areas at 95 percent of their market value. A minimum bid therefore will be expected. Typically, sellers will target at least 80 percent of the home's market value as a minimum for an auction. Their hope is to get more, and most importantly, to move their inventory quickly.

How Auctions Are Set Up

No auction would be complete without an auctioneer. Actually, in the current age, auctions are normally staged by companies that specialize in this function. Auctioneers must be licensed in many states. Three national companies tend to dominate the market: Sheldon Good & Co. of Chicago, Illinois, Hudson and Marshall of Macon, Georgia and Auction Company of America, of Miami, Florida.

These companies, and others, provide a range of services in setting up the auction. They can advertise it. They can arrange set minimum bids on houses. They can choose the site for the auction and equip it with whatever it needs—loudspeakers, overhead projectors and a lectern with a hammer, of course! Auction marketing companies can create bidding packages and brochures for the homes they market. They can make themselves available to brokers who wish to refer prospects. Finally, on the night of the auction, they will provide the needed personnel, which will probably consist of bid takers, a "watcher" and the auctioneer.

Bigger Is Often Better

The modern auction usually groups as many as a hundred houses to be sold on one or more nights. The houses may come from mortgage companies or S&Ls with unsold REOs from private mortgage insurance companies that have exercised their right to acquire properties from the lender in exchange for covering the lender's loss, or from large secondary market companies, similar to FNMA, that have purchased loans that went into default. The auction marketing company will very likely arrange a number of houses from various sources to be packaged in one large auction. That way, the company's fees, the advertising and the other auction expenses can be defrayed over a larger number of properties. A big auction may look like it will draw such a large and rich crowd that a hotel may even provide a banquet hall for free. Size helps an auction to obtain higher bids, too.

Preliminary Marketing

Most auction marketing companies will arrange at least two forms of advertising:

1. Newspaper ads near the time of the auction
2. Direct mail to known auction bidders

The way to get a place on a mailing list is to attend an auction held by one of the large companies. Don't be a mere bystander. Register to bid, produce an earnest money check to flash at the door upon entry, check out a bid card and enter the bidding part of the room. Do that once, and you'll be on that company's auction mailing lists for quite some time to come. Some mailing lists that can be purchased prior to auctions include the names of people who have asked to be included or whose name found its way onto an investor list. There are even real estate investment clubs. Join one, and your name may very well wind up on a mailing list. Brokers or brokerage firms are likely to be on the list. Otherwise, you'll have to watch the newspapers for ads about upcoming auctions.

Showing the House

Many auction companies make it possible to see the house before the bidding. Most auctions consist of houses that may be seen through open houses and brokers.

The dates and times for open houses are usually in the flyers that are mailed out before the auction, as well as newspaper advertisements. At the open house, there may or may not be personnel on site who can show the house effectively, but there will be someone around and the house can be entered and inspected. This is a big advantage compared with buying at the legal foreclosure sale, where prior inspections of occupied properties are very difficult. Often, the homes are repaired and spruced up before their presentation in an open house.

Brokers can obtain access to a house—usually through a lockbox the broker can get a key or combination to—and show it to the investor buyer.

Brokers—The 1 Percent to 2 Percent Solution. Brokers who show the house will usually be expected to register their prospective bidder before the auction. The auction company will need a registration letter on the auction company's form, signed by the prospective bidder. The broker will be identified in the letter, which must be turned in by a strict deadline.

With an advance deadline, the broker can't just find a friend who would have gone to the auction anyway and arrange to get a commission by supplying the party's name as a bidder to the auction company. Of course, it could happen anyway, but it would have to be arranged further in advance. Also, brokerage commissions are usually not paid if the bidder already contacted the auction company before the broker or salesagent did.

The broker will normally get a commission on the order of 1 percent to 1.5 percent of the bid price at the auction. There is no fixed, standard, suggested or recommended commission for licensed persons. Also, any attempt by the broker or salesagent to split the commission with any person not licensed as a broker or active salesagent is illegal. The broker is often asked to attend the auction with the prospective bidder as a prerequisite to collecting the commission. Finding a ready, willing and able bidder is not enough to earn a commission. Normally, the sale must be not only signed in contract form, but completed through the closing in order for the broker or salesagent to receive a commission. The broker may also be asked to sign an affidavit that he or she is acting as a broker and not as a principal, namely a buyer, in whole or in part, at the auction. Otherwise, every bidder with a license would demand a commission, which would defeat its purpose: to find a buyer that would not have otherwise bid.

Many auctions, including FNMA auctions, often pre-arrange special financing for auction buyers. Lenders are so often the sellers that some type of financing might be possible. Otherwise, the bidder will be expected to come up with cash to buy the house at the auction or shortly thereafter. At the auction, the bidder must give up the earnest money check and sign an earnest money contract agreeing to buy. If the party does not buy, this earnest money, typically $2,000, will be forfeited. This will probably be true regardless of whether the bidder obtains a loan to buy with or not.

The sales are usually made on an "as is, where is" basis without any guarantee as to the condition of the property. Alternatively, some sort of limited warranty may be offered. Sometimes the homes will be fixed up prior to sale. Sometimes not. However, the prospective bidder must be absolutely sure to take advantage of any opportunity to inspect the property prior to any bid. Occasionally, people bid at auctions because the price is low, without inspecting the property. Such bidders almost always regret their decision.

The companies that are contributing properties to the auction will normally reserve the right to pull them out of the bidding at any time before the auction. The terms for sales announced by the auctioneer at the time the auction begins will take precedence over prior written or advertised terms. That fact is usually disclosed in the advertising to reduce the likelihood of anyone bringing charges of deceptive trade practices.

The Night of the Auction

The prospective bidder must normally sign in and produce a $2,000 cashier's check for inspection by the auction company's door officials. A bid card is normally obtained. The bidder walks into the bidding area, takes a seat and the auction begins. In any auction sale, prospective bidders should do their homework. They should know exactly how high they can go and not bid a penny more, no matter what insulting comments the auctioneer makes or how frenzied the bidding becomes.

Sometimes auctioneers start out low and chop off the bidding at a price that is unusually low to encourage bidding.

When the auctioneer's sing-song calls out a price, the bidder normally holds up a bid card to raise the price by increments that have been preset by the auctioneer. The bidding might be by $500s, for example. If the bid is open, and bidders can call out their own figures, it is best to bid in small increments to avoid paying a big increment ($1,000) over what it takes to beat the competition, which might be only $50. Once a bid card is raised or a bid is called out, a bid taker's fist will shoot up. A watcher below the podium may also shoot a fist up and shout "yo!" or something similar. At that point the pitch on the auctioneer's sing-song will shift; he or she will go up an increment and will bang the gavel. Some auctioneers use a wooden block to get the same effect as a hammer.

Once the high bid is reached, the successful bidder will be asked to sign a contract to buy the property. It is possible that loan application papers may be signed at this time, if financing is available on auction properties. The earnest money check must be turned in. Sometimes, second or backup contracts are signed at an auction. This would give the successful bidder the right to buy the property if a first and prior bidder, who bid more, fails to close on the purchase.

Closing

Normally, the closing is held at a title company designated by the auction company or the lender whose property was sold. The closing takes place in a relatively normal manner. A title policy is purchased. Closings are frequently quite swift, sometimes requiring only two or three weeks after the auction for homes on a loan or faster still for cash purchases.

AUCTION PROCEDURES FOR BUYERS

Most bidders at auctions would be well advised to review what are fairly standard procedures for bidding. Here we mean not just the physical procedures, but the way buyers should undertake buying a house at an auction.

Before the Auction

1. Check out financing.   Usually it's best to prequalify for the financing offered on auction homes first, rather than later. In particular, if financing is offered, make sure it does not consist of balloon notes, rollovers or other financing that may be undesirable.

2. Always inspect the property before buying.   The most skilled bidders at real estate auctions know their property well before they ever bid. A bit of advice: it's almost never wise to bid on an unknown house at an auction, even if the price looks so low that the bidder can "steal" the house. Once you've seen a bidder get a house at $15,000 and want to give it back as soon as he or she has seen it, you too will become a believer. Always look at real estate before buying it.

3. Estimate the value of the property before bidding.   If possible, obtain an appraisal. If not, then get a Broker's Price Opinion, which may cost $50. This is the area where the smartest bidders do the most work. They know not only value, but resaleability as well. They buy properties that they know what to do with. They will resell them as is, rehabilitate them and get a big increase in value or hold them for later resale when the market improves. All strategies depend critically on knowing the value of the real estate before buying.

4. Set a price you're willing to pay, and never go higher.   Most bidders should have a price limit. They should go up to that price and stop, no matter how tempting it is to go higher in the heat of the moment. Auctioneers try to create a feverish, frantic, competitive atmosphere. They will appeal to your ego. I can recall one auctioneer who looked straight at a bidder who was just outbid by a nearby bidder and shouted, scornfully, "You're out of there, you're out of there!" as though that person were nothing financially. It can be bruising to one's ego. It might be tempting to respond with a higher bid. *Don't do it!* Know how much you're willing to pay and stop bidding at that point.

5. Get the paperwork well in advance.   That way, you'll know the rules for the auction. If possible, get copies of tax statements, surveys, a legal description and viewing information. Obtain a copy of the sales contract; that should always be available.

6. Be sure title is clear. Sometimes auctions are held to get rid of properties with questionable titles. They may be hard to resell quickly. Do not accept the seller's mere guarantee that title is good: ask for a title insurance policy. If a written guarantee is available, get that in addition to the title insurance. All guarantees should be in writing, preferably in the deed, and with abundant written representations as well. If none of these things are available, get a legal description and have a title searcher search the title to look for trouble. It may be worthwhile to pay for a full abstract and have it reviewed by an attorney. Title protection always costs money; title does not often fail, but when it does, the costs in the real estate business are staggering.

Special Tips at the Auction

1. Use written bids if possible. Some auctions allow written bids. In such instances, a bidder may submit a letter bidding up to a set figure, such as $150,000. If the bidding at the auction reaches that figure, the bid will be introduced at the appropriate point. If the bidding reaches an even $100,000, but will go no higher, many auctions will allow the auctioneer to introduce a portion of the written bid in an amount equal to the next higher increment, let's say an additional $1,000 for a sale price of $101,000. Even though the written bid would have gone as high as $150,000, the bidder gets the house at $101,000. Written bids prevent the frenzy of the moment at an auction from getting the better of the buyer's judgment. They also eliminate the hassle of trying to wave a popsicle stick with a bid number on it at the appropriate moment.

2. Watch the timing. It is hard to predict the exact period at which the best prices can be had during an auction. Sometimes prices are high at the beginning, but most often they are lower. Sometimes auctioneers will deliberately start a house at a low figure. They will then cut off bidding at a price well below market value, or the point at which the smart money would begin bidding. There may be a flurry of bids at the last second when people realize what's happening, but it may be too late. Someone just stole a house. After that, the auctioneer guesses that bidding will be mean and fierce right from the start.

On the whole, bargains are more likely to be had early in the auction rather than at the end. Probably the best time is during the middle of the auction. This is particularly so if there are a lot of properties and not very many bidders. They may start to run low on funds relative to what's for sale. Toward the end of the auction, prices usually rise as bidders decide to get something rather than nothing. They don't want to leave empty handed, so they bid harder.

AUCTION TERMINOLOGY

Shill. A shill is introduced by the auction company or sponsor to bid on property in order to force the bid to a higher level, although that person has no intention of buying. Shills can be hard to spot. Someone who bids often in all price ranges, but never wins, may be a shill.

Buyer's premium. A buyer's premium is usually a sales commission paid to the broker. It is important to note whether the commission is added to the high bid or paid from the high bid proceeds by the seller.

Auction with confirmation. An auction with confirmation normally gives the seller the right to accept or reject the high bid. Hopefully, the seller will pay a damage fee to the buyer if the bid is rejected.

Upset price or reserve. This is a price below which the seller will not sell the property at an auction.

Hand in money. Successful bidders may be asked to show their good faith by making a good faith deposit on the order of 5 percent to 20 percent of the high bid figure. Some auction companies take personal checks, but others demand cashier's checks for the purpose. If so, make out the cashier's checks to the bidder, rather than the auction company. That way they can be redeposited easily if they are not used. Have them made out in a variety of denominations, let's say $10,000, $5,000 and $1,000. Count out the checks the same way a cashier at a checkout counter does, by tens, fives and ones. Be sure to keep a record of which checks were used, by serial number, and for what house. Have the recipient sign a receipt containing that information before handing the checks over. Some people keep a roll of $100 bills for smaller increments. Cashier's checks are not much safer than cash. Effectively, they are cash when they hit the floor and are stolen by anyone who can forge a signature. Be careful with all that money!

CONCLUSION

Auctions are among the fastest and most effective ways for a small investor to buy foreclosed real estate. Financing is regularly available at many auctions. It is often possible to preview the property before bidding on it. However, there is likely to be competition in bidding for the best houses at an auction, and there are games that auctioneers play, such as starting out bidding too low on one sale, and selling the property at a very low price before the smart money tries to dive in on the auction. Smaller investors may do well with an auction, provided they know how much to bid and won't bid a penny more no matter what the auctioneers say or do.

CHAPTER 10

Fannie Mae and Secondary Market Foreclosure Sales

Companies that buy loans from mortgage companies and banks (which actually made them to real homeowners and borrowers), are called the *secondary market* in the lending industry. When the loans that secondary market companies, such as the Federal National Mortgage Association (Fannie Mae or FNMA), buy go bad and have to be foreclosed on, the secondary market company may choose to take the house instead of being paid off on a mortgage. Once FNMA gets a house, it sells it. The secondary market sellers do not fool around in down markets: they hire crack agents and crack marketers to sell off properties with skill and speed. However, there are plenty of ways in which the skilled investor can win big, particularly if the investor takes full advantage of the incredible financing that is frequently offered. When interest rates are low, these sound houses, bought at good prices with low interest loans, make wonderful rental properties.

Federal National Mortgage Association (FNMA or Fannie Mae) homes have several advantages over other types of foreclosure resale properties: they are kept in the best condition of almost any foreclosure property held for resale, they are sold with excellent financing and they are easy to purchase. FNMA usually puts houses it acquires under the care of a broker who must fix up and maintain the property. FNMA arranges for new carpet and new paint and repairs any obvious damage. Once fixed up, FNMA homes are easy for brokers to show to prospective buyers. FNMA usually arranges for low down payment financing to both investors and regular buyers, at very competitive interest rates and terms. FNMA sells either through very skilled brokers or through auctions. It is easy to see a FNMA home before buying and easy to actually buy a FNMA home. The big disadvantage of FNMA for investors is the prices charged for homes. It's harder to get a FNMA house at a bargain, but it's a safer bet than almost any other purchase. Even then, it's not risk free. FNMA sells on an "as is" basis and there can be problems with the physical condition of some properties.

Investors should know that the FNMA is a government chartered corporation that buys mortgages. Typically, a mortgage company lends a homebuyer the money to buy the house. The rights to that loan are then resold to FNMA. The homebuyer may not know a thing about the resale and continue to make monthly payments to the mortgage company. However, the mortgage company in turn will remit the money to FNMA. The mortgage company acts merely as a *servicer* for the loan, that is, it collects payments and passes them on. It will also send out late notices and handle the foreclosure, if one is necessary.

Sometimes the homeowner whose loan has been sold to FNMA goes into default due to divorce, job loss or bankruptcy. If so, the mortgage company will hire the trustee and arrange the foreclosure. At the foreclosure, the title will go directly to FNMA from the foreclosure trustee by means of a trustee's deed. Of course, third party buyers, such as wealthy investors, could outbid FNMA at the legal foreclosure sale and take title, but this is unlikely, unless the property is worth 20 percent to 50 percent more than what FNMA is owed on the loan, which happens about 1 percent of the time. As a result, FNMA usually owns the house. FNMA will then sell the house for closer to a market price to smaller investors and regular homebuyers.

THE FNMA PROGRAMS

Investors and homebuyers should expect to buy a FNMA home through one of two resale programs: Brokers or auctions.

FNMA Brokers

FNMA uses both large and small independent brokerage firms to fix up and market its properties. Investors and homebuyers will work with a FNMA broker, but the lower level decision maker at FNMA is usually a sales specialist. The sales specialist in turn works with independently owned and operated brokers who have been approved by FNMA. These are known as Fannie Mae brokers. Generally, FNMA chooses reputable, aggressive and capable brokers, which makes it easy to buy a FNMA home, but harder to get a great bargain. A small bargain is not so hard to get, but a big one is. Some brokers have made a great deal of money selling FNMA homes. The sales specialist will also give the FNMA broker the name of a contact with the old servicer.

The investor buyer may not necessarily deal directly with FNMA's larger brokers. The large brokers undertake the extensive repairs needed for a property because they have the money to let subcontracts for completing repairs without the need for quick reimbursement by FNMA. They can complete the repairs promptly, then bill FNMA later. They can also obtain bargains on materials and repairs, which helps put value in the houses investors buy, for a much lower cost than the investor could arrange. For example, large brokers can buy carpet directly from the factory in huge quantities. This is the source of the infamous FNMA brown carpet in so many FNMA resale homes. It's good carpet, but it's the same carpet!

Many investors will buy FNMA homes through smaller brokerage firms, which deal with investors and regular homebuyers. These firms have proven very useful to FNMA for resales of houses: they are aggressive and often have outstanding sales talents. They may also be large enough to handle at least some of the repairs and maintenance needed. Better still, since the people selling the houses directly are responsible for managing the repairs directly, there tends to be a higher degree of coordination between the maintenance and the sales than would otherwise be the case. The repairs that are really needed to market the house are done and done quickly.

FNMA Listing Contract Requirements

FNMA listing contracts are exclusive-right-to-sell listings, which give one broker the exclusive right to market a FNMA property for a limited time. FNMA brokers are usually under pressure to sell homes quickly. The listing usually lasts only 90 days. FNMA pays commissions only on actual sales; it won't pay a commission just because a broker finds a good buyer. Moreover, investor buyers should recognize that FNMA can terminate a listing contract quickly for a variety of reasons over which the investor, homebuyer or broker has little control. A FNMA listing may come to an end because

- the property is deeded over to the mortgage insurance company that insured the loan;
- FNMA is unable to obtain clear title to the house;
- FNMA requires the original lender for the loan that was foreclosed on to repurchase the house (this is nasty; it means that the original loan should not have been made);
- the property is suddenly sold as part of a package deal with many other properties in a bulk sale to a buyer; or
- the property is made available for sale by auction.

MARKETING FNMA HOMES

Investors and homebuyers should recognize that FNMA requires its brokers to perform certain marketing activities, such as

- putting a For Sale sign on the property when the practice is legal;
- listing the property in the MLS computer system; and
- listing the home in the MLS with the following language: "SPECIAL FANNIE MAE FINANCING AVAILABLE."

Of course, these simple, rudimentary measures hardly begin to describe what a broker will probably do to get a sale. FNMA offers good deals on houses, and they expect their brokers to be experts at marketing. Generally, they are. I have seen FNMA brokers obtain signed earnest money contracts within 24 to 72 hours after they begin marketing, even in a down market. It is very competitive to become a FNMA broker.

In practice, investor buyers and homebuyers will find FNMA homes to be among the easiest to keep track of. Most Fannie Mae brokers are expected to use a combination of newspaper ads, open houses and networking to obtain sales, as well as all the conventional tools, such as signs and the MLS. FNMA actually sends out checkers to see what the broker is doing to market the property.

If the home is occupied, FNMA only permits homes to be shown when an appointment is obtained in advance from the occupant. However, FNMA will not allow occupants to be in the house unless they have agreed to cooperate with FNMA's marketing program. They must agree to move out on 30 days' notice. All mortgagors (former borrowers who were foreclosed on) will be evicted expeditiously by FNMA. They may not stay.

Investor buyers and homebuyers should expect a very fast response on an offer to buy a FNMA house. If a response is not obtained quickly, there may well be a problem with the broker. Once the broker gets an offer on the property, FNMA will want to see it immediately. FNMA will generally respond to an offer within 72 hours or less. Some FNMA officials claim that listing brokers should be so efficient that a cooperating broker who produces a buyer can take off for Acapulco and expect the commission check will be waiting when the vacation is over. FNMA can even arrange the financing, usually through selected mortgage companies.

FNMA Earnest Money Contracts

An offer by a prospective buyer will normally consist of a filled in and signed FNMA earnest money contract, accompanied by an check made out to FNMA, usually for $1,000. The contract names FNMA as the seller. The contract is a standard earnest money contract, but with a significant addendum. Here is a list of some of the matters covered in the addendum, with an analysis of each provision.

1. FNMA does not guarantee it is selling the right house. FNMA sells so many houses, it could sell the wrong one. Don't laugh. It can happen. Admittedly it is embarrassing to find out that the wrong address was used in the paperwork and that FNMA didn't have the house for sale after all, but if that happens, then the buyer's remedies are limited to recovering the earnest money and FNMA has no further liability.

2. FNMA will only give the buyer a special warranty deed. All FNMA will give is a weaker deed, called a special warranty deed. In a special warranty deed, FNMA guarantees that it has kept its title clean as long as FNMA has been the owner, but it makes no guarantee against title problems that arose prior to the time FNMA acquired title. Thus, title problems that occurred during or before the foreclosure are not covered by a deed warranty.

3. FNMA may refuse to sell at the last minute.   It is not unconditionally obligated to sell the property. FNMA may withdraw the home from sale under the contract for the following reasons:

- FNMA decides the lender did such a bad job with the original loan that the lender will have to buy the house from FNMA. However, it might be possible to negotiate a quick sale from the lender after it buys the property from FNMA.
- The mortgage insurance company wants the house after all.

4. FNMA's loan underwriting guidelines apply to any loan.
FNMA is not guaranteeing financing for the sale. The buyer must have the ability to pay (income and assets) and willingness to pay (a good credit rating), as defined in FNMA's extensive underwriting guidelines. If the buyer doesn't measure up, FNMA won't do the deal.

5. FNMA does not guarantee that the property is in good condition.   FNMA has a paragraph in its addendum that disclaims warranties not only on the house itself, but on all fixtures or equipment sold with the house, such as air conditioners, built-in stoves, dishwashers and so on. FNMA then gives the buyer two options regarding property condition:

- Sale "as is" with no inspections. Under this option the buyer does not even demand an inspection of the home.
- Sale "as is" with inspections. Under this option, the buyer can have an inspection. The buyer has ten days to get an inspection or otherwise determine that a repair is needed and to notify FNMA of any repairs the buyer wants. If FNMA accepts, then the repairs will be made by FNMA. They should be listed on a special addendum to the addendum. If the buyer stays silent for ten days after the date of the contract, then the buyer is accepting the property in an "as is" condition with no repairs.

Investor buyers and homebuyers should take caution that FNMA may not fix every problem with a house. If a problem is readily visible, FNMA will usually get it fixed. Deeper, harder to detect problems may be missed. It's still a very good idea to get professional inspections on FNMA homes, even though they appear to be in great shape.

6. The buyer pays for the appraisal unless the sale closes.   The buyer agrees to pay for the appraisal initially. FNMA will only reimburse the buyer for the appraisal cost if the deal closes and the property sells.

7. FNMA gives up possession no sooner than it has to.   FNMA does not allow any move-ins before closing. Any sale is made subject to the rights of anyone currently leasing the property. Generally, tenants have 30 days to move out.

8. FNMA does not have any liability for delays.   FNMA may elect to hold an interest rate constant for 72 hours, but it has no liability for delays due to loan processing or title problems.

FNMA FINANCING

Normally, a buyer would be expected to meet all the FNMA underwriting requirements. Sometimes special financing will be made available, but it is increasingly unnecessary. In a normal, nonauction sale, the buyer would normally be expected to pay all the closing costs related to the loan. This would include costs for any appraisals, inspections and credit reports. The buyer would be expected to pay prepaids, such as advance escrow deposits for property taxes and hazard insurance and any mortgage insurance premiums. The buyer would normally be expected to pay points.

If the offer is accepted by FNMA, and financing is approved through a FNMA lender, then the FNMA home is sold at a regular closing at a title company, which is conducted in a normal manner. FNMA, of course, wants a copy of the HUD-1 settlement statement.

PROPERTY MANAGEMENT FUNCTIONS

Investor buyers and homebuyers should realize that FNMA properties are likely to stay in good shape because of the fairly elaborate program established for maintaining the house during foreclosure, which is when a lot of damage is done, and after foreclosure, while it is being sold.

During the foreclosure process, FNMA's loan servicer, which is often the original lender, must maintain the property. This includes mowing the grass, removing trash, winterizing the property and securing the property. The lender should continue utility services. In Houston, Texas, the rekeying function may be performed by the FNMA broker. All exterior locks should be changed and all windows and exterior doors should be secured, but the property should not be boarded unless absolutely necessary to prevent vandalism.

Investors and homebuyers often buy FNMA homes through smaller brokers. These brokers are expected to inspect, repair and maintain the properties FNMA lists through them. In particular, the duties are as follows:

- Rekey the house.
- Coordinate access to the house by all interested persons, whether they are buyers or contractors.
- Conduct inspections twice a week, report any damage and maintain an 80 degree summer and a 60 degree winter temperature.
- Arrange and pay for maintenance, lawn mowing and maid service. Utilities are left on in a FNMA house, in FNMA's name, at the broker's expense, although FNMA will reimburse the cost, eventually. Brokers in that position need funds, and a fast sale, which investor buyers should keep in mind when dealing with FNMA brokers.

Good Condition—A Key FNMA Selling Point

Unlike bid properties or many auction properties, FNMA homes are almost always in an attractive condition. On the other hand the FNMA repair system has been criticized for performing repairs that are cosmetic rather than complete. Buyers should be warned that appearances can be deceiving. FNMA properties are still sold strictly on an "as is" basis. The condition is not guaranteed, despite the good looks.

Sometimes repair problems can and do arise after the sale, for which FNMA claims it is not responsible. FNMA may still have liability for property condition problems under the Texas Deceptive Trade Practices Act, which cannot be disclaimed, even by an "as is" agreement. The DTPA has an express antiwaiver clause. It depends very much on the circumstances whether such liability may attach or not.

FNMA AUCTIONS

Investors and owner-occupant homebuyers may well obtain a FNMA home through an auction. A broker can register a buyer for a FNMA auction, which costs the buyer nothing, although the broker gets a small commission. The homebuyer or investor can also just read the newspapers and directly attend a FNMA auction.

FNMA auctions are efficient and well run. They are truly a spectacle to behold. FNMA auctions are typically held at large hotels, in a great ballroom with hundreds of people. Some are scheduled for two or three nights. The audience is often a sight in itself. Investors from all over the world attend. A prospective buyer walks up to the table set up just outside the entrance to the ballroom and presents a $2,000 cashier's check for examination by one of the auction's checkers, who examines the check carefully to make sure it is real, and then hands the buyer a folder. Inside the folder is a bid card to be held up to make a bid on a property. Also, the prospective buyer receives a program guide, something like a football program, with which to follow the sales at the auction.

At one auction, an organist was playing as prospective buyers entered the hotel ballroom. The organist handled an organ much the way it is done at a baseball game. Apparently the purpose is to whip up the crowd into a bidding frenzy. The auction was handled by Asa Marshall of Hudson and Marshall, a well-known auctioneering firm. Asa Marshall himself was on the podium. He is from Macon, Georgia, and he told all the folks in soft southern tones, to "sit back, reeelax and ENJOY the auction!"

The arrangement of personnel deserves some mention here. The auctioneer stands on a great podium many feet above floor level. Lower to the floor is a person nicknamed the watcher. The watcher does not stand idly by with hands folded, but crouches down as though ready to tend goal at a hockey game. In front of the watcher are a flock of bid takers.

If you haven't already done so, open your program guide. Ideally, sharp bidders should know exactly which homes they plan to bid on, and the maximum price they will pay for each. They know how to handle the situation if they succeed with more than one bid. The program guide gives a number for each house for each night. The property address is listed, and whether it comes with tenant, or without. If it came with tenant, then the dollar rent figure is listed. Anyone who wanted to could have inspected the homes prior to the auction, during set days and times when open houses on the property were held. Only a foolish investor would buy a house sight unseen.

The organ begins to whoop up the crowd. The bid takers assume their angry looks. The watcher crouches. Asa Marshall picks up the hammer. When he brings it down, an overhead projector flashes a picture of the house with the number keyed to the first house in the program guide. The auctioneer begins his fast talking auctioneering banter. The bid takers fan out and walk right up to members in the bidding audience. They jab their fingers right in people's faces with each finger corresponding to a ten thousand or a one thousand on the other hand. Bid cards go up, and bids are taken.

The auctioneer may try any of a variety of tactics. Sometimes he or she starts the bidding low, then brings it up. The smart money hangs back because they know the right price is still much higher. But this slows bidding, and the auctioneer can deal with that! The auctioneer might bring the bidding to a very fast close at a very low price, "going once, going twice. . . ." Suddenly, there may be a flurry of bids as bidders realize what's happening—he's going to sell! Sold! Too late for many. They should have had their bids in. A house just sold for many thousands below what it should have. The auctioneer might take a few backup contracts just to rub it in. The next time the auctioneer starts the bidding, it will be faster and more furious.

Once bidders start to bid, the auctioneer may shift to other tactics, perhaps trying to pit one bidder against another. He or she will point to one, then the other. When one bidder raises the bid, the auctioneer will wheel and turn to the other and virtually shout in an obnoxious tone, "you're out of there, you're out...." Would you take that as a bidder? No way. You shout out a bid that's higher just to "show 'em." The auctioneer smiles and takes the bid. Go to the price level you know you should go to, and no higher, no matter what anyone says or does. Play it cool. Never, never bid in an ego-driven frenzy. But it's hard not to do so when one is in front of a roaring crowd!

If a bidder wins a bid, then a svelte, sharply dressed person saunters down the aisle, hands the bidder a contract to sign to confirm the bid and takes the $2,000 earnest money cashier's check. At a FNMA auction, they'll let you bid for five houses with only $6,000 in cashier's checks; otherwise it's one $2,000 check per house. What a way to sell real estate! It's quite a spectacle, tinged with a bit of sadness. Is the poor young couple whose job was lost and whose home is being sold on the block among the frenzied crowd? Probably not.

SOME ISSUES CONCERNING FNMA AUCTIONS

Contracts

FNMA auctions generally use a special earnest money contract that is similar to standard forms used in a given state, except that all the terms described previously are incorporated into the contract or put in an addendum. The auction contract also deletes most of the normal financing provisions in place of the current auction-oriented financing FNMA will be providing. The contract is normally filled out immediately after a successful bid in a special contract room, unless the successful bidder wants to continue bidding on other homes. In the past, the contract would be signed; title could only be taken in the name of an individual. Trustees, corporate names or assigns are not normally permitted on FNMA auction contracts. Corporations can make arrangements to buy, however. As always, the contract makes the sale strictly "as is, where is" without the addendum's opportunities for inspections and agreements concerning repairs. Auction properties are very much an "as is, where is" affair, no holds barred.

Financing

FNMA auctions usually have a prequalification room that can be visited before the auction. A prospective bidder can walk into the prequalification room and the able personnel can determine almost immediately how much financing the bidder can handle, under the terms FNMA's lenders offer that night. Typically, FNMA will assign selected mortgage companies to handle the financing for the sales at that night's auction. Typically, three lenders will be needed for a three-day auction, with one lender providing each night's financing exclusively. The financing will always be FNMA-based financing, with no FHA or VA loans allowed. If financing is not arranged through one of FNMA's lenders, then buyers have to either arrange their own financing or bring cash. It is not uncommon to close in two to three weeks. The interest rates are usually quite good, often a half-point below the normal market rate.

FNMA financing usually splits up the closing costs with FNMA paying the broker's commission, the cost of a tax certificate, which shows that property taxes have been paid, and the preparation of the deed. Other than that, FNMA may set a limit on closing costs, such as 3 percent, and offer to pay anything above that limit. However, FNMA usually excludes prepaids, mortgage insurance and escrow deposits for taxes and insurance that have to be paid at closing.

Bidding

FNMA auctions are under the control of the auctioneers, who settle all disputes. They determine who makes the high bid. Each bid made on a FNMA home would be separate from other bids, and not made contingent on winning or losing any other bid. FNMA normally reserves the right to add or withdraw properties from the auction at any time. Any announcements from the podium at the auction would normally supersede any contradictory written or advertised material.

Closing

Closings on FNMA auction homes typically have to be within 40 days of contract date, unless $500 is paid for one ten-day extension. FNMA also typically refuses to do a closing strictly from escrow. Otherwise, there will be an obvious risk that an investor buyer may try to improperly obtain owner-occupant financing on favorable terms; they will avoid revealing their identity by not showing up at the closing. FNMA typically picks the title insurance company for the closing. The standard title policy will be available at or after closing.

CONCLUSION

FNMA is the best housekeeper in town for most foreclosed homes. FNMA takes the high road by fixing up properties before offering them for resale. It matches a strong fix-up program with an active effort to find good brokers and get a regular sales program going. It's easy for the investor to learn how to make a basic bid at a FNMA REO auction. Financing is almost always available, making it easy for the small investor to borrow money to buy a FNMA foreclosure home. Some buyers like the terrible frenzy of the moment when auctions take place. It's not a scene for the faint-hearted, but many, many properties are sold under the hammer, even if they are a little bit lower than expectations on the price.

CHAPTER 11

HUD Home
Sales

When an FHA loan on a house has to be foreclosed, then the Department of Housing and Urban Development (HUD), an arm of the federal government, will very likely get the title to the house out of the foreclosure and then sell it by its own procedures. HUD home sales constitute a special type of foreclosure home resale. They are normally sold "as is" with no special financing. The condition of the property may vary greatly from house to house. However, HUD insists its homes are not distressed! HUD homes may be without power or light, water or heat, the ceiling may be on the floor instead of above it, the commodes may be ripped out, the sheetrock may be damaged, but they are beautiful homes in the eye of a knowledgeable investor who knows what to look for. There are some very nice HUD homes as well, which may require a little different approach at a HUD sealed bid opening. We'll discuss HUD's sealed bid strategies and the ways to beat the competition. The keys are a good preview, a good HUD broker, a knowledge of HUD's bidding procedures and a little bit of luck.

This discussion of HUD home sales is broken down into the following categories:

- Overview and background for HUD home sales
- HUD and the foreclosure process
- HUD bid sales
- HUD closings and closing attorneys
- HUD brokers and brokerage

- Financing the HUD bid sale
- Problems with HUD homes and winning bid strategies

OVERVIEW AND BACKGROUND FOR HUD HOME SALES

Terminology—HUD versus FHA

The FHA or Federal Housing Administration is part of the Department of Housing and Urban Development, called HUD. Just as the U.S. Army is part of the Department of Defense, the FHA is part of HUD. In the real estate business, the terms FHA and HUD are often used interchangeably. For example, people may say "HUD homes" for sale or "FHA foreclosures for sale." It's the same program.

HUD Homes—What They Are

Some prospective homebuyers ask how HUD came to be the owner of so many foreclosure homes. HUD doesn't make loans; it insures loans made by private lenders. HUD acquires most of its foreclosure properties from private mortgage companies that have foreclosed on a borrower who had an FHA-insured loan. FHA loan insurance pays off the private mortgage company, usually for every penny they were owed by the borrower, and the mortgage company in turn deeds ownership of the property to HUD. By taking over ownership of the property and reselling it, HUD accomplishes two things: (1) lenders are more willing to make FHA-insured loans because they know HUD will handle the problem of reselling foreclosed homes; and (2) HUD reduces its potential losses from insurance payouts—if the lender sold it, with HUD covering any loss on the resale, then there wouldn't be much incentive for the lender to sell the foreclosed home at a good price.

HUD buys loans from private mortgage companies when the loan is in trouble through a procedure called *assignment*. Occasionally, HUD will foreclose on one of its assigned loans. Otherwise, HUD pays off a private lender to obtain title. HUD gets title after the foreclosure. Buying a HUD home that is listed for sale in the newspaper is nothing more than buying a home HUD owns and wants to resell. HUD bid openings are not true foreclosure sales; they are merely resales of homes HUD acquired from lenders who in turn acquired the homes through foreclosure. Once the FHA has acquired the house, it will sell it. The FHA's objective is to complete the entire sale in four months, broken down to 60 days to market the home and 60 days to close.

FHA Losses—What's Behind a Good Deal for the Buyer

Each day the FHA has to hold a home, it costs $20-$25. HUD may lose $20,000 and more per foreclosure in a city with a down market. So HUD will price a HUD home low, even though this means a sale at a loss. (To the extent that a home sells for less than what the FHA bought it for, plus any holding costs, the FHA sustains a loss.) Just because the FHA loses money on a sale does not necessarily mean the buyer gains. A buyer should look for a home priced at or below fair market value, regardless of the FHA's own losses. However, a person who wants a home to live in may be happy with a good home at or below fair market value.

FHA or HUD Sales Through HUD Brokers

The Property Disposition (PD) offices of an FHA field office usually handle sales to prospective homebuyers. However, a small staff alone cannot be expected to sell large numbers of homes every month without help. As a result, FHA will not deal directly with homebuyers, but rather through HUD brokers.

HUD doesn't hire full-time staff brokers to sell houses. Instead, regular brokers who desire to sell HUD properties must qualify as HUD brokers. Then, when the broker sells a HUD property, he or she collects a 4 percent to 8 percent commission. Because HUD lists its properties as an owner, it gives the full commission to the broker who finds a buyer. HUD only pays brokers who find buyers.

HUD AND THE FORECLOSURE PROCESS

HUD acquires properties from lenders that made FHA loans to borrowers who are now in default. The lender, usually a mortgage company, hires an attorney who is appointed to handle the actual legal foreclosure in accordance with state law. The lender buys the home at the true legal foreclosure sale, after which the mortgage company will go through what is called a *claims with conveyance* procedure. The home will be sold to the FHA, usually for the original loan balance plus the costs of foreclosure. A general warranty deed is used to convey title from the lender that got the house in foreclosure to the FHA. The lender usually recovers any and all possible losses. The FHA receives title to the house in the process. HUD will then market the property.

The AMB

Once a lender forecloses on a house which had an FHA loan, the lender must notify HUD and the local Area Management Broker (AMB), who will manage the HUD homes in a specified area of town until they are sold. The AMB will promptly change the locks, put up the FBI warning sign to scare vandals, install lockboxes so that HUD brokers can get in and arrange for inspections and appraisals. The AMB will inspect but do no more than fix any problems that are imminent hazards to the public. The property is not ready to be shown yet. Such homes must not be shown by any HUD broker until they are properly advertised in the newspaper. However, an examination of the REO lists from a local foreclosure listing service could alert a homebuyer, or a HUD broker who can help a homebuyer, to the addresses of any upcoming HUD homes.

Unfortunately, HUD homes in the care of an AMB are often damaged or vandalized before sale. AMBs bid competitively for work, so they can't afford to spend much on a HUD home. They generally will not be paid to do serious fix up work on the property. HUD homebuyers must remember the saying *caveat emptor*—let the buyer beware.

Initial Steps

The AMB is responsible for checking for occupants, obtaining appraisals and removing junk in the house. If occupants are found, then the local field office must be notified immediately. If the people who were foreclosed on are still in the house, HUD will arrange for their eviction. If tenants are in the house, they will usually be evicted as well, except under special circumstances. If the property is vacant, the AMB must check for personal belongings that have been left on the premises. The personal property may be removed when the field office approves it. The AMB must obtain three appraisals, which can't be more than six months old, of the value of the property. The AMB will also shut off the power and water. A spokesman for the FHA estimates that a flooded house might take as much as $15,000 to repair. To avoid this, the water is turned off, as are the electric power and the natural gas. The AMB must also test for items that may be subject to freeze damage.

Initial Inspections, Appraisals and Forms

Once the AMB inspects the property, he or she must file an initial report on the inspection and condition of the property, which includes the total estimated cost of repairs, with a breakdown by general category, such as the structure, including the roof, foundation and walls; and the systems, including heating and air conditioning, electrical and plumbing. This information is on file at the HUD office, and it may be possible for an investor to obtain it, which could be very useful.

Protecting the Property

On the initial inspection the AMB is responsible for securing and protecting the property by

- securing all openings (i.e., locking the doors and windows);
- notifying local authorities of the change in ownership;
- posting signs on the property, including a warning sign, an FBI warning sign and a HUD foreclosure sale sign; and
- installing lock boxes.

These measures are not especially effective. HUD homes are routinely vandalized. Keys are not particularly difficult to obtain. Every HUD broker has one and entirely too many other people have them as well. HUD brokers can check out many keys for use by sales agents. Some keys slip into the wrong hands.

HUD and Title

Anyone buying a HUD home has reason to be concerned about title problems left over from the foreclosure. HUD can at least convey as good a title as it gets, and it takes measures to get good title. The foreclosing lender is responsible for conveying good and marketable title to the property to HUD. The lender must furnish satisfactory title evidence when the property is conveyed to the Secretary. This may be done either by procuring a title insurance policy or by obtaining a certificate of title from an attorney, which indicates that the attorney has examined the records and found that good title exists.

In general, HUD is able to solve most of its title problems before resale. However, it is advisable for any buyer of a HUD home to purchase a policy of title insurance. HUD no longer pays for the title insurance policy, but the buyer should do so anyway. This is particularly true because HUD only issues a special warranty deed, which gives little protection to the buyer. Moreover, a lawsuit against HUD is governed by the Federal Tort Claims Act, which makes HUD a very difficult target. HUD cannot be sued under state laws. HUD brokers should be particularly careful in this regard because while the government is hard to sue, the HUD broker has no such sovereign immunity.

HUD BID SALES

HUD's Preferred Method of Sale: The Sealed Bid

HUD homes are offered to the public throughout most of the United States by a sealed bid system that is operated out of the HUD field offices for a given region. The United States is broken down into regions, and each region has several field offices. A HUD broker fills out a 9548 Earnest Money Contract with the buyer's bid, which is turned in to the HUD office in a sealed envelope and opened in public during a weekday at a special bid opening, usually held in an auditorium or hotel ballroom. The high bid wins the house.

From time to time in the past, HUD offices have sold properties through an auction. However, the feeling in some HUD offices has been that the auction system has significant problems. Speculators often obtain houses at exceedingly low prices, while unsuspecting first-time homebuyers pay too much. The sealed bid system, which uses HUD brokers, offers the best solution, from HUD's viewpoint. HUD brokers can warn potential buyers about the physical problems with the homes. This is particularly important because HUD cannot afford to fix up its properties the way other sellers can. Auction sales lack this protection because brokers are usually not involved in an auction. Moreover, HUD brokers will help obtain a good price for a buyer. As a result, HUD has persevered with its sealed bid system with considerable success.

HUD Newspaper Ads—How Homebuyers Can Learn about HUD Homes

HUD properties must be listed for sale in a newspaper ad within a few weeks (typically two weeks) of acquisition. In addition, a printed list may be distributed to sales brokers and investors. The list is distributed every week or so with supplements as required to give notice of additions and deletions. The newspaper ads provide the information needed to begin the bidding process.

The newspaper ad itself will list many homes for sale each week. Each home takes up a line of space that typically includes the following information:

- A sequence number
- A key map number—keyed to a privately published map dividing the city into numbered zones
- An FHA case number
- The street address of the property
- A list price
- The number of bedrooms, bathrooms and garage spaces
- The number in parentheses indicating the closing area

Possible additional items include the following:

- LBP, which stands for Lead Based Paint—for pre-1978 homes
- FL after the street address, which indicates the property is within Zone A of the Federal Emergency Management Flood Map System 100 year flood plain.

The *list price* represents HUD's appraised value for the property. The property is appraised at fair market value. The listings are grouped according to the way they are to be sold, namely "uninsured," "insured" or "insured with repair escrow." The newspaper ad also describes how HUD homes are sold and may also give additional information about changes in HUD procedures. HUD brokers should read the paper to learn about shifts in HUD policies.

Newspaper Ads—When To Look

HUD foreclosure listings usually appear in the Friday edition of a city's newspaper. These ads contain the new listings under the New Listings Heading.

EXAMPLE: (Check your local HUD field office for exact dates and times, or just read the real estate section of your newspaper)

Fri	*Sat/Sun M T W Th F Sat/Sun M*	*Tues*	*Wed*
Newly		Sealed	Bids
Listed		Bids	Opened
Houses		Due	
1st Ad			

No bids may be submitted on the new listings until ten days after the ad appears, typically a Monday or Tuesday. This time may be used to show the house to a prospective homebuyer. A suitable bid should be worked out.

If at First HUD Does Not Succeed, It Will Try, Try Again

If a house is not sold the first time through, then it is put in the Extended Listings category and advertised as such. Please note that it is called an extended listing and not a "rerun" or a home that didn't make it the first time. HUD is sensitive to marketing considerations. The Extended Listings will run for several more weeks before the home is pulled.

The HUD newspaper ads are the appropriate source of new HUD home listings. If the house is not listed in the newspaper for any reason, then it is not for sale. Unadvertised HUD homes are not to be entered or shown to potential buyers by HUD brokers. In short, the HUD sales process does not start until the ad runs.

The HUD Bid

HUD bids are submitted by HUD brokers. Individual members of the public are not, in virtually all areas of the country, permitted to write up their own bids and submit them to HUD. The fact that the homes are for sale by an agency of the U.S. government in no way bypasses the need for a state broker's or salesagent's license in offering, appraising or otherwise dealing in HUD homes for others for a fee. All HUD brokers hold a real estate broker's license.

The HUD bid takes the form of an earnest money contract that must be filled out and taken to the area's HUD office. The form 9548 Standard Retail Sales Contract is produced by the U.S. government for use nationwide. This form may have to be supplemented to comply with specific state and local requirements for sales contracts.

"Thunked" and in the Box

Once completed, the HUD earnest money contract (or sales contract in some states) must be signed by the broker and the buyer, sealed up in an envelope with special markings, and then "thunked" with a date time stamp at HUD's office and tossed in the box for bids. Later on, typically a day or so later, the envelopes will be lined up, opened and read. The high bid gets the house.

Lender Prequalification

In some cities, HUD offices require the buyer to be preapproved by a HUD lender for a loan up to a certain figure, which must be greater than the bid price. That way, HUD knows the bidder can really buy.

The Envelope, Please

The HUD bid envelope should be marked on the outside with the case number, property address and return address of the broker. Fig. 11.1 depicts how HUD wants the envelope marked.

Some HUD offices impose additional requirements. The regular or extended listings will be one or the other on an actual envelope, and a choice of only one of the following: "insured," "uninsured" or "insured with repair escrow" will be on the envelope. HUD demands compliance with its submission requirements, or the bid will be rejected. Investors who will not occupy the property must be distinguished from those that do; in a tie bid, HUD will favor the owner occupant.

HUD brokers may submit an unlimited number of offers on an individual property, provided that each offer is from a different prospective purchaser. This practice is not recommended. Any HUD broker who submits multiple bids on the same house runs the risk of being accused of dishonest dealings, bad faith or untrustworthiness in dealing with the buyers. It is hard to fairly serve several buyers with obviously conflicting interests.

FIGURE 11.1   HUD Bid Envelope

Company Name	Bulletin Number
Name and address of broker	Date to be Opened
Broker Code Number	Regular or Extended Listing

SEALED BID DO NOT OPEN

Purchaser's Name	Property Sequence Number
	Case Number & Property
	Address
	(Insured, Uninsured or Insured
	with repair escrow)

The sealed bids must remain sealed and safeguarded until the specified public opening, which is usually the day after the submission deadline.

And the Winner Is . . .

At the time for the sale, the sealed bids will be opened. They are arranged on a table at the front of the large ballroom. Hundreds of HUD brokers, investors and onlookers are usually around. At the appointed hour, the HUD officials will begin opening the envelopes and reading the bids aloud, in the same order as the houses are listed for sale in the newspaper. Each bid envelope that is marked for a given house will be opened. Then the *net to HUD* figures will be compared, and the bid with the highest figure will be announced as the winner. In the event of a tie between two offers, then an owner-occupant bid will be given priority over an investor bid.

All offers will be announced when the bids are opened and the *tentative acceptance* made of the highest net to HUD offer. Comparisons must be made to see if the high bidder on one house was also high bidder on another house that had no competition. If so, the later bid, the one in which there was no competition, would be the one accepted and the former would be rejected. HUD will keep a careful record of the bidding.

HUD brokers (or bidders) can learn about whether or not a bid was successful in one of three ways:

1. By personally attending bid openings;
2. By calling HUD's phone numbers; or
3. Visiting a HUD field office, if you can't attend and the phones are always busy.

Acceptance

HUD accepts a bid by signing the 9548 bid contract. Any broker whose offer has been accepted must be so notified and instructed to take whatever actions are necessary to conclude the sale. If the earnest money check was not included in the bid, it must be sent over promptly to the HUD closing attorney, or the bid will be rejected. Some offices will reject such bids automatically.

HUD brokers are responsible for submitting earnest money to HUD, regardless of whether or not the money has actually been collected from a buyer. Failure to come up with the money could disqualify the broker from the HUD program. So many HUD brokers will demand money, up front, from any buyer who wants to submit a bid.

Rejection

All offers that have been rejected will be returned by HUD by certified mail, including any earnest money check. If the broker gets the earnest money, then it must be returned promptly to the buyer, not held for another bid without the bidder's consent.

If at First You Don't Succeed—Try, Try Again

The first and best shot any bidder has on a property is at the main bid opening that occurs after the house is first advertised in the newspaper. Many of the best houses receive multiple bids and disappear on the first bid opening. However, some houses are not bid on at all. Or all bids on the house are rejected as too low or improperly submitted. If so, the house is still available for sale.

Extended Bid Openings

In cities with down markets and a large number of HUD foreclosures, HUD may offer homes that were unsold on the main sale day on a daily basis. Each day, the HUD bid submission procedure will be repeated. The same envelopes, the same amount of earnest money and the same procedures will be required, except that the bids must be in by a set time for a bid opening that day or the next. Although the best shot at a good HUD home is the regular bid opening, extended listings can be a source of HUD homes at good prices. If the house doesn't sell as an extended listing after three weeks or so, HUD will reprice it and offer it again in the main bid opening.

No Time To Lose—Only a Few Weeks To Close

Once a bid has won, then the buyer has a set time to close from the date a HUD official signs the 9548 earnest money contract, usually a few days after the high bid is won and often on the bid day.

The buyer may now wish to apply for title insurance and inspect the property. However, a buyer who backs out of the contract because of problems with the property's condition will lose the earnest money. At the end of the time period, the buyer must either close or pay a delay fee.

BYOF—Bring Your Own Financing

HUD sells its foreclosure homes for cash. It does not offer financing as an integral part of its foreclosure resale scheme. A buyer may apply for an FHA loan with which to buy the HUD home, use any other financing or pay in cash. Also, if the house is listed as "uninsured," FHA loans aren't available, so private financing or cash must be substituted.

The broker may arrange for the buyer to meet with a loan officer from a mortgage company, particularly one who has experience with HUD home purchases. In many cities, HUD now requires a buyer to submit a preapproval letter from a HUD-approved lender giving the amount a borrower is eligible for. If the bid is won, the buyer should go to the loan officer to fill out the application form for a loan. The broker can pick up a copy of the signed earnest money contract from the Property Disposition counter at HUD headquarters. The contract and the prequalification information should be enough for the lender to start processing the loan application.

Buyers of HUD homes are not required to use FHA financing, but a majority do. Although FHA loans are available to the average bidder/buyer, it does not influence the bid.

Inability To Get a Loan after a Successful Bid

HUD offices often permit successful bidders to recover some or all of their earnest money if they cannot obtain financing on "insured" or "insured with repair" escrow homes, although bidders on "uninsured" homes lose their money. However, to ensure prompt return of the earnest money, bidders should make certain that they can document their inability to obtain financing. In the event a HUD loan was applied for, the documentation is fairly simple because either HUD rejected the loan when it was submitted by a private mortgage company for approval, or a private mortgage company who is a D.E. (Direct Endorsement) would have rejected the loan, then written HUD to request regular processing through the HUD office, and the Mortgage Credit branch of HUD would have rejected the loan as well, thereby producing a HUD 92900.4 form with the rejection noted thereon. That would be excellent documentation.

Failure To Close—In General

There are many reasons why the top bidder at the regular bid opening will not be able to close. Among the most common is the inability to obtain financing, which has been discussed already. Other reasons include problems with the property's condition that came up after the initial walk-through which led to the bid submission. As one HUD official once put it, the situation might be one where "the air conditioner sprouted legs and ran off." What the buyer sees before the bid is not necessarily what he or she will get after the bid. Much can happen to the property during the 60 days of waiting for a loan to close, not all of it good. Some HUD brokers even pay a neighborhood youth to watch over the house prior to closing. It's not a bad idea. Of course, a buyer might simply get cold feet. But what happens if the buyer has difficulty in closing, whatever the reason? There are two problems in particular: the first is paying extension fees to get the house; the second is coaxing HUD into returning the earnest money if the deal won't go through. Neither alternative is very pleasant for the buyer.

Return of the earnest money?—the answer is usually NO!   If a buyer can't buy a HUD home because the loan application is rejected by a lender due to lack of income or creditworthiness, then the buyer may recover the earnest money submitted with a bid. Without such a rule, bidders would be more reluctant to bid. Otherwise, however, HUD offices can be very hard-nosed in some areas about giving back the earnest money to a successful bidder who doesn't close. HUD wants the money because it needs to cover the cost of holding a home in inventory. If the house suffers damage beyond what the buyer expected after the initial inspection, HUD will not return the earnest money if the buyer backs out, nor will it pay for the repair. HUD is not completely inhuman, even on "uninsured" bids, but the answer is almost always "no" to investor buyers who back out of buying and seek return of earnest money, regardless of the reason.

Hope beyond hope.   HUD does provide a very limited policy of returning the earnest money under conditions of great hardship. Here is what HUD says officially: "In the event of extreme theft or vandalism to the property, HUD will use its discretion and may refund the earnest money. There may be other isolated cases where HUD will agree to refund earnest money which will be reviewed on a case by case basis."

Buyers should be advised that their earnest money is very much at risk when it is submitted and a bid is accepted.

HUD CLOSINGS

The sales closing must occur within two calendar months of HUD's acceptance of the sales contract, which is the date the contract was signed by the appropriate HUD official. Usually this is done the day of the bid opening. A sale is considered officially closed on the date of funding, that is, once the money may actually be deposited into the HUD closing agent's account.

Because HUD loses money every day a HUD home is not sold, it will charge extension fees if the buyer attempts to close past the closing date. A 15-calendar-day extension may be granted for a fee. The broker must forward the extension fee to the closing agent prior to the expiration of the two calendar months HUD gives to close the sale. Extension fees are nonrefundable and will not be applied to the purchase price. However, extension fees can be prorated (refunded) at a successful closing at $10+ per unused day. HUD counts fast, however; weekends and holidays count as days.

HUD closes the sales of its foreclosures through HUD closing attorneys or title companies. HUD normally divides a city into districts, each with its own HUD closing attorney. The closing attorney wins the position by competitive bidding. Even if another special attorney is used, HUD will pay no more than the regular closing attorney bid. Once HUD signs the 9548 sales contract with the high bidder, it will send a closing package to the HUD closing attorney (not the lender), which includes the sales contract, tax and title information, a letter to the AMB and a repair escrow list if the home is being purchased as an insured, repair escrow home.

The HUD home closing at an attorney's office is similar to a title company closing, except that the seller, the FHA, does not appear. HUD closings often occur toward the end the month and toward the end of the week. HUD closing attorneys usually have a staff member who handles the closing in a small conference room. The buyer may be asked to sign documents that will satisfy a lender, if one is involved. A HUD-1 Uniform Settlement Statement will be prepared, showing who pays what. HUD has some special policies regarding funding, locks and keys and final settlement.

HUD and Lenders—Papers Please!

HUD home foreclosure resales are normally financed by an outside lender. HUD sells homes for cash, in contrast to the VA or FNMA, which provide financing for qualified buyers. Investor buyers of HUD homes simply pay cash for the homes. If the bid winner of a HUD home arranges financing through a regular lender, which is likely, then the paperwork must be sent to the HUD closing attorney in order to close. Lenders should be encouraged not to send in papers at the last minute in order to avoid problems.

Locks, Board Removal and Possession

On closing and funding (cash delivered), HUD will normally provide new locks once a door lock change fee is paid. Under no circumstances are HUD keys to be given to prospective purchasers. Buyers must not occupy a residence, begin repair work or turn on utilities before closing and funding. HUD will remove boards and replace any broken windows on "insured" or "insured with repair escrow" properties on closing and funding.

HUD BROKERS AND BROKERAGE

As indicated earlier, only HUD brokers can submit bids or obtain HUD keys. Salesagents who work for HUD brokers may submit bids and use keys, but they do not have any special license or designation.

In cities with many foreclosures, regular, state-licensed brokers usually become HUD brokers by taking a short training course.

Buyers Can Bargain Broker Compensation

Many brokers are used to signing some kind of exclusive listing agreement giving that broker the exclusive right to be a broker in the sale of a given house. Such listings are not available for HUD homes. All HUD homes are sold as open listings, which means any HUD broker can sell a HUD home. The first broker to find a buyer and submit a winning bid wins the 6 percent commission, and it's winner take all. The winning broker does not have to share the commission with anyone. Even if another bid was close, the losing bid wins no commission.

HUD agrees to pay a sales commission of up to 6 percent of the sales price (in very selected circumstances, even more) to the selling broker. Brokers may waive all or part of their sales commission to enhance the competitiveness of a bid for a house. By reducing the HUD brokerage commission, more money goes to HUD, giving a higher net to HUD figure, which actually wins the bid, rather than the sales price. The commission is listed in item 6 of the HUD Sales Contract (HUD 9548). The commission will be paid to the broker on closing and funding.

In the past, some HUD brokers were involved with operations that charged *bid submission* fees to potential buyers of HUD homes. HUD brokers are not permitted to charge such fees, which were often disguised as mortgage loan application or processing fees. Some of these operations were heavily advertised. They would charge the buyer $300 or more to prepare a bid for a buyer or check out the buyer's credit. Once again, a broker may not receive such fees because HUD does not allow it. If the HUD broker is associating with or benefitting monetarily from unlicensed persons who are charging these fees, then the broker is violating HUD policy.

Broker Advertising

HUD brokers commonly advertise HUD homes. However, a knowledgeable buyer can get information about HUD homes directly from the newspapers or from HUD itself. HUD brokers often advertise to get business for themselves, rather than to sell a specific house. HUD brokers are restricted in that they cannot advertise HUD homes as distressed, or say that a particular broker is the exclusive agent for HUD homes. Ads to sell HUD homes must comply with Fair Housing and Truth in Lending laws.

For Sale Signs

Investors can identify a HUD home by the sign, which is put up by HUD itself. HUD brokers can't put signs on or about a HUD home, unless authorized by HUD, such as for an open house. Otherwise, hundreds of broker's signs would appear on one HUD home. However, if a HUD broker sells a HUD home, then that broker may install a "sold" sign.

Open Houses

Investor buyers can attend HUD open houses. HUD-approved brokers may hold an open house provided the following guidelines are adhered to. Typically, the first broker on the property in the morning gets to hold the open house, so interested buyers can generally tour HUD homes early in the morning.

FINANCING THE PURCHASE OF HUD HOMES

Although HUD does not provide financing as part of its foreclosure resales system, successful bid winners may arrange any type of loan the buyer chooses, such as an FHA-insured loan from a private mortgage company or other FHA-approved lender. Most major residential lenders are DE (Direct Endorsement)—these are lenders who can approve loans directly without sending papers to be double-checked by HUD.

Loan Approval

Ordinarily, if a DE lender rejects a loan, that's it. However, if the loan was to be used to buy a HUD foreclosure home, then a DE must send the paperwork to HUD for review. HUD/FHA's Mortgage Credit branch may decide to approve the loan anyway, even if the DE disapproved it. If HUD approves the loan, then HUD issues a commitment to insure the loan (effectively loan approval) and the loan and closing will soon follow.

Investor Loans versus Owner-Occupant Loans

An owner-occupant loan is for a home (just one) that the owner will live in as a principal residence. Investor loans are for homes that the owner will rent out, but not occupy as a principal residence. All but a few types of new investor loans were stopped on December 15, 1989. HUD's investor loans for foreclosured HUD home purchases survived HUD's December 1989 massacre and live on, at least as of 1993. However, the post-December 1989 investor loans for foreclosure properties are not assumable without credit approval of the buyer by the lender, which is new. This makes HUD homes less desirable for investors because they will be harder to resell if a buyer has to meet a lender's credit standards. In any event, HUD has always favored the owner-occupant loan. Owner-occupant borrowers must live in the home, although it may be sold or leased under hardship circumstances.

Down Payments for HUD Homes

When a bid is turned in to HUD for a particular home, the calculations on the earnest money contract should show a down payment. The minimum down payment will vary, depending on whether the home will be bought by an owner occupant or an investor. A buyer who will live in the house may make a lower down payment than an investor.

HUD Minimum Bids

HUD hopes to sell a home at the price it lists in the newspaper. This price is HUD's appraised value. However, it will accept lower bids in weaker markets, to a specified minimum. The minimum may be as low as 91 percent for an owner-occupant buyer purchasing a house listed as "insured" in the newspapers, or 75 percent for a cash-as-is home purchased by an investor. However, if bidding is strong, a house may actually be sold at more (not less) than the newspaper price. The best HUD offices average sales at 100 percent of newspaper list price or above.

Certain specialized newspapers or data services may have to be consulted to see what the minimum bid appears to be, which they do by tracking successful bid prices in a given area. That's why a good HUD broker who knows the bid prices in an area can help win a bid. An astute buyer can still win by bidding at a price HUD will accept at a minimum for the property, or by bidding high enough to win against many bidders.

HUD SALES CATEGORIES—"INSURED," "UNINSURED," "INSURED WITH REPAIR ESCROW"

The financing for any property is also affected substantially by which of the three bid categories the HUD home is sold under. All the categories normally offer no warranty, require a $1,000 down payment and must be closed in two months. However, some terms and conditions of sale vary for each category. There are three important groups: "insured;" "insured with repair escrow"; and "uninsured."

HUD Homes Advertised as "Insured"

A home listed in the "Insured" column in the HUD newspaper ad means that it's eligible for FHA-insured mortgage financing. An FHA loan is not guaranteed, but the house meets minimum standards to allow a qualified buyer to use an FHA loan to buy it. The buyer will have to apply for the loan and be approved, in terms of income and creditworthiness, by a private lender. Bidders may use either FHA or conventional financing to buy the home. HUD will also take cash.

Property condition.   To HUD's knowledge, the property meets the minimum property standards that an FHA loan normally requires. An FHA-insured loan could therefore be obtained as far as the property condition is concerned, at the time that HUD looked at the property before listing it for sale. Please note, however, the property is sold in an unrepaired condition. There could be many things wrong with the property that need repairs; even worse, the property might deteriorate after a bid is submitted. Since an FHA appraisal has already been obtained, property condition problems that come up after the bid is won should not affect the lender, but the buyer may be crazy to buy the house unless he or she can afford the repairs.

HUD Homes Advertised as "Insured with Repair Escrow"

FHA-insured loans are available on properties offered as "Insured with Repair Escrow" in the newspaper. These loans are available for owner occupants only. The properties in this category require certain repairs to make them eligible for FHA-insured loans. FHA/HUD uses the repair escrow procedure only with HUD/FHA financing; it isn't done with other types of financing. The buyer must have sufficient income and creditworthiness to qualify for an FHA "insured with repair escrow" loan.

Property condition.   Unlike the insured category, the "insured with repair escrow" properties need repairs before they can be financed with an FHA-insured loan. The property is sold in an unrepaired condition. To HUD's knowledge, the property needs $5,000 (this figure has been rising) or less in repairs to meet HUD's minimum property standards for an FHA-insured loan. HUD does not guarantee that the property is without defect or that the cost to repair all defects will be less than $5,000.

A list of the known repair requirements is supposed to be posted in the house by the Area Management Broker (AMB). Unfortunately, these lists are purloined quite often. Calling the Area Management Broker to get one doesn't always seem to work either. It can be quite frustrating. A call to HUD's main office is recommended, but that doesn't get the list. The solution is to go down to the Property Disposition counter at a local HUD office, where a copy of the repair sheet is kept on hand. It's a hassle, but it's better than not having one.

The newspaper listing will indicate a repair amount of 110 percent of the figure shown on the repair requirement list posted in the property and at the HUD office. The 110 percent amount will show up on the HUD 9548 sales contract. Remember, the actual repairs on the repair sheet will be 100 percent (let's say $3,000, for example), but the newspaper list and the contract form will add 10 percent (making it $3,300 in the $3,000 repair situation). Also, the full repair escrow figure must go on the contract or HUD will reject the bid.

Generally, the repairs are light ones such as carpet, paint, etc. Heavy repairs, such as foundation work, are usually not included in the "insured with repair escrow" category. Such situations might justify a 203(k) loan, explained in Chapter 2, which begins at $5,000 in repairs, but such loans are tricky to work with in some situations.

FHA financing is available through FHA approved private lenders, provided that the borrower qualifies. Part of the FHA loan will be put into a repair escrow at closing for this type of property. The money will then be spent, under the lender's supervision, so that FHA can be sure that the needed repairs are completed. A final inspection of the repairs will be made for the FHA.

Some, but not all, contractors demand cash for as much as half the repairs up front from the homebuyer. The contractors who do not charge up front are probably more familiar with HUD procedures to begin with. If a buyer pays the contractor for part of the repairs up front, then the contractor can still be reimbursed from the lender's escrow as the work is done. The homebuyer will then have to get his or her cash back from the contractor!

Investor buyers may buy "insured with repair escrow" homes, but they are not available to investors with HUD financing. Hence, for the investor such homes are much like buying uninsured properties, except that the damage is lighter.

Repair escrow provisions.   The escrow repair amount entered on the sales contract will be escrowed at closing. Repairs should be completed within ten days of closing. After a compliance inspection has been performed, payment of the actual costs for the repair will be made to the contractor who did the work. Of course, the purchaser may also make the repairs, but if so, only the cost of the materials will be reimbursed. No labor cost will be paid. Any unused amount in the escrow after all repairs have been paid for will be used to reduce the outstanding principal balance on the loan. Any repair costs in excess of the amount escrowed will be the sole responsibility of the buyer. The repairs will be done after the sale is closed, so they won't delay matters.

HUD Homes Advertised as "Uninsured"

These properties are sold in an unrepaired condition for cash. The sales contract is not contingent upon the buyer's ability to obtain financing. HUD will offer no assistance in obtaining any financing. HUD wants cash at the close, or it will keep the earnest money, but it will not sue for specific performance. HUD expects to close these cash sales quickly. These properties may have a low price, but they may be a poor buy if the condition is so bad that the price is really justified. Buyers should use due caution in purchasing such properties.

Property condition.   The property is unrepaired. Its condition is such that it cannot meet the property condition standards for an FHA-insured loan. The property may also violate local building codes. HUD won't even make repairs required by building codes. Any requirements that a lender has for repairing the property cannot be undertaken until after the purchase. It would be advisable, therefore, to arrange to buy the property for cash, rather than count on a loan, because a lender may not want to make a loan until repairs are done. This is not possible with a HUD home.

Financing.   HUD will provide no assistance in obtaining financing, and FHA-insured loans are unavailable to buy this type of property.

Buyers should carefully consider their ability to obtain financing before they submit a bid on the property.

Down payment.   No down payment is required because the entire purchase price is due in cash at the close. However, if a buyer uses a conventional loan of some kind (an unusual one, given the poor property condition) to buy the house, then the buyer would have to satisfy the lender's requirements for a down payment.

PROBLEMS WITH HUD HOMES

Property Condition Problems

One of the largest single drawbacks to buying HUD homes is the property condition: these structures often have many problems. Commodes may be ripped out. Walls may have damage. The rug may be growing fungus—underneath. There may be "slime in the ice machine." Most importantly, the foundation and roof may be in poor shape. These two items are routinely the largest repair projects.

HUD makes few repairs.   Early in the development of its foreclosure program, HUD decided to make very little in the way of repairs to the homes. There were several very good reasons for this policy. First, the initial Property Disposition staffs were far too small to operate and manage any repair program. Second, the repair of a HUD home would involve contracting with the federal government, which is a complex process that would inhibit fast sales. Third, HUD officials took the sensible view that the U.S. government is inherently less efficient than the private sector at making repairs. HUD's theory, and one that has proven correct, is that private buyers would purchase HUD homes, look at the condition of the property and calculate how best to make repairs with all the creativity, cost savvy and ingenuity that the private sector has.

HUD simply put the homes on the block, and let the market settle the price with due consideration to the repair problem. One problem with this policy is the ignorant buyer who tries to buy a HUD home thinking the agency warrants its condition. HUD hasn't, HUD doesn't, and HUD won't guarantee a home in good condition to a buyer.

HUD may make very limited repairs to the property for security purposes. Broken windows, missing doors and missing locks may be replaced. Eager employees in HUD's Property Disposition Department often figure ways to get a little bit of money to fix the house. For example, if the ceiling has fallen, HUD may have the money to sweep up the floor, but not to replace the ceiling.

Damage after bid submission.   Between the time the HUD contract is signed and the time the HUD home is purchased, the house may suffer further damage. The air conditioner compressor may vanish. Pipes could be frozen and break. A leak in the roof might cause the attic to accumulate water on top of the ceiling, resulting in a collapsed ceiling. A foundation that looked good initially might break or suffer further damage by the time of purchase. A buyer who fails to close because the house at closing is not the same house as the one when the bid was submitted, will nevertheless lose the earnest money.

Vandalism.   There is no telling who vandalizes a HUD home. The FBI warning sign does not stop them. Vandals may include mischievous neighbors, vengeful former owners, professional bandits, juvenile delinquents, drifters and all persons with a HUD key, which is an all too large portion of the city's populace. Some HUD brokers pay a neighborhood youth to watch the property that was successfully bid on until the closing.

Buyers—be careful.   In sum, the HUD home may present some problems for first time buyers. The questionable condition of some of the homes, combined with the risks of losing the earnest money if the bidder walks, make the HUD home less desirable for certain types of buyers. HUD homes may not be suitable for persons who are withdrawing their life savings and cannot afford to lose their $1,000 earnest money deposit. HUD home buyers must accept risks or not buy at all.

Price Problems—Bid Pricing and Competition

A really nice house in a rising market may require a bid 20 percent over the HUD newspaper price figure to win. Investors won't pay that much. However, a couple that wants a home at a reasonable price can certainly obtain one through HUD. On the other hand, the lower-priced homes will often have their share of problems. Some houses sell for less than the newspaper list price, but others sell for more. When market prices rise, so do HUD home prices.

HUD's competition.   A really nice HUD home may receive several bids. On the other hand, HUD homes with few bids often have problems. It's best to bid the first time a nice HUD home comes on the market. Competition makes it hard to assure a buyer that a particular home can be obtained. Wise HUD brokers sell the program, not the house. Wise buyers buy the HUD program, rather than get their hearts set on one house. However, all buyers can get their hopes up, only to see them dashed with an unsuccessful bid. To be assured of winning, a very high bid may have to be submitted, but that won't feel good if you find out that you could have got it for less! Any bid system has such problems.

WINNING BID STRATEGIES

Naturally, the HUD homebuyer wants an outstanding deal. The buyer would ideally like to buy a property at a price below fair market value. On the other hand, HUD wants to realize, on average, the fair market value for its properties. However, HUD needs to sell its homes. There are several ways to win the game as a buyer:

- Bid near the minimum acceptable level and hope perseverance at that level will pay off.
- Submit bids at a below-market price with the idea of being tapped as a backup.
- Aim to buy a house under the HUD program, rather to buy one particular house.

HUD sets a minimum bid on its properties, but it is not an official figure that is rigidly set. Normally, it is 80 percent of list price. HUD can raise the figure if the circumstances warrant. For example, in one city, HUD raised its minimum bid to knock out a particular investor's low-end strategy. The investor, presumably, was bidding consistently near the minimum level and getting too many homes. The minimum bid could be calculated by an astute HUD program watcher, so HUD officials will usually tell about what the minimum will be, but they don't guarantee it. HUD can also drop its bid. For example, in Houston,

HUD once engineered the great Thanksgiving "Turkey Sale" during November, by dropping the minimum bid to 70 percent.

Potential buyers can submit bids with the idea of being tapped as a backup. Although buyers still fail to get financing, HUD's new prequalification procedures make that less likely to happen, but if it does, or if the buyer can't buy for another reason, HUD may offer the house to the second highest bidder at that point. HUD may call only once, and there may be no follow up. The second highest bidder, after being called, should accept within a day or the opportunity may be lost. This strategy can get a house at a below market price.

HUD's list price is its estimate of fair market value. However, these appraisals are not always precise. However, some of the most knowledgeable people in the HUD business will tell you that HUD's estimate of value is not right all the time. The inspection that accompanies the appraisal may be minimal. One way to be sure to get a good buy is to appraise the property very carefully to look for one with a better value than HUD gave it. Some of the most astute investors actually maintain professional appraisers to do this, but a knowledgeable broker or salesagent who knows the area may be able to beat the odds and find that good buy.

A careful analysis of HUD home prices in an area is highly desirable. A broker who plans on submitting a bid should consult the HUD office computer printouts to review the bid prices for successful HUD home bids. This may be done free of charge at the HUD headquarters where bids are turned in. Alternatively, many brokers prefer to hire a consulting service, such as the HUD "Yellow Jacket" (or other specialized newspaper), which prints lists of HUD bid prices, so HUD brokers can tell what they are up against. A winning bid can then be calculated and submitted.

CONCLUSION

HUD acquires properties from lenders who acquired them from defunct borrowers at a foreclosure. HUD will pay off much, if not all, of a lender's loss in an FHA foreclosure situation. Once that happens, HUD needs to resell the home. Here are a few characteristics of HUD foreclosure resales:

- HUD sells by sealed bid on the theory that this forces the bidder to bid a high price for fear the property will be lost unless the bidder bids all he or she can.
- HUD closings may take place at title insurance companies or approved HUD closing attorneys.
- HUD sells through brokers and salesagents who work for HUD brokers. A licensed broker can apply and become a HUD broker who sells and trades in HUD houses. Regular buyers cannot submit bids on houses; all bids must go through a HUD broker.
- Various bidding strategies can be used to buy HUD homes, such as turning in a low bid in hopes that the first successful bid will be rejected, and the house will fall to the second bidder. It doesn't happen automatically. People must ask.
- HUD may help sell its own properties by a loan, which are commonly available to investor purchasers at a bid opening.
- HUD homes vary tremendously in quality, from being in very good condition to being run down.

The number of HUD homes grows as foreclosures grow, and fall as the number of HUD home loans declines. HUD will not last in its current form forever, but it has a usable and very useful set of procedures for such matters. HUD homes may be great candidates for fixer-upper strategies and speedy resales.

CHAPTER 12

VA Home
Sales

When a VA loan goes into foreclosure, the VA itself will most likely get the title to the property. Once the VA gets a home, it will resell it, through its own unique resale procedures, which may parallel HUD's, but differ in certain respects. VA-foreclosed home resales have a few advantages over other programs in the area of financing such as zero or low down payments, VA loans for nonveterans and low closing costs. No one else can match such financing. VA sales are normally organized through sealed bids or auctions, but the sales strategies can vary in a bureaucracy that must struggle mightily to cope with foreclosure problems. A sharp investor may be able to find a good opportunity to take advantage of a VA foreclosure resale.

THE BASICS OF THE VA FORECLOSURE
RESALE PROGRAM

What VA Foreclosure Homes Are

VA resales operate in a manner similar to FHA resales, which were described in Chapter 11. The Department of Veterans Affairs or VA is a government agency which guarantees that qualified mortgage loans made to veterans will be repaid to the private lenders who made them. If the borrower defaults and fails to pay, then the private lender will foreclose and almost always acquire title to the property from the legal foreclosure sale. After that, the private lender will file forms with the

VA much like insurance claim forms, and ask the VA to repay the lender the full loan balance unpaid by the veteran, in exchange for a deed to the property. Once the lender deeds the property to the VA, the VA will resell the house to the general public under a special program. Small investors and homebuyers are the target market for these homes. Basically, the interested buyer will have to:

1. locate a VA broker,
2. find a house,
3. submit and win a competitive bid on the house,
4. get a loan and
5. finalize or close the purchase.

Selecting a VA Broker

Like the FHA, the VA uses special brokers to handle its bid submissions. In order to become a VA broker, a regularly licensed broker normally attends a free workshop/seminar on selling VA homes, which is sponsored by the VA. Such seminars are usually open to the public and are the best place to learn about VA sales procedures. Unfortunately, in some parts of the country, brokers aren't required to attend any workshop in order to sell VA homes, so be careful which broker you use. Not every VA broker in a down market is skilled at the job.

A prospective homebuyer would probably have the best luck submitting a bid through a VA broker who regularly deals in VA properties. In a rising market, bidding is competitive, but in a down market, not every house is a good or safe investment. Brokers who keep up with the VA stand the best chance of advising a buyer about the best houses and bid figures. In addition, an increasing number of computer services or newsletters are available to help with VA bids. Another problem confronting the VA buyer is the condition of the property. A broker who does the homework on a VA house is likely to provide better service to the homebuyer.

VA brokers work directly for the VA, which pays only for a sale and not for a listing. Therefore, the VA broker who finds a buyer can keep the full commission. The VA will pay up to a 6 percent commission, but the commission is added to the buyer's bid on the VA house. It reduces the net to the VA, thereby reducing the buyer's chances of success on the bid. The broker may agree to reduce the VA commission if it will assist in winning the bid. The VA also may pay bonuses to VA brokers who find cash buyers or work hard to sell properties. VA brokers are subject to VA regulation and must work in the VA's best interest, rather than the buyer's, if the two interests are in conflict.

Selecting a House To Bid On

The VA acquires homes regularly in every VA region. It also has a substantial inventory of unsold homes. However, not every VA-owned home is for sale. Those that are for sale and that a prospective buyer may bid on are listed in the VA's weekly ad, which is usually carried in a city's major newspaper. A bid may be submitted after the house first appears in the newspaper. The bid will be opened on a set day of the week, which is usually advertised in the paper. More desirable homes will often go at the first available bid opportunity. Therefore, it pays to watch the papers and move quickly to make a decision submitting a bid. Here is an example of a typical VA time schedule to run an ad and take bids on a house:

Thur	*F S SM T W Th F S S M*	*Tues*	*W*	*Thur*
House 1st Appears in Newspaper Ad		Bid Due VA Office		Bid Opening VA Office

Here's the basic plan for buying a VA home advertised in the paper:

- Finding out about a particular VA property
- Selecting a VA property
- Submitting and winning a bid

FINDING OUT ABOUT A VA PROPERTY

Basically, a VA property is listed in the newspaper. If it's not in the newspaper, it's not for sale. A VA broker may only offer advertised properties for sale, even if the VA owns the unlisted homes. Other than the papers, the VA has two methods of finding out about properties: a "hot line" phone service and a computer bulletin board.

The phone service can tell interested persons whether a house is still available for sale. Some VA regions have experimented with computer bulletin boards as a medium to advertise houses. A buyer calls in, connects to VA's computer program by modem and sees a list of VA homes for sale on the buyer's home computer.

VA Newspaper Ads

VA newspaper ads contain several columns each of which contains either a number, a code or some other bit of information. Below is an explanation for each item:

Sequence Number—This is the order in which the bids will be opened on the bid opening day listed for that ad. The ads may be run in different newspapers, often one paper for a broad city area.

Key Map Number—(a.k.a. "Kmap" in the newspaper). This handy map system breaks cities into key map zones, which make it easier to locate specific addresses. Each key map zone has its own number, which is listed in this column of the VA ad. Key maps are available in book form (rather than as a single foldout map) at many local bookstores. These maps are extremely useful when investigating real estate.

Address—This is just the street address of the house.

PM Number—This Property Management number is used on all the VA's documents to identify the property. It must be on the bid, the loan papers and any correspondence concerning the property. The VA may know nothing about the property unless you know the PM number.

Zip—This includes the last three digits of the U.S. Postal Service zip code.

Listing Price—(a.k.a. "LPrice" in the newspaper). This price represents the VA's estimate of the property's value. The VA will accept bids at less than this price, but generally not below 80 percent of the figure. It varies. On the nicer properties, a bid in excess of the list price will probably be needed to stand a reasonable chance of success. An *asterisk* next to the LPrice *indicates that financing is not available* from the VA for the property. It is probably not available by other means either. This is a property that will very likely require a cash bidder.

The "M" Column—This indicates whether the property meets Minimum Property Standards. The VA has extensive standards for properties. They must have sound foundations and be in generally good condition. If the property "is believed to meet" minimum property standards sufficient to obtain a VA loan, then the "M" column is checked Y for Yes.

Rooms—The format is Bedrooms/Bathrooms/Garage. Baths can be full or half baths.

Remarks—Remarks about the property are written out. They should be studied to learn some of the problems that exist with the property. It also includes the AR number.

AR stands for "Acknowledgment Required." This means the prospective buyer will have to initial a checksheet next to the listed AR number. Each AR number corresponds to a problem with the property. By initialing an AR number, the prospective buyer is acknowledging that he or she understands a particular problem exists with the house. Here is a brief list of some of the AR numbers:

- **AR-1 "As Is".** The property is being sold "as is." No repairs will be made by the VA to the property on plumbing, heating or electrical systems.
- **AR-2 Pool.** The VA will make no repairs of any kind to the pool, its machinery, equipment or operation.
- **AR-3 Foundation.** The property shows signs of foundation settlement. The VA does not warrant the foundation or repair of damage resulting from foundation movement. This is probably the most serious expense a homeowner can face. A bad foundation may cost up to $20,000 or more to repair.
- **AR-4 Flood.** The property is in a special flood area that requires flood insurance.
- **AR-5 Sewer.** Water and/or sewer service is on a private system. No other information is known and the VA makes no warranties, express, or implied, regarding these systems.
- **AR-6 LPG.** A Liquified Petroleum Gas (LPG) system serves this property. The adequacy and stability of the system and the ownership of any tanks is unknown.
- **AR-7 Maintenance Assessment.** Maintenance assessment is to be paid directly to the homeowner's association and is not included in the mortgage payments.
- **AR-8 Rot/Termites.** Damage has been caused to this property by one or more of the following: dry rot, rot and/or

termites. Hopefully, an inspection will show that the damage from termites does not require tenting the house, that is, putting a big tent around the whole house and pumping it full of deadly insecticide, preferably after all people and pets are outside.

- **AR-9 Lead Paint.** Due to the widespread use of lead-based paints prior to 1950, we understand the potential danger to children that may exist in this house if they eat the chipping or peeling paint.
- **AR-10 Appliance Ownership/Condition Unknown.** Ownership and operability of all free-standing appliances, window air conditioners, burglar bars, ceiling fans and gas grills, etc. are unknown. Possession is 9/10ths of the law in these situations, but beware the enthusiastic former owner who simply removes the appliances without the home-buyer's permission. I was once told by such a person that calling the police to stop their repossession was pointless because they would remove it faster than the police could arrive on the scene to stop it!
- **AR-11 Other.** Other problems, or good selling points, should be filled out exactly as they appear in the newspaper.

Last Week's Listings—The newspaper ad may include last week's listings, which have not been bid on.

Extended Listings—These properties were offered for sale the last time, but no one wanted them. They're not listed as "rejects" but rather as "extended," which means that for a limited time only, their availability for sale is extended! These can be bid on during the week without having to wait until the main bid opening.

Visiting a VA Property

A person who sees a newspaper listing that looks interesting should visit the property before submitting a bid on it. There are at least three ways a prospective buyer can see a VA house:

1. Drive by it.
2. Have the broker show it.
3. Attend a broker-sponsored open house.

Drive by.   There is nothing in the VA regulations to prohibit an enterprising purchaser from driving past the outside of a VA house. Readers who might do this are cautioned not to enter the property, as this would probably be illegal trespass. A VA house will be identified by the VA's own sign. Buyers need a VA broker to get inside the house.

VA broker escorted visits.   A broker can help a prospective buyer in many ways, by skillfully selecting and presenting the best VA listings for a buyer, by helping the VA buyer find a lender and be prequalified or preapproved and by submitting, winning and closing a bid. A good broker will fill the buyer in on problems with buying VA properties, as required by the VA, and recommend the best ways to bid on them.

VA brokers have the keys. A VA master key, which can't be duplicated, is needed to get into a VA house. VA brokers have these, but can't give them out and must accompany the buyer on a house visit. A few years ago, a broker prepared a special package that included a description of the property and a master key. The broker was suspended. VA brokers must accompany the buyer and sign in.

Check the property inspection record. Home buyers may want to look at the Property Inspection Record, which will be posted inside each VA property. The VA broker or salesagent must sign this form and provide the broker's name, firm, date and purpose of the visit. The form lists the home's Area Management Broker.

Vandalism. The VA itself states: "Vandalism to our properties is a continuing problem." A sign will be posted on all VA properties indicating the name and phone number of the firm or individual assigned by the VA to maintain and care for the property pending its sale.

Expect rough visitation conditions. The VA home buyer should be prepared for rough conditions in the house. The power is out. The water is off. The broker will show the house by flashlight, because it will be dark. There's no water, so restrooms can't (or shouldn't) be used. Ugh! The VA expects buyers to use good sense and not further trash the property by tracking in dirt or litter.

Open house.   VA-registered sales brokers and management brokers may hold open houses. The open house will be held by the first broker or salesagent on the scene with a key for a given day. Some brokers bring ice chests, folding chairs and flyers, which is nice for buyers. A broker or salesagent, not a hostess or custodian to help buyers, must remain on the premises at all times.

Property Condition Problems

One of the biggest problems facing the prospective purchaser is the poor condition of many VA properties. Unlike FNMA, which has the funds available to completely rework the property and put it in good condition, the VA properties often sit and deteriorate. The property may have suffered from (various brokers have their favorite expressions) the "tire iron treatment" or "karate chop stuff." Sometimes the damage is senseless: air conditioners are frequently missing, commodes are ripped out, the ceiling may suffer from water damage. Anyone who wants a VA property should be prepared for such sights. A house may look bad, but it may not be a bad buy, depending on repair costs.

The broker should inform the buyer about VA house problems. The buyer should expect some problems and be prepared to deal with them. Many brokers and salesagents market rundown properties as "handy-man's specials," which can be a good deal for someone who can repair the property. This means buyers should be sure to have the extra cash it takes to put the property in good condition, and they should expect to spend the time and effort to correct the problems. VA properties may not be the right type of house for first-time buyers who have not yet developed the knack for spotting value behind a trashed out appearance.

Not all VA properties are in bad condition. The buyer should tell the broker what he or she wants and be sure to visit the property. Never purchase such homes sight unseen. Pay particular attention to foundation problems, roof problems or missing equipment, such as heaters and air conditioners. Problems with the utilities really can't be explored because service has been turned off. That doesn't mean there are no problems. It's part of the risk of the purchase.

Liability for Property Problems

The VA sells its properties strictly on an "as is" basis. Some effort is made to disclose the problems with the property by means of the AR

"Acknowledgment Required" system. Nevertheless, problems will occur. Worse still, the property condition may not be the same at closing as it was on the initial inspection. Once again, the VA does not accept liability for problems with the property. It's tough to sue the government. The buyer should depend on catching the problem before purchase, rather than correcting it afterward by a lawsuit.

SELECTING A VA PROPERTY—WHAT YOU SEE IS NOT ALWAYS WHAT YOU GET

Just because a prospective homebuyer wants a particular home does not mean that the homebuyer will be able to get that particular home. Prospective VA homebuyers should be cautioned about two things concerning these listings:

1. Bids are competitive. It's best to buy a VA home as part of a larger plan to buy the best VA home you can get rather than to get one's heart set on a particular property. Another bidder may win the desired home.
2. Properties drop off the list. Even before the bid opening, properties can be pulled back from sale for a variety of reasons. Sometimes the old owner declares bankruptcy and pulls the house back from the listings.

The VA program does not guarantee that any prospective buyer will get a particular house. VA brokers are encouraged to sell the program, not just a particular house.

SUBMITTING A WINNING BID

In order to buy a VA house, the procedure, after inspecting the property, is to prepare a bid. A contract, an addendum and an AR statement are placed in a sealed envelope. The envelope is either hand carried, or, if the region permits it, mailed to the nearest VA office that can accept bids. The bids are opened on a set day at a set hour, as shown in the VA's newspaper ad. The bids will be opened in the same order as they appear in the newspaper. All bids for a given house will be opened and read publicly. The high bid on a house wins. Three aspects of the bidding process deserve careful consideration:

1. The competitive nature of the bidding
2. The mechanics of submitting a VA 6705b contract bid
3. The follow-up on the bid in order to close the sale.

Bidding Is Competitive

It is not necessarily an easy matter to win a VA bid. A good house, in good condition, in a good neighborhood may attract many bids. VA brokers are encouraged to bring prospective buyers to a bid opening just to see the fervor of the competition. One way to gauge the interest of the public and competitors is to carefully study the sign-in sheet at any VA house to see who's been looking at it. The broker or sales agent's name can also be checked against past bid submissions to see what he or she might do on this house. Specialized information sources such as private newsletters can be used to analyze bidding on such houses.

The VA may accept less than the newspaper list price, but usually has a floor, such as 85 percent or so. Any lower bid will be tossed, even though it was the highest dollar figure bid on the property. The VA reserves the right to raise or reduce this figure without prior notice. Even a bid above the VA's floor may be unacceptable. The VA reserves the right to reject any bid that is deemed not to be in its best interest. The VA does not run a sale absolute, which would be to sell the house at the lowest bid, regardless of how low the bid is.

Submitting the Bid—The Paperwork

A bid on a VA house consists of filling out a VA Form 26-6705 (be sure to get the most current edition of the form), called an Offer to Purchase and Contract of Sale, and its Addendum to Purchase Offer, and placing it in a specially marked envelope that will be hand carried or, in some cases, mailed to the VA office that will accept bids. It is normally date-time stamped. The bid is due by a set time about two days before the actual bid opening. At a set hour on a set day, advertised in the paper, the bids are opened.

The bid contract. The contract should be properly filled out and submitted in a timely fashion. An original of the contract and addendum and one copy of each, with original signatures, should be submitted to

FIGURE 12.1   VA Bid Envelope

Broker's Name   Listing No._____
_____   Sequence No._____
                                                 Bid Opening Date _____
                                                 Regular or Extended _____

SEALED BID—DO NOT OPEN

                                                 PM No. _____
                                                 Address _____
                                                 _____ TX _____
Bidder Name(s)

Some regions require the broker's registration number and expiration date below the broker's name on the upper left hand side.

Broker's Name
_____

Broker's Registration Number
_____

Expiration Date
_____

---

the VA. The VA may reject incomplete forms. Cash sales could take extra paperwork.

The envelope please.   All required forms must be inserted into a specially marked envelope. Different formats may be required in different regions around the country. A fairly common format is shown in Figure 12.1.

According to the VA "An incorrectly completed envelope may be cause for disapproval of an offer even if it is discovered the offer is the highest net return to VA." Which means the bid was the high bid for that house.

The envelope should be an standard business envelope, not a large manila envelope.

Bid submission—main bid.   Bids must be submitted before they are opened. Here are the bid submission procedures:

The day: A set day of the week, advertised in the paper.

The time: A set hour, such as 1:00 P.M.

The place: In most cities, the regional headquarters for the VA region.

The manner: Hand carried for properties.

The box: Put each envelope in the proper container.

The stamp: Each bid must be stamped no later than the set hour, such as 1:00 P.M.

Submissions on homes outside of the city where the VA is headquartered will go either to another city's VA office or may be submitted by mail.

Put the regularly marked bid envelope in a separate mailing envelope and send it to the above address.

Bid Submission—mini-bid.   The VA also holds a mini-bid opening every day, except the day of the main bid and holidays. A mini-bid works like a main bid, except that all houses in the mini-bid were not sold at a main bid. This could be because the bid was incorrectly submitted or failed; or because no one wants the house; or because VA is holding out for a higher bid.

Earnest Money

The earnest money deposit for a VA home is usually about $1,000, which must be in the form of certified funds. In some cases, for cities that lack a regional or field VA office, brokers may hold the funds in an escrow account until bid opening.

In cities with a regional or VA office, the check and contract may have to go to an Agent Cashier, who will issue a receipt on the spot. The VA may require such a receipt to refund the money if the bid is rejected. If there's no VA office in the city, then an escrow agent may have to be used to hold the check pending the bid opening. Any VA broker who acts as an escrow agent may wisely demand a cashier's check from the buyer, and must promptly refund the money if the bid fails.

The Non-VA Contract—Non-VA Financing and Cash Offers

When VA uses the term *cash offer* we have to be careful to define it. There are actually two types of cash offers. The first is a true cash offer, in which the buyer, who is probably rich or an investor, literally puts up cash to buy the house. In the second type of cash offer, to use VA terminology, the buyer of the house arranges financing without using the VA vendee loan arrangement. Sometimes an investor prefers another type of loan.

A non-VA conventional (private) loan must be closed within 45 days. FHA loans may be allowed extra time, such as 60 days, to close. The earnest money is forfeited for failure to close on time.

THE BID OPENING

The Main Bid Opening

Bids must be submitted before they are opened. The sealed bids consist of the envelopes that contain the VA 6705 form contract, the addendum, the AR statement and any state-specific addendum. The sealed bid does not contain the earnest money check. Rejected sealed bids land in the shredder. If the bid envelope contains a valuable cashier's check, it too is shredded. This can generate problems in trying to get a refund of the cashier's check funds from the bank.

Last Minute Problems

Confusing VA and FHA bids.   This is a sad problem that catches all too many brokers. They plan to bid on an FHA house on, let's say, Tuesday, and VA houses on, let's say, Thursday. Unfortunately, the envelopes are sometimes mixed and the VA bids are turned into the FHA and the FHA bids are turned into the VA. Unfortunately, this will result in losing the bid. Some brokers are now color-coding their envelopes to be sure to get the right bid to the right agency!

Withdrawing a bid. Before the opening, bid offers that have been submitted may normally be withdrawn at any time, literally even moments before the bid opening process begins.

The procedure is to turn in a written withdrawal request signed by the broker and the buyer prior to the Thursday bid opening or the mini-bid opening. In outlying areas, brokers may fax a withdrawal to the VA with written confirmation signed by the broker and the borrower to be mailed immediately to the VA regional office (VARO). The withdrawal should contain the same information, such as PM number, that is present on the outside of the bid envelope.

Attempting to withdraw a bid after it is accepted by the VA will very likely result in a forfeiture of the earnest money. The money will be forfeited if the VA determines the broker has not acted in the best interests of the VA or the buyer.

Newspaper List Order—The Highest "Net to VA" Bid Wins

The bid envelopes are arranged in newspaper list order. All the bids on a given house are opened. If the form of the bid is not correct, then the bid is tossed out. Too many bids are eliminated for defects in form, unfortunately! For example, contracts are turned in that are not signed originals. These bids are thrown out even if they are higher than other bids! If the bid is in acceptable form, it is called out and lined up in comparison with other bids on the same house. The highest net to VA bid wins the house. This figure is found in the VA addendum.

The Runner Up—Bids Accepted as Backup Contracts

If the box on the VA 6705 form has been checked to authorize the use of the contract as a backup, then it may be called out as a backup contract. This means if the winning bid fails to close, such as through a buyer's inability to obtain financing or a similar problem, then the backup offer will be accepted in its place. The VA may take up to two backup offers per house. These would be the runner-up bids, and the next runner up, provided the boxes are checked authorizing their use as backups.

Some bids do not authorize the use of the contract as a backup. Such buyers want to get in and win a bid on a particular house. A backup bid price is usually lower than the bid price announced as the winner at the public bid opening. It may be substantially better. It is one good way to get a really good price on a house. Backup bids are hard to monitor. About the only way buyers will know about a backup bid figure is to listen carefully to the actual bid openings. This information is not normally made available to the public in more readily usable form.

Bids on More than One Home

A bidder could easily lose on a given bid. That's why it makes sense to submit more than one bid. However, the buyer/bidder may be able to afford only one house. That doesn't stop the bidder from bidding on more than one house, however. Assuming the buyer/bidder desires an owner/occupant house, then the VA will accept one bid on such houses. This is true not only for this one bid opening, but for future bid openings as well. The VA will accept the first owner/occupant bid it receives. The VA will trash every subsequent bid offer made by the buyer who just won one. As a result, a bidder should be careful to submit bids for houses in descending order of desirability. The house the buyer wants most may be the first bid, then the next most desirable, assuming it is later on the list, would be the second bid and so on. Unfortunately, there is no way to back-track and rebid on an earlier house. Once it's bid, it's gone. VA prefers owner/occupants to investors if it can get them. The VA is set up to provide housing, not make anyone rich from investments.

Multiple Bids—With the Intent To Buy More than One House

Investors can bid on as many houses as they like. The first house the investor buys can have a VA vendee loan with only 10 percent down. A vendee loan is a loan made to help sell a VA foreclosure home. The second and any later house the investor buys require 20 percent down payments, unless a satisfactory payment record can be shown on the earlier houses. If the investor can demonstrate a satisfactory payment record for six months following the date the first payment is made, then later VA vendee loans can be approved. If after an initial sale, the investor wants to buy more homes on a VA vendee loan basis, then additional sales may be approved.

Finding Out about the Winning Bid

The quickest way to find out if one has won or lost a VA bid is to attend the bid openings. This can also provide useful information about backup bids. The VA also has a phone line that can be called to hear the latest information about which bids won. A given day's bid information should be available on the phone by that evening. If a bid is lost, a bidder who wants a particular house might attempt to bid on the property, if it has not already been sold, at the next mini-bid opening. All may not be lost.

AFTER THE BID OPENING

Acceptance. If the bid is in good form, and represents the high bid, then the VA will accept the bid and sign the contract.

Collapse of the sale—"sale fails." The buyer should be aware that a VA broker must tell the VA as soon as the broker learns the buyer can't buy.

Return of the Earnest Money—A Tough Question

The VA manual states that it will instruct the broker on how to dispose of the earnest money after an offer is withdrawn. The manual states clearly that "After an offer has been accepted, VA will normally not authorize the refund of earnest money except when the purchaser is disapproved for financing."

The VA's policy is to direct brokers to keep one-half of the earnest money deposit and remit the remaining one-half to the VA. Sales brokers should not return the earnest money to purchasers until they receive specific instructions to do so from the VA on any offer that has been accepted. Should the broker return the purchaser's deposit without VA approval, and the VA decides it wanted the deposit, the broker has the responsibility of sending the VA its share of the money.

After the bid is accepted, and loan processing is underway, if the lender finds the buyer is unqualified for the loan, then the earnest money can be recovered. The buyer, through the broker, should submit a copy of the "adverse action letter" from the lender indicating that the loan was denied due to poor credit, inadequate income or a similar loan-related reason. Without such documentation, the VA may not consent to the return of the earnest money.

Sometimes buyers discover that the condition of the property has changed after they submitted a bid on the house. If so, the buyer may want to back out of the purchase but he or she still loses the earnest money. The VA will probably keep the earnest money if the buyer will not close for any reason that is not loan related. This is particularly true of problems with appliances. Free-standing appliances are not even considered in the VA's appraisal figures, nor are they given weight by a regular lender. However, the buyer may want to pull out of the purchase if the appliances are stolen. It's too late!

VA FINANCING

The basic information about VA financing holds true for both the northern and southern VA regions. A key characteristic of these fore-closure resales is that the VA provides financing. The VA refers to this procedure as a sale *on terms* or a *vendee loan*. Either way it is the VA selling someone a house on credit. The VA will, of course, sell a house for cash or the buyer can arrange his or her own financing, provided it is done within 45 days of winning a VA bid. However, the VA vendee loan is the most commonly used arrangement.

The two basic areas to be discussed in VA financing are:

1. Characteristics of VA vendee loans
2. Qualifying for VA vendee loans

Characteristics of VA Vendee Loans

VA vendee loans behave in a fairly similar manner to other VA loans, but there are a few differences. Here is an analysis of VA vendee loans characteristic by characteristic.

Assumability.   VA vendee loans require VA approval before the property is transferred unless the loan is paid in full as part of the deal. All VA vendee loans may be assumed on a "full" assumption basis if the buyer qualifies. The VA may charge a one-half of 1 percent funding fee and a processing fee to approve the transfer. VA vendee loans may no longer be assumed on a simple assumption basis in which the VA does not have to approve the assuming buyer's income and credit to make sure he or she "qualifies" for the loan.

Regular VA loans have not been assumable on a "simple assumption" (no approval, no qualification) basis since March 1, 1988. VA vendee loans made after March 1, 1988, but before January 9, 1989, are assumable on a full or a simple assumption (no approval) basis.

In all new VA vendee loans made after January 9, 1989, the buyer's credit and income must be checked and approved in order for the loan to be assumed. However, if the buyer qualifies, the assumption must be approved, and the existing interest rate will be maintained. A $300 application fee is permitted. If approved, a 1 percent funding fee on the loan balance may be charged.

Down payments.   The minimum down payment to be made by purchasers of VA-acquired properties is specified in the sales listings. Some VA properties will have low or no down payments. On VA vendee loans, there are at least four categories of down payment:

1. Typical owner-occupant bidders making a bid of less than $100,000 will not have to make a down payment.
2. Investor bidders will have to make a 10 percent down payment.
3. Bid offers (not newspaper listings, but the bid offer) in excess of $100,000 will normally require a 5 percent down payment from owner occupants and 10 percent from investors.
4. After the first non-owner occupant investor bid is successful, further sales to investors involving VA vendee loans require a 20 percent down payment. Later purchases may be restricted to five houses at a time with a good payment record.

As a bidding strategy, a bid that ties with another bid (net to VA is the same) will be awarded to the bid with the higher down payment. As a result, some bidders put in a small down payment (a few dollars) just to wipe out tie bids.

Maximum loan amount.   There is no maximum loan amount on a VA vendee loan.

Minimum loan amount.   The VA cannot sell smaller loans into the secondary mortgage market. Therefore, houses sold at less than $15,000 are generally not available with VA vendee loan financing.

These are cash sales. The VA may also insist on "all cash" for homes even above $15,000. Check the newspaper ad for details.

Shorter-term loans.   VA vendee loans have a term of 30 years. Terms of less than 30 years are permissible only if the sales listing permits them and the buyer specifically requests such terms. Other than 30 years, the only terms VA will permit are 10, 15, 20 and 25 years. A bid involving a loan term of less than 30 years will not be given any preference over other bids.

Interest rate.   The VA interest rate is no longer set by law. VA buyers may pay points since November 1992. Offers in process will be closed at the interest rate that was locked in at the time the bid offer was accepted for processing.

Prepayment.   VA loans, including VA vendee loans, may be pre-paid in full or in part at any time, but may not be less than the monthly principal and interest payment, or $100, whichever is less.

Installment due dates.   Installments are due on the first of the month. There is no grace period.

Funding fee.   VA vendee loans involve a 1 percent funding fee, but the funding fee is waived for certain exempt individuals, who are

1. veterans receiving compensation for a service-related disability;
2. veterans who are eligible to receive disability compensation but have elected military retirement benefits instead; or
3. surviving spouses who have been approved for loan benefits.

Disclosure of outside assistance.   If a buyer obtains outside assistance, such as cash advances for expenses, from sales brokers or anyone else, this must be fully disclosed to the VA. This category includes trades, equity purchases, loans, gifts or any other financial assistance. Salesagents and brokers must be sure this information is disclosed, if they know about it, or they can be excluded from further participation in VA foreclosure resales.

VA LOAN VENDEE LOAN QUALIFICATION

There are three basic aspects of VA loan qualification that merit discussion:

1. Who is eligible for VA loans
2. Standards to meet for a VA loan and
3. How the VA procedures work

Who May Apply for a VA Loan?

Almost anyone with adequate income and creditworthiness can apply for a VA loan. The VA vendee loans for foreclosure resales use the same qualification and income ratio standards as ordinary VA loans, with some important exceptions, which are described below.

Non-veterans may apply for the VA vendee loan. Ordinary VA loans are restricted to veterans, except on assumptions. Investors may also apply for VA vendee loans. Ordinary VA loans are for owner-occupants. There are, however, some important restrictions on investor loans. The investor's first loan requires no down payment, but the second or later loans require either a 20 percent down payment or a satisfactory payment record for six months.

Who May Not Apply for a VA Loan?

VA affiliates may not apply for a VA vendee loan. VA affiliates include the following:

1. VA employees involved in pricing VA homes
2. VA Management Brokers who try to buy a home they manage
3. Appraisers who buy homes they've appraised for the VA

Processing the VA Loan

Many VA regions use mortgage companies to preprocess vendee loans. The key to VA processing is a system in which the VA vendee loan application is filled out and preprocessed through a VA-approved mortgage company. In most areas, VA brokers no longer take loan applications and process loans, which frees them to do what they do best: sell. The system permits the VA to sell its vendee loans on the secondary market to GNMA (which buys about 95 percent of all VA loans) or other loan buyers. At that point, it is arguable whether such a loan is even a VA vendee loan anymore. The VA's standards for such loans are usually the same as those for a regular VA loan, but with the exceptions outlined above.

The Broker's Responsibilities

Brokers are responsible for getting buyers to make a loan application with an approved Vendee Processor Lender soon after the VA accepts a bid offer, usually three days. Brokers should monitor the loan processing and assist in getting the documentation the lender needs. The VA broker must make sure that VA home buyers will have a fire and extended coverage or homeowner's insurance policy, effective as of the closing date, with a paid receipt for the first year's premium. The actual policy, not a binder, must be furnished. The face value must be equal to or greater than the loan amount. The loan must be identified, and it must be made payable (Mortgagee Clause section) to the Secretary of Veterans Affairs, his successors or assigns, c/o the Director.

The broker must also provide a flood elevation certificate so that a flood insurance policy can be obtained in time for the closing. In outlying areas, brokers are asked to familiarize themselves with the local procedure for obtaining the needed flood elevation certificate. In any area, the broker should also verify that the master insurance policy is in effect for condominiums.

Vendee Loan Paperwork

The VA still needs its traditional loan application form to get started, which is the Credit Statement of Prospective Purchaser. In some regions, this form can be filled out by a mortgage company representative or loan officer, who may be very experienced and capable. Otherwise, the application is submitted by the broker who submits the bid on the house. After the loan application form is filled out the loan processing may use regular or expedited processing.

In some regions, if a buyer desires a VA vendee loan, then the broker who submits a bid on a VA house must also submit loan application materials along with the earnest money contract, such as a Credit Statement of the Prospective Purchaser (VA Form 26-6705), verification of employer income through pay stubs or tax returns and a VOE (Verification of Employment form) sent to the employer. The employer should be asked to supply a letter verifying the employer's name, address and telephone number, and the employee's name and address. It should include

- the date the employment began;
- the employee's title;
- the probability of continued employment;
- the current base pay, indicating hourly, average weekly or annual pay earned during the current and past year;
- the year-to-date earnings, past year's earnings and the likelihood of continued overtime or bonus pay;
- the name and position of the person verifying employment.

Various types of income require various types of verification:

Self-employed income—verify by tax returns and an audited profit and loss statement.

Military income—Active duty personnel should include an Original Leave and Earnings Statement no more than 90 days old.

Rental income—Verify by tax returns and an audited profit and loss statement, and a copy of all rental/lease agreements.

Social Security income and retirement income—A copy of the most recent letter, military retirement statement or last year's W-2 form should be submitted.

Appropriate Verification Must Be Submitted

The VA will selectively verify employment on a random or spot-check basis. Brokers should follow up on employment documentation.

Some regions use a 22-day figure. When an offer is selected for processing, the required employment/income verifications must be received by the VA no later than 22 days after the end of the simultaneous period, or 22 days after the purchase offer is received, if that is later. If the information is not received in 22 days, the offer will be automatically rejected and the prospective purchaser will be required to forfeit his or her earnest money.

If regular processing is used, the loan credit application and supporting documentation must be submitted to the VA by lenders in a file folder organized in a format provided to Vendee Packagers through the

VA. Lenders are to include two preaddressed stamped postcards addressed to the broker and the lender packager. VA underwriters will complete and sign the postcards to indicate VA's action: (1) approved; (2) rejected; or (3) suspended in the event additional information is required from the lender/packager. The VA underwriter will call the lender and allow five business days for receipt of the additional documentation; otherwise, the application will be rejected. As stated on the VA Net Addendum, VA vendee packager has a maximum of 30 calendar days from the date the offer is accepted to submit a complete credit package to the VA. The VA makes the final credit decision and funds the loan on term sales financed by VA.

Expedited processing allows reduced documentation to be submitted to gain loan approval.

Alternative Region Arrangements

Different regions make different arrangements. While the arrangements so far described are used in many areas, alternative arrangements are sometimes used in others. Here is a fairly typical alternative set of arrangements to those just described above.

Earnest money.   The earnest money deposit does not have to be mailed in with the contract, but it should be retained by the sales broker until the VA decides whether it will accept the offer.

VA offices that handle offers.   Once the regional VA office receives an offer, it will evaluate it by the closing date stated in the newspaper listing. This period is sometimes called the simultaneous period because that's the period in which multiple offers on the property may be submitted by various brokers:

SIMULTANEOUS PERIOD

|—————————————————————————————|

House offered   Closing date
in newspapers

During the simultaneous period, all purchase offers will be considered as received by the VA at the same time and no purchase offer will receive final acceptance. Even if a submitted offer is acceptable to the VA in price, conditions and terms, the VA will nonetheless hold the offer until the closing date for that house, which marks the end of the simultaneous period for that house. The simultaneous period will not end on a Friday, but will be extended, if necessary, to the next work day for the VA after the weekend. The offer made during the simultaneous period that best serves the interests of the VA will be processed for acceptance at the end of the simultaneous period.

VA's Criteria for Acceptance

The VA will determine the best offer by applying the following criteria in the order listed:

1. 10 percent above list price. The highest offer to VA that exceeds the list price by 10 percent or more.
   - If all cash, the amount shown as "Net Cash to VA" in the Addendum to the Offer to Purchase wins out.
   - If on terms (VA financed), the amount shown as "Purchase Price" in Item 9 of the main contract, VA Form 26-6705, wins out.
2. Highest net all-cash offer over 90 percent of list price. The net cash offer is computed after deducting loan discount points, and normal buyer's closing costs. If it's 90 percent or above list, it wins.
3. Highest purchase price offer for a VA-financed house that is 3 percent or more above list price. The highest price that is 3 percent or more above list wins.
4. Highest purchase price offer for a VA-financed house, the offer which exceeds 3 percent of the list price, and exceeds any VA required down payment at the same time by that 3 percent of list price figure.
5. Degree of acceptability of credit risk.
6. Purchase for own occupancy and use.
7. Veteran over nonveteran.
8. First in time among offers otherwise equal. The time of receipt by the VA will determine acceptance among otherwise equal offers. Even if the VA's interest rate for foreclosure homes changes during the simultaneous period, the shift will be disregarded in ranking offers. However, once the simultaneous

period ends, and the house does not sell and is relisted, the interest rates on new bids must be those for the relisting.

9. For RO (reasonable offer) properties only—highest offer even if below list price. If the newspaper ad lists a property as RO, Reasonable Offer, then the VA will consider offers below list price. Cash offers below list price have no special priority over offers involving VA financing that are below list price.

Bid Acceptance

The VA will accept the bid that it determines to be in the VA's best interest. Once accepted, the broker who submitted the winning bid for a buyer will be requested to send in the earnest money check and a VA earnest money agreement signed by the purchaser. The check and form must be sent in immediately.

The buyer should deposit the earnest money with the VA broker prior to submitting a bid. The amount varies from region to region, but typically $500 to $1,000 is enough. The deposit should be retained by the broker until a bid is accepted. The check should be accompanied by a VA earnest money agreement signed by the buyer.

Return of the Earnest Money—Be Careful

If a bid is unsuccessful, the broker may return the earnest money to the buyer, unless the buyer plans to promptly submit another bid. Except for below list price offers, a buyer may withdraw a bid that has been submitted to the VA, but not yet accepted, and receive a refund of the earnest money from the broker (not the VA). However, the buyer is not entitled to a refund of the earnest money if the bidder tries to withdraw a bid that is below the VA's list price. According to the VA: "Once the VA has accepted an offer to purchase and the prospective purchaser either cancels or fails to perform, there will be no refund of the earnest money." A wise broker will collect the earnest money check from a prospective buyer before submitting a bid of any kind to the VA. Once the bid is submitted, the VA broker is responsible for remitting the earnest money if the bid is accepted by the VA. That's true whether the buyer ever gave the broker the earnest money or not.

CLOSINGS

The VA recommends that all preparations for closings be made in time to avoid any postponement or delay beyond the date established for closings, which is normally 45 days from the date the VA Form 26-6705 is received by the VA.

Closer Functions

In any sale.   The closer will prepare the necessary documents and paperwork needed to organize and complete the closing. The closer will do the following:

1. Furnish and have the buyer sign a Hazard Insurance Renewal Authorization (see below for more on insurance).
2. Furnish a manually prepared Mortgage Collection Card and return envelope; the collection card will be completed to show the first installment due date, the loan ID number, and the total installment amount. The buyer must use this card to make the second month's payment if the VA fails to send a computer bill in time. The interest from the date of closing to the end of the month, plus the first month's loan payment must be made in cash at the closing, as is traditional in Texas for most loans. That interim interest (about 1/30 of the monthly payment multiplied by the number of days from the closing to the end of the month) can be quite substantial if the closing is near the beginning of the month, but quite small if it's near the end of the month. As a result, closing schedules can become very crowded near the end of the month.
3. Give the buyer advance notice of the approximate payment to be made for adjustments and other closing costs, including
    • document preparation fee,
    • sales closing fee,
    • transfer fees,
    • recording fees,
    • funding fee,
    • tax certification fee, and
    • credit underwriting fee.

4. Collect all funds at closing in the form of a cashier's or certified check.
5. Prepare all the standard VA forms and instruments required to close the sale, including the deed and, for VA financed sales, the loan forms and documents.
6. Record the deed of conveyance, which the buyer pays for in these sales!
7. Calculate the prorations. If the net adjustment is in favor of the VA, it must be paid by the buyer at closing. If the net adjustment is in favor of the purchaser, then it will be deducted from the purchase price at closing.
8. Prepare the Sales Closing Statement. The closing statement the VA normally uses is a standard HUD-1 Uniform Settlement Statement. It must show all essential phases of the sales closing in order to provide the VA and the buyer with a precise record of the transaction. The closer will prepare an original and three copies, which must be signed by both the closer and the buyer. One copy goes to the buyer.

Insurance in VA-Financed Sales

In VA financed sales, the insurance matters described below must be attended to by the closer.

Hazard insurance. A policy effective the day of closing naming as the insured mortgagee (lender) the Secretary of Veterans Affairs, his successors, or assigns must be paid for by the buyer. In addition, there must be acceptable evidence that the buyer paid for the policy directly to the insurance agent by means of a cashier's check. The purchaser can choose the insurance agent. One-year policies are the minimum the VA will accept; three-year and five-year policies are preferred.

Flood insurance. If the house is in a flood hazard area, then the buyer must obtain flood insurance under the National Flood Program.

NEW CLOSING POLICIES

In 1990, the VA announced major changes in the method and manner of handling closings. Under the old system, VA closing attorneys were key figures in the VA home sales system. This will no longer be true. Instead, VA home sales will be concluded in one of three places:

1. At a title company of the buyer's choice
2. Through an attorney approved by the VA
3. At the VA's main office

The purchaser will have the option of closing the sales transaction at the VA Regional Office (at no charge) or choosing to close with a title insurance company or licensed attorney. The purchaser or broker will pay all costs charged by the attorney or title company for holding the closing.

The VA will pay for an Owner's Title Policy, up to a limit, typically $500 (which may be low) if requested by the purchaser, on all sales. All amounts above the limit must be paid by the purchaser.

CONCLUSION

VA acquires homes from lenders who got them from delinquent borrowers at a foreclosure sale. The Department of Veterans Affairs operates in a manner similar to the FHA, but important differences exist. The VA will generally finance purchases for investor buyers with a great zero down payment vendee loan, while in contrast, the FHA does not provide for it. The VA normally sells homes by a sealed bid auction. It also closes its sales through either title companies or specialized HUD closing attorneys. Procedures vary at different offices around the country, but VA is normally very concerned to advertise not only the availability of a property for sale and its estimated price, but also the condition of the property through its commonly used AR system, which not many other foreclosure sellers use. If a nice one can be found, a VA home can be an excellent buy.

CHAPTER 13

RTC and
FDIC Sales

The Resolution Trust Corporation (RTC) is the result of changes in the S&L industry and the problems lending institutions have had with down markets in many parts of the United States. The RTC itself also changes, frequently, and often, significantly. It's hard to keep up with what's going on. An astute investor or homebuyer who takes the time to figure out what is happening with the RTC, or even appears to know more about what's happening with the RTC than other people can buy these properties and win big. This market may grow immensely, so the time spent with such sales may really pay off.

The RTC is a government-chartered and government-owned operation. It was set up by FIRREA, the Financial Institutions Reform, Recovery and Enforcement Act of 1989, which was passed by the U.S. Congress in response to the mounting S&L crisis. More and more S&Ls are becoming or have become insolvent. As they are shut down, their assets will be given to the RTC, which will sell them off. For a time, the RTC will become the largest landholder in the world and will set more real estate than any other corporation in history.

This chapter on the RTC can be divided into four areas:

1. Overview—the S&L crisis, FIRREA and the RTC
2. How RTC arranges to acquire and sell S&L assets
3. RTC sales of real estate
4. Low income properties and the RTC

OVERVIEW—THE S&L CRISIS, FIRREA AND THE RTC

The savings and loan associations in the United States are undergoing a crisis. S&Ls operate by taking in money as deposits, then lending the money out. The problem occurs when the money is not paid back. The S&L generally forecloses on the real estate, thereby adding another REO to its balance sheet. The problem is that the real estate the S&L forecloses on is generally not worth as much as the original loan. A case in point would be a Texas-based S&L that loaned over $12 million to renovate a building into a multilevel shopping mall. The shopping mall never leased as much space as it needed to, which turned the project into a financial disaster. It was later sold for a little over $3 million. When an S&L lends $12 million and later gets $3 million back, the resulting loss can significantly damage its balance sheet.

Most S&Ls are capitalized rather thinly, at around 3 percent (a figure that has been increased to 6 percent). This means that there are roughly $97 in deposits and other liabilities (a deposit is a liability to the bank) for every $3 contributed by the owners of the S&L or retained from profits. A $1 billion S&L would have about $30 million in capital. A $9 million loss eats deeply into the capital. When an S&L loses all its capital, then it is insolvent.

Further losses come from deposits, which were insured by the Federal Savings & Loan Insurance Corporation (FSLIC) or by the Federal Deposit Insurance Corporation (FDIC). Once deposits are being lost, the bank or S&L should be shut down by FSLIC or FDIC. This tends not to happen in practice. The FSLIC, which once had the responsibility for insuring S&L deposits, lacked sufficient funds to pay off depositors whenever an S&L had to be shut down. So the S&Ls continued to operate, losing money all the while, and the nation's S&L crisis grew deeper.

FIRREA

Although the U.S. Congress tried passing laws to fight the S&L crisis several times in the 1980s, by 1989 it was apparent that only strong legislative medicine could deal with the problem. This legislation was passed in the form of FIRREA, or Financial Institutions Reform, Recovery, and Enforcement Act of 1989. Admittedly, the name sounds like an acute stomach ailment, but the legislation is arguably the most significant effort to restructure the U.S. banking industry in half a century. FIRREA made the following key changes.

- dissolved FSLIC, the Federal Savings & Loan Insurance Corp.;
- gave the FDIC the old S&L insurance functions FSLIC had;
- created the FSLIC Resolution Fund to take over the assets and liabilities of the FSLIC, other than those given to RTC;
- created the RTC, or Resolution Trust Corporation, which will become the largest landholder in the world; its purpose will be to take over assets from defunct S&Ls and the Federal Asset Disposition Administration, or FADA.
- abolished the FHLBB, the Federal Home Loan Bank Board;
- created the Federal Housing Finance Board to oversee Federal Home Loan Banks;
- created the OTS, the Office of Thrift Supervision, and gave it regulatory power over state savings associations; federal savings associations; and savings and loan holding companies.

Purchase of Real Estate from Federal Agencies/Corporations

Under FIRREA, there will still be at least two institutions that will sell real estate: the RTC (Resolution Trust Corporation) and the FSLIC Resolution Fund, which will be managed by the FDIC. The FSLIC Resolution Fund consists of all the assets and liabilities of the FSLIC, which were transferred to the fund upon FSLIC's dissolution, other than those that go to the RTC. Assets that go to the FSLIC Resolution Fund, rather than RTC, include all assets and liabilities for which FSLIC was appointed receiver prior to January 1, 1989. In addition, FSLIC's assets and obligations under the Southwest Plan (a special plan to help Texas and Southwest area S&Ls) will go to the FSLIC Resolution Fund.

The RTC will receive assets from defunct S&Ls. Specifically, the assets that RTC is to manage, sell, merge, reorganize or otherwise resolve will come from two sources:

1. All S&Ls for which a receiver is appointed between January 1, 1989 and August 9, 1992 (a little over three years)
2. All the assets of the old Federal Asset Disposition Administration (FADA), which got its assets from defunct S&Ls.

The RTC itself is scheduled to come to an end by December 31, 1996, but it will likely be in existence for some time after that. RTC has the same powers as the FDIC in dealing with its set of defunct financial institutions as FDIC has with respect to currently insured financial institutions.

RTC should get a considerable amount of business. By the middle of 1989, about 390 S&Ls insured by FSLIC were insolvent by GAAP standards (Generally Accepted Accounting Principles). Another 394 had zero to 3 percent in capital by GAAP standards, which makes them essentially "brain dead." Their days are numbered, and by 1996, they should be taken over by the RTC. About $200 million in property could pass through the RTC in the early 1990s, making RTC the largest owner of real estate in the world. However, it is a self-destructive field because the RTC is expected to sell a lot of the real estate it acquires. Raw land and very troubled properties could remain on the RTC's inventory for a very long time.

RTC and the S&L Crisis—A Battle with No Tomorrow

The RTC has only limited resources with which to work. It long ago ran out of its original $50 billion and has continually requested, and received, more money. The RTC can use the power of the U.S. government to guarantee bonds. Once guaranteed, the bonds are sold and the money is raised. Hopefully, a lot of the money will be repaid from resales of properties the RTC acquires when it shuts down S&Ls. However, it is almost hopeless to fight a $500 billion S&L crisis with the funds the RTC has received. Sooner or later, the RTC will run out of money and require more. Sooner or later, the RTC program will have to be revised. Until then, the RTC, together with FDIC, will be fighting the mounting S&L crisis.

It may get worse before it gets better. The projections for the total loss from the S&L crisis do not consider what can happen if real estate prices plummet in parts of the country other than Texas. Although some cities, such as Denver, Phoenix and now Boston have experienced sharp downturns in real estate, many more could be hurt as well. The bricks and mortar or cost of construction component of the value for homes in many parts of the country is relatively small and the speculative part of the value is relatively high. This ratio is as high as six to one for California waterfront properties or older homes on valuable sites. Therefore, a downturn in real estate in other parts of the country could be quite serious. The high prices are maintainable only in a seller's market in which everyone wants to buy and no one wants to sell. In such a situation if prices start to fall, there is no real floor. Such problems in parts of the country other than Texas could lead to staggering losses. These losses would surely make the S&L disaster even worse. On top of that, banks and perhaps even insurance companies could suffer some of the same problems as S&Ls. Although this pessimistic scenario may not occur, very real evidence suggests that the S&L crisis could get a lot worse before it gets better.

HOW RTC ARRANGES TO ACQUIRE AND SELL AN S&L'S ASSETS

The RTC will handle defunct S&Ls at several levels:

1. Conservatorship, or government management
2. Receivership, or government liquidation
3. Asset manager, which is private management under RTC auspices. Approximately two-thirds of the RTC's assets are in conservatorship and approximately one-third of the RTC's assets are in receivership.

Conservatorship

Institutions that are open and operating, but under government supervision, are in conservatorship. A Managing Agent who works for the RTC is put in charge of the operation. The Managing Agent replaces the board of directors. The RTC will bring in an Asset Specialist who will look at the assets in place. In consultation with the Asset Specialist, the RTC will approve sales and other transactions while the entire institution's affairs wind down. The institution will normally continue to make residential loans, but not commercial loans. Very few of the personnel involved in the conservatorship are RTC employees. A key goal of conservatorship is to shrink the size of the institution. If the institution must be shut down and liquidated, the smaller the institution is in terms of loans outstanding and real estate owned (properties obtained from foreclosure), the better.

Receivership

Once an S&L has collapsed as a business, the government will step in, revoke its charter to do business, shut it down and put it into receivership. A Liquidator in Charge (LIC) or Resolution Assistance Contractor (RAC) will be put in charge. Typically, the assets are transferred to another institution on relatively favorable terms. Residual assets will be disposed of by the RTC.

Once an S&L goes into receivership, contracts between the old conservatorship S&L and customers may be disavowed by the S&L. Tenants may be told that they have to move to a new property owned by the receivers or their leases will be terminated and they will be asked to leave. They may get a ten-day notice. It's rough, but the effect may be to concentrate tenants in form viable, saleable assets.

Earnest money contracts signed by persons to buy real estate owned by the conservatorship may be disavowed when the S&L passes into receivership. Hopefully, if the earnest money contract was at a good and reasonable appraised value, it will be honored by the receivership, but it may terminate the contract without penalty. Remember, receivership is bank bankruptcy and the powers of the receiver to disregard debts are very formidable.

Asset Management

One approach the RTC will take in dealing with institutions in receivership is to contract out the management functions to asset managers. The owner of the institution and its assets will be the RTC, but the asset managers will manage and sell the assets.

Asset managers may be set up for the different types of assets, such as commercial loans or single-family residential housing. The manager may also obtain a group of assets, such as multifamily residential (apartments) combined with single-family residences, to manage as a group. Or one asset manager can be delegated the authority to handle all the assets.

Asset managers will normally be given varying degrees of authority to deal with the assets they manage. For smaller assets, such as single-family residences, the asset manager may be given blanket authority to dispose of the asset without direct approval from the RTC or even an RTC representative. The blanket authority may include certain guidelines, such as a minimum price that must be obtained when a house or other small asset is sold, but otherwise, the asset manager is probably free to sell it on such terms as he or she determines are best.

RTC SALES OF REAL ESTATE

Let the Sales Begin

The RTC has been selling properties for several years. Originally, most of the properties (17,000 out of 35,000) were in Texas, but now they are much more widely distributed around the United States. All of the RTC's properties are available for sale.

Theoretically, all of the RTC's properties can be bid upon by the public. First, however, an interested buyer must find out what's available. It's not that easy. The RTC will make information about its properties available in the following ways.

A printed list.   There are several volumes of listings for the RTC properties. The residential list is available to the public for a low price. The lists show the properties RTC has for sale, including a contact person for every property in case you want to submit a bid. By law, the RTC must update this list semiannually. More frequent updates are available on other media.

The CD-ROM system.   CD-ROM, a computer information storage device, with information about RTC properties, is available from private sources. The RTC likes this technology, which has tremendous storage capacity and a simple system for retrieving property descriptions in an organized manner. This technology stores the RTC information on a laser disk and plays it back through a computer.

The RTC data are updated at least semiannually. However, some of the systems, such as the CD-ROM and the floppies, may be available with updated information on a more frequent basis, probably at least quarterly. RTC's listings are available by calling the RTC.

Seminars.   From time to time, the RTC has offered seminars in major cities around the country to explain its procedures. Hopefully, the RTC will continue to run its seminars into the future. Call the nearest RTC office for more information.

Property Types Held by RTC

The RTC holds at least three types of real property:

1. Residential
2. Commercial
3. Land

Although residential properties are the largest component of the RTC's inventory in terms of numbers they are only a part of the whole, which includes many commercial properties.

RTC Sales Methods

RTC properties are sold by the following means:

- Open listing
- Exclusive listing
- Auction
- Sealed bid
- Direct sales

The RTC's properties are to be sold on a commission basis. The normal and customary commissions that are paid in an area will be paid by the RTC. Unfortunately, due to the antitrust laws, the normal and customary brokerage commissions shouldn't exist, but to the extent that they do, the RTC will use them. Properly speaking, the prevailing market rates should be used by the RTC.

Open listing. Most of the RTC's properties will be offered on an open listing basis, which means that any RTC-approved broker can offer a bid on the property. No one broker has the exclusive right to offer the property. All offers by any RTC broker are welcome. The first one to find a buyer receives the full commission. However, brokers must be approved by the RTC. It is fairly easy to be on the RTC's contractor list.

Exclusive listing. The exclusive listing will be used sparingly by the RTC for hard-to-sell properties. In most instances, broker cooperation will be required. The list broker who gets the exclusive listing must be registered as a contractor with the RTC.

Auctions.   The RTC has been very enthusiastic about auction marketing as a means of selling RTC properties. It is anticipated that the RTC will sponsor a number of large auctions as a method of selling its real estate. Most likely, established auction marketing firms will be contracted with (see RTC contracting procedures) to run the auctions for the RTC and the properties will then be auctioned off to the highest bidder.

Sealed bids.   Other agencies such as the FHA and the VA have used sealed bid systems with great effect. It remains to be seen exactly what the RTC plans to do in this regard. So far, the RTC seems to want to work through existing brokerage firms or asset managers and forego running a large-scale sealed bid program. However, other agencies have had such success with sealed bid procedures, particularly in Texas, that the RTC may have to seriously consider such methods in the long term. In the meantime, the RTC tends to show its banking influence by handling sales and management of its properties in a manner somewhat like the REO department of a savings and loan association would handle sales.

Direct sales.   The RTC will probably try to put together a number of bulk sales packages because it would like to sell off its inventory in large blocks rather than piecemeal. Blocks as large as $100 million have been actively discussed, which would include real estate and other assets as well. Already the RTC is blocking up tiny groups of assets in which a number of very desirable properties are mixed with a few less desirable properties and sold as a package. The RTC is still experimenting with methods to package its sales.

RTC Welcomes Offers

All of the RTC's properties are available for sale and all offers are welcome. Anyone who wants to bid on an RTC property may do so. It will be necessary to find the contact person to submit the offer to or from whom information about submitting a bid can be obtained. The RTC lists always include a contact person, brokerage company or firm for each property in its rolls.

Right now, the RTC is still working on its forms for submitting offers. However, for low-income sales, special forms are in use. Otherwise, standard contract forms or other commonly used contracts may be submitted until the RTC comes up with a full set of its own forms. Once the offer is submitted, it can be sent back.

Repeat offers are likely to be necessary. Sometimes, the RTC just likes to receive offers without acting favorably on them. It tends to give a feel for the price and saleability of the property. If a first offer does not succeed, try again. Also, the RTC is free to counteroffer and may very well do so.

Unfortunately, the RTC will not pull a property off the market just because a letter of intent has been submitted. The RTC may also take in more than one contract offer and wait on them: it has up to 30 days to respond. By the way, that's too slow for most residential brokers. However, the RTC plans to respond more quickly than 30 days. Active bargaining and brokering are to be expected. Once the RTC signs a contract, it can take the property off the market, but it will not do so before then.

RTC Sales—One RTC, but Many Sellers

The RTC is the umbrella organization for a variety of actual sellers. Many sellers will actually be S&Ls in conservatorship as opposed to receivership. Some may be listed directly by the RTC; many others will be listed through an RTC asset manager, or even by a real estate broker on an exclusive basis. The RTC's asset inventory should include the name of the institution that owns the property and the contact telephone number. Be sure to check with the contact person for an RTC listing to find out the status of the real estate (i.e., conservatorship or receivership).

RTC Pricing

The RTC must establish two types of market prices The first is a pure market value for resale. The second is a net realizable market value, which means the pure market value minus holding costs that a quicker sale eliminates, such as real estate taxes, insurance and professional service fees for brokers, auctioneers and attorneys.

Fair Market Value. The RTC defines fair market value as the value that can be obtained in "A fair sale wherein buyer and seller are prudent and knowledgeable and not affected by undue stimulae." The RTC requires fair market value to be set by an appraisal.

Net realizable market value.   The RTC defines *net realizable market value* as the current fair market value (see above definition) minus "extended holding and marketing costs." These costs will include taxes, insurance, maintenance, management fees, marketing, advertising, brokerage or auctioneer fees, security and the time value of money. Maintenance expenses may include repairs to get the property ready for sale and to keep it up while being rented prior to the sale. It is not clear exactly how the RTC will define the reasonable holding and marketing costs involved. In fact, it can vary quite a bit depending on the property in question.

RTC's Sales of Real Estate—The 95 Percent of Fair Market Value Rule

The provision that the RTC will sell properties at not less than 95 percent of market value is rapidly becoming a complicated rule, with some important exceptions, such as a new 80 percent rule. In general, the 95 percent rule is an antidumping rule to keep the RTC from unloading so many properties so quickly that it would worsen the local real estate market. Actually, the 95 percent rule is set as follows:

1. The board of directors of the RTC may set the minimum disposition price (sales price) for the RTC's properties.
2. Unless the board sets it at something else, the minimum disposition price in distressed areas is set at 95 percent of fair market value.

Distressed areas.   RTC will be restricted in its sales of real estate assets in *distressed areas* of the United States, which currently include parts of the Southwest, the West Coast and New England. These areas have large inventories of unsold properties that were obtained by the FSLIC or FADA from insolvent or barely solvent S&Ls. There has been much fear and speculation that the liquidators will come to town and sell off these properties at firesale prices with ruinous effects on the local real estate markets concerned. In order to keep this from happening, the RTC must sell its real estate holdings for at least 95 percent of market value, established by a proper appraisal. However, the RTC may appraisal. However, the RTC may change the 95 percent rule if it determines that sales in general or specific sales can be made without undermining RTC's basic objectives, namely minimizing the impact on the area's real estate market and maximizing the RTC's returns.

It will be interesting to see how the fair market value can remain unaffected once the supply of saleable real estate is greatly increased when the RTC begins to market its properties. Another problem area will be the method and manner in which appraisals are undertaken. In the commercial field, where income properties predominate, the income capitalization approach to appraisal might lead to some very low figures for the sale of shopping centers and office buildings that lack tenants. Likewise, there are often few reliable comparable sales in an area from which to develop a good fair market value appraisal. The RTC/FDIC is scheduled to develop its own special appraisal standards. Hopefully, good sense will prevail. If it doesn't, the Oversight Board may have to intervene.

The 95 Percent Rule Doesn't Apply to All Homes

Even in the specified distressed areas of the country, the RTC is not restricted by the 95 percent rule, if the real estate meets the criteria outlined below for low- and middle-income properties. In particular, RTC may sell below net realizable market value (which is market value minus holding and marketing costs) to enable a lower-income family to buy a house or enable a nonprofit agency to comply with a low-income occupancy requirement. However, homes may not be sold at less than net realizable market value to enable a for-profit purchaser to meet lower-income targeting requirements. Other types of residential real estate, namely those outside the distressed areas, are apparently not covered by the 95 percent rule, although that rule can be modified as outlined above.

Technically, FIRREA only requires the 95 percent rule to be applied to properties owned in fee simple by the RTC in its corporate capacity. Real estate loans which are sold as loans are not subject to the 95 percent restriction. Perhaps it would be possible to buy a loan that is in default, at a sharp knockdown price, then foreclose that loan on a valuable home, which could thereby be acquired at a substantial discount. However, the RTC is voluntarily applying the 95 percent rule to the many properties owned by thrifts which are in RTC receivership or conservatorship, even though the RTC does not technically own such properties. Also, the 95 percent rule has to be applied only to real estate over a certain dollar figure set by the RTC's board, but this figure has not been set. Therefore, most of the RTC's properties must be sold at 95 percent of fair market value, but read on to find out some of the current exceptions.

The New 80 Percent Rule

The RTC has softened its earlier approach to the 95 percent rule. Certain houses will be offered by the RTC at a 15 percent discount rather than the 5 percent discount (95 percent rule). If the property does not sell after 90 days of marketing, the RTC will sell the house at a total discount of 20 percent. It is not discounted from a 95 percent figure, but rather from 100 percent of fair market value. The 80 percent figure, however, may be taken against net realizable fair market value figure. Further discounts beyond 20 percent will require a reappraisal of the property before it can be offered for sale again.

Hard Costs Can Reduce the RTC's Price to Lower Levels

When the RTC incurs *hard costs* to continue ownership of a property, such as property taxes, it may be possible to reduce the bid price on RTC property by these anticipated costs. Here is an example given by the RTC itself:

Fair Market Value		$100,000
Less		
Documented and verifiable holding costs		
Savings on commission	6%	6,000
Taxes	2%	2,000
Insurance	1%	1,000
Maintenance	3%	3,000
Holding costs	8%	8,000
(Subtotal) Holding Costs		$20,000
Adjusted Fair Market Value		$80,000
Sales Price at 95% of Fair Market Value		$76,500

Once again, it may be possible to apply a figure less than 95 percent of the fair market value under the new rules.

RTC FINANCING

Seller Financing

The RTC is legally permitted to provide seller financing in the form of a first or a second mortgage for all or part of the purchase price of either a home or a multifamily complex. However, the RTC will sharply restrict the availability of seller financing on non-low-income housing. RTC's seller financing will only be available

1. when local financing is not available;
2. to expedite the sale of hard to sell properties; or
3. in situations in which the present value of the financed sales price exceeds the highest and best cash offer.

In case 1, loans are virtually unavailable in some cities. The RTC can make financing available. In case 2, the RTC has yet to define what it regards as a hard to sell property. Many of its properties are hard to sell, particularly land. In case 3, the present value is a finance term. If a property to be sold at $100,000 with a 10 percent interest loan of $100,000 were rated as to its present value, including financing, that value is $100,000, provided the market rate of interest is 10 percent. If a cash offer on the property is for $90,000, then that offer would be less than the present value of the financed sales price. Essentially, the present value is the unfinanced value of the property.

On multifamily and rental homes, subsidized interest rates will be available to nonprofit organizations that provide low-income housing, but not to for-profit investors.

RTC Sales—Some Extra Rules

Down payments. The RTC may require down payments of 15 percent, but it prefers 25 percent if it can get it.

Deposits for a bid. The RTC will also require a 5 percent deposit on all offers to buy RTC properties.

Offers in writing. The offer to buy an RTC property must be in writing. The RTC national office is working on standardized forms, but in the meantime, the regional offices are making up their own.

Special warranty deed. The RTC will convey title by means of a special warranty deed, not a quitclaim deed. It is not possible to obtain title insurance in Texas with a quitclaim deed as the main transfer of title document.

Title insurance. The RTC anticipates selling its properties with a standard title insurance policy.

Title in general. It appears that RTC titles will be a little less reliable than FDIC titles. The RTC will sell as a receiver or as a conservator without actually acquiring title in its own name as the FDIC does.

First lien. The RTC's seller finance loans must be first lien loans.

Conflict of Interest Rules—A Key Feature of FIRREA

Because of the tremendous HUD scandals, the problems involving FADA (where the chief officers were paid up to $300,000 and more a year), and the reputation FSLIC had for doing inside deals with the former customers, owners or officers of the S&Ls that were being "resolved," the FIRREA instituted some rigorous conflict of interest requirements. As a general rule, conflict of interest rules are so strong that it would be better not to be both a manager and a purchaser of RTC properties, for example. Anyone who has been previously connected with the government agency or the S&L that has been taken over should be extremely cautious in dealing with the RTC or the FSLIC Resolution Fund. There are actually criminal penalties in some cases. An *institution affiliate* may include attorneys, accountants or consulting firms that worked with a defunct S&L. It pays to be careful.

Direct Purchases of FDIC Properties at Foreclosure

Generally, FDIC sales directly at the courthouse in Texas are to be viewed with great caution. Please read the section on direct foreclosure sales in Chapter 5 to learn more about the problems involved.

LOW-INCOME PROPERTIES

Special Restrictions for Homes Less than $67,500 in Value

In the course of its operations, RTC will have to dispose of homes that were foreclosed on by institutions ultimately taken over by the government, and whose inventory in turn will pass to the RTC. The RTC will sell off such homes, but there are some special restrictions imposed by FIRREA. Only homes that appraise at a value of $67,500 or less will be eligible for the special restrictions. During the first three months after a single family property is made available for sale, the RTC may sell such homes to only two groups:

The first is homebuyers who meet two criteria:

- Their income must be less than 115 percent of the area median; and
- They must intend to live in the property as their primary residence.

The second group consists of public agencies and nonprofit organizations that agree to either

- resell the units to lower-income families or
- provide rental housing affordable to lower income families for the home's remaining useful life.

After three months, if there is no offer to buy an eligible home, then anyone (including investors) may buy it. The RTC will set up guidelines for the settlement and closing of the sales of such homes.

The RTC will also be required to make available information about houses it acquires, even before it has clear title, to *clearinghouses,* organizations that will provide information about RTC's available houses to prospective low-income homebuyers. The clearinghouses will include state housing finance agencies, the Office of Community Investment and any national nonprofit organization that the RTC believes has the ability to be a good clearinghouse. Such organizations will almost certainly include the Council of State Housing Agencies, the National Low Income Housing Coalition, the Neighborhood Reinvestment Corporation, ACORN, LISC and the Enterprise Foundation.

The special restrictions have been criticized in terms of their usefulness in the southwestern parts of the United States, where the greatest number of RTC houses is likely to be found. In these areas, unlike the northeastern United States, very few public agencies and nonprofit organizations provide housing for poor or low-income families. As a result, there will be some difficulty in renting or selling eligible homes to their targeted buyers. Properties sold through the FSLIC Resolution Fund, unlike RTC properties, will not be subject to the low-income sales restrictions and procedures.

The low-income rules will apply to any property the RTC acquires fee simple title to in its corporate capacity. They will also apply to properties for which the RTC is the receiver, although ownership remains with a distressed thrift institution. Interestingly, the 501(c) rules apparently do not apply to properties that the RTC will hold under a conservatorship arrangement with a thrift that actually holds title.

CONCLUSION

The RTC and FDIC, which were born from the S&L disaster, offer many foreclosed properties for sale. Ironically, the same foreclosures helped create the S&L crisis by dragging S&Ls and banks into bank bankruptcy. After being taken over by a federal agency, S&Ls and banks give the FDIC and RTC the inventory of foreclosed properties that these lending institutions acquired. Smaller investors can find a wide variety of homes and other properties for sale, but the procedures for resale change very quickly. Investor buyers must watch for properties to come onto the market that might be good deals, which will be sold by auctions and special brokers. Alert buyers will also watch the shifts in procedures to catch a profit opportunity that others might easily miss. The key is often just to know what's going on with such sales before too many other people find out about how to buy an RTC or FDIC foreclosed property. Those who learn fast can mint money from the S&Ls, banks and the government in the form of the FDIC and the RTC.

GLOSSARY

abandonment   The situation in which a homeowner leaves a house with no intention to return.

abstract of judgment   An abstract is a summary; an abstract of judgment is a summary of a judgment; a judgment is the end result of a lawsuit. A judgment may run many pages. An abstract of judgment typically runs one or two pages. It just shows who won the lawsuit, who lost, how much is owed, what court made the decision, the date of the judgment and the attorney for the winner of the lawsuit. Once the abstract of judgment is recorded (filed with the county clerk or county recorder), it creates a general lien on the judgment debtor's property, including the real estate. An abstract of judgment will be discovered by a title company whenever a landowner tries to sell the land. Most title companies will demand that it be paid off as a condition of insuring the resale.

acceleration   To make the future payments on a loan due immediately. That way, when a borrower misses payments the lender will not have to sue for each missed payment one by one until the end of the loan. Instead, the lender can sue the borrower for the entire amount of the principal balance that remains unpaid on the loan. However, the lender may not sue for future interest. Once accelerated, the entire unpaid portion of a loan is due.

adjustable-rate mortgage   A loan that has an interest rate that can go up or down at certain intervals, called periods, and within certain limits, called *caps*. The loan is secured by a house, on which the lender will foreclose if the loan is not paid.

AJ   *See* abstract of judgment.

amortization   A method of calculating the payments on a loan such that, at a given interest rate, a loan payment of a set size will repay the loan over a certain period of time.

as is   When a property is sold as is, the seller does not warrant or guarantee that the property is free of defects. The buyer accepts the property in its present condition, without modification.

assignment   A procedure in which a loan can be turned over to the Secretary of Housing and Urban Development. This means that the loan, which started out as a privately owned but FHA-insured loan, will become a HUD-owned loan.

assignment of rents   A procedure in which a borrower gives a lender the right to receive the rents collected from a tenant in a house owned by the borrower.

assumes and agrees to pay   A clause in a deed or related document under which a buyer who takes over payments on the seller's old loan also agrees to pay the old loan. The buyer will normally receive title and make the payments. The *assumes and agrees to pay* language is often found in the consideration section of the deed that transfers title from the seller to the buyer in such an assumption. The seller may or may not be released from liability, but in either case, the buyer is responsible legally to make payments on the loan.

assumption   A procedure in which a buyer takes over payments on the seller's old loan. Title is transferred from the seller to the buyer.

auction   The process of selling property at a public sale to the highest bidder. The person conducting the sale will call out the initial asking price and each price that anyone in the audience bids until no one will bid a higher price. The auctioneer then calls out "going once, going twice, sold to the highest bidder!"

automatic stay   A bankruptcy court order. When bankruptcy is filed, the bankruptcy court will issue a court order that prevents any creditor from attempting to collect any debt from the person who declared bankruptcy. Creditors, even though they are owed money may not undertake foreclosure, repossession, eviction or seizure, or even call or write the debtor demanding payment. Instead, they must all come to the bankruptcy court and seek the money they are owed together with other creditors.

balance owed on the loan   The part of the original loan that remains unpaid by the borrower at a given point in time.

bankruptcy   A specialized court proceeding in which a person who owes more than he or she owns and lacks the resources to pay obligations on a current basis can either restructure the payments or have all but a few debts discharged. The person filing bankruptcy must in turn give up all but a few exempt assets in an effort to pay creditors what they are owed.

bill of complaint   The initial paperwork filed in many states to begin a foreclosure. It is part of the process of filing a lawsuit.

bond   A set sum of money or assets that are available if needed to pay to a court or other named person upon a certain event.

BPO   *See* broker price opinion.

broker price opinion   A real estate broker's estimate of the price for which property can reasonably be sold. The broker price opinion is often much cheaper than a professional appraisal, but often just as good, or even more useful because it tells the owner at what price the property can successfully be marketed.

buydown   An arrangement in which the seller of real estate pays some or all of the buyer's loan costs, usually measured by increments of 1 percent of the loan called *points*. The seller pays enough points to the lender to permit it to offer the buyer's loan at a reduced interest rate, which reduces the monthly payment. The cost to the seller is small, but the reduction in payments to the buyer is often quite substantial. Buydown arrangements are often structured to focus the entire reduction in interest rate, and therefore monthly payments, in the early years of the loan. In a 3-2-1 buydown, a seller will pay enough points to reduce the buyer's interest rate by 3 percent, such as from 10 percent to 7 percent, the first year, then by 2 percent the second year and by 1 percent the third year. In the fourth year the loan interest rate and the monthly payments would return to the normal market rate of interest as set when the loan was first obtained.

certificate of reasonable value   A VA appraisal.

certificate of sale   A document indicating that a property has been sold to a buyer at foreclosure, subject to a right of redemption for a set period after the foreclosure sale. In an IRS sale, the redemption period is 180 days. The redemption period is different in other types of foreclosures. Many foreclosures take place without any certificate of sale. Instead, the sale is final, or near final, and the buyer gets a deed rather than a certificate of sale.

Chapter 7   One of the chapters in the federal Bankruptcy Code. Chapter 7 is liquidation bankruptcy in which a debtor's nonexempt assets are gathered together and given up or sold for the benefit of creditors in order of their priority. Priority creditors get much of the cash, if any. Their debts are not discharged. Secured creditors receive continued payments or the asset that served as collateral for the loan. Unsecured creditors are usually given little or nothing in a Chapter 7 bankruptcy.

Chapter 13   One of the bankruptcy chapters in the federal Bankruptcy Code. Under Chapter 13, a wage earner can reduce debt payments through a bankruptcy court order according to the terms of a plan that will allow the debtor to pay much or even all of the original amount.

clear title   Ownership rights to a piece of real estate that are not diminished by liens, leases or other types of encumbrances. No other ownership claims exist.

collateralized mortgage obligation (CMO)   A type of security sold to investors to raise money to buy mortgages.

collections   An activity in which lenders or their agents employ various techniques to put pressure on borrowers to pay what they owe.

compromise sale   A sale in which the balance owed on a VA loan is greater than the house's sale price. The difference, or loss, may be partly covered by the VA.

condominium   A land ownership arrangement in which one owns an individual unit and a percentage of common areas.

conforming loans   Loans that meet FNMA standards.

conservatorship   A state of affairs in which a bank or savings and loan association has been taken over by the FDIC or RTC and is being managed by these federal institutions, either directly or through hired managers. The institution will be preserved in its existing form until it can be sold complete or broken down into its major components. The institution is run on a caretaker basis until it can be sold.

consideration   Something of value exchanged between the parties to a contract. It may consist of goods, services or promises.

contingency fee   An employment arrangement commonly used by attorneys in which the attorney is paid a percentage of whatever money damages are awarded at the final judgment in a lawsuit.

contract for deed   A sales arrangement in which the seller holds title until the buyer finishes paying for the property. The terms of the sale and the payments are set in a written contract signed by the buyer and the seller. At the end of the payment period, the buyer gets title to the real estate by means of a deed.

conventional lender   A lender that makes conventional loans.

conventional loan   A loan that is not insured or guaranteed by any agency of the federal government. It is a private loan.

conveyance   The process of transferring title or some interest in real estate to a new owner.

coverage   The amount of money an insurance company will pay in response to a claim.

cram-down   A Chapter 13 bankruptcy arrangement in which a plan to repay lenders and creditors, which was developed by the debtor's attorney, is ordered into effect by the bankruptcy court. It is crammed down on the sometimes unwilling creditors.

credit   The willingness of a borrower to repay borrowed money. It is usually measured by a borrower's past record of payments on loans and debts, which is kept in a credit report.

credit doctor   An individual who specializes in stealing or otherwise fraudulently (and criminally) obtaining good credit for a noncreditworthy borrower.

CRV   *See* certificate of reasonable value.

cured default   Correction of a borrower's failure to make payments or meet the terms of a loan to the lender's satisfaction.

damages   Monetary compensation set by a court for a loss suffered by a party to a lawsuit.

debt collector   Under federal law, a person or entity, including an attorney, that regularly collects debts for others. Debt collectors must give certain notices and follow certain procedures under the Federal Collection Practices Act.

decree   The final order of a court in many states.

deed   The legal document commonly used to transfer ownership of real estate from one owner to the next.

deed in lieu of foreclosure   Instead of waiting until the lender forces the sale of the house in foreclosure, usually to the lender, the borrower just deeds the property to the lender.

deed of trust   In spite of its name, this document is not really much of a deed or a trust. Instead it is more proper to regard it as a three-party mortgage arrangement between the borrower, the lender and a trustee. If the borrower fails to pay, the trustee is preauthorized by the borrower to sell the house and apply the sales proceeds to pay off what remains unpaid on the loan secured by the deed of trust or to give the deed to the lender in exchange for cancellation of some or all of the borrower's debt.

default   Nonperformance or breach of one's obligations under the legal documents that control the loan arrangement.

defeased   In medieval times ownership rights constituted a *fee*. To be defeased meant to lose the fee, or today, to lose ownership.

defendant's original answer   The first responsive pleading of a defendant in a lawsuit.

deficiency   Money a borrower who has lost real estate in foreclosure still owes to the lender because the foreclosure sale failed to generate enough to pay off the loan. Frequently, lenders acquire title to real estate at foreclosure, in which case they most often give credit only for the fair market value of the property against the balance due on the loan. Any unpaid balance on the loan after all just credits are applied is the usual amount of a deficiency. Many states limit or restrict deficiencies.

deficiency judgment   A court judgment that a defaulting borrower owes a deficiency.

delinquency   The state of affairs when payments on a note or other loan obligation are past due.

d'Oench, Duhme doctrine   A legal doctrine that holds that when the FDIC or RTC take over a lender, they may disallow almost any counterclaims by borrowers against such fallen lenders. The name is taken from the original law case that created the doctrine.

Department of Veterans Affairs   The arm of the federal government that guarantees loans and performs other services for veterans. This agency was formerly known as the Veterans Administration (VA).

depository institution   A bank or S&L that accepts deposits.

discharge of indebtedness   A lender tells a borrower that a loan doesn't have to be paid back, also called discharge of debt.

discovery   The phase of a lawsuit in which respective parties are permitted to ask each other formal written and oral questions, obtain copies of documents and in general find out the facts related to the lawsuit.

double whammy   Some lenders refuse to permit assumptions, which is one blow, while at the same time insisting on a hefty prepayment penalty when the nonassumable loan is paid off early, which is a second blow.

down payment   The initial cash a borrower pays to the seller to purchase a property. It does not include closing costs.

due on encumbrance   A clause in a mortgage that prevents a borrower from encumbering title to the property with liens, leases or other encumbrances without the lender's consent.

due on sale   A clause in a mortgage that demands that the borrower pay off the loan in full if the house is ever sold. The lender can't prevent the sale, but it can demand payment in full on the loan balance, which often has the same practical effect. In the absence of a due on sale clause, the loan is assumable without the lender's consent. Older FHA and DVA loans are assumable without the consent of the lender.

early sales   When a borrower faced with foreclosure tries to arrange with the lender to sell the house as early as possible in order to minimize any losses that would result from a normal foreclosure and subsequent resale of the home.

earnest money contract   A contract in which the seller agrees to sell and the buyer agrees to buy.

ejectment   A common-law action to obtain a court order commanding the occupant of land or a house to leave.

entitlement   The amount of money the Department of Veterans Affairs will pay on behalf of a defaulting veteran on a VA loan.

entry and possession   A method of foreclosure used in some states in which the lender, who already owns the property, reenters it and takes possession away from the borrower, either peacefully or by court order.

equity   The excess of fair market value over the outstanding loan balance.

equity of redemption   *See* redemption.

equity skimmer A scam artist who assumes a loan and collects money up front, and possibly rents, then refuses to pay the payments on the assumed loan while keeping the cash paid up front.

escrow A deposit held ready for some use, such as to pay taxes and insurance on a mortgaged property.

eviction The legal procedure to have a tenant forcibly removed from a dwelling.

execution sale The sale of property by a sheriff pursuant to a court order.

extending the loan term Giving the borrower more time to repay a loan.

Fair Credit Reporting Act A federal law that regulates credit bureaus and credit reports and gives persons certain rights regarding both.

fair market value The value that a willing and knowledgeable buyer would pay, and a willing and knowledgeable seller would accept, in an arm's-length transaction for a property.

Fannie Mae *See* Federal National Mortgage Association.

FCL The abbreviation a lender puts on a borrower's credit record to indicate a foreclosure.

FCRA *See* Fair Credit Reporting Act.

FDIC *See* Federal Deposit Insurance Corporation.

Federal Debt Collection Practices Act A federal law that regulates the manner in which debts are collected. It requires that certain notices and opportunities to dispute debts must be given to borrowers when debt collectors attempt to collect money.

Federal Deposit Insurance Corporation The corporation set up by the federal government to insure deposits in banks and S&Ls.

Federal Home Loan Bank Board A former agency of the federal government that regulated S&Ls.

Federal Home Loan Mortgage Corporation A government-chartered but privately owned corporation that buys mortgages from S&Ls. Also called *Freddie Mac.*

Federal Housing Administration An agency of the federal government that regulates many aspects of the real estate industry, and that insures repayment of certain home loans.

Federal National Mortgage Association A government-chartered but privately owned corporation that buys mortgages from mortgage companies. Also called *Fannie Mae.*

Federal Savings and Loan Insurance Corporation A corporation formerly run by the federal government that insured deposits in S&Ls; FDIC took over this function. FSLIC deposit insurance funds, what were left of them, were transferred to an FDIC fund called *Savings Association Insurance Fund,* SAIF for short.

FHA *See* Federal Housing Administration.

FHA guidelines   Rules that specify income and credit requirements for a borrower, and the condition and value of a property to allow an insured loan of a particular size.

FHA insurance   Federal Housing Administration insurance that compensates lenders if a borrower fails to repay an insured loan.

FHLBB   *See* Federal Home Loan Bank Board.

FHLMC   *See* Federal Home Loan Mortgage Corporation.

financial counseling   Advice to a borrower from an expert on how to better manage the family budget.

Financial Institutions Reform, Recovery and Enforcement Act   A federal law that abolished FSLIC and FHLBB and created RTC. This law made the most sweeping changes in U.S. banking laws since the depression.

FIRREA   *See* Financial Institutions Reform, Recovery and Enforcement Act.

first lien   The initial claim against a piece of real estate that gives a lender the right to force its sale to pay a debt.

"fizzbo"   *See* for sale by owner.

FNMA   *See* Federal National Mortgage Association.

forbearance   A lender voluntarily accepts payments that are lower than originally agreed in the loan documents for a limited period of time in order to allow the borrower to recover financially. The borrower must eventually repay the missing or reduced payments, as well as all the other remaining payments on the loan.

foreclosure   The forced sale of a piece of real estate to repay a debt.

for sale by owner (FSBO)   A property being marketed by its owner without the help of a real estate broker.

fraud   Intentional false statements that were believed and relied on by a person, who suffered loss as a result.

Freddie Mac   *See* Federal Home Loan Mortgage Corporation.

freeze order   *See* automatic stay.

FSA   A designation for Federal Savings Association.

FSBO   *See* for sale by owner.

FSLIC   *See* Federal Savings and Loan Insurance Corporation.

full assumption   An arrangement in which a buyer takes title to the house and takes over the payments on the seller's old loan with the full permission of the lender, which evaluates the buyer's ability to show adequate income and creditworthiness by the lender's traditional standards. The process of obtaining lender approval is called *qualifying*.

Ginnie Mae   *See* Government National Mortgage Association.

GNMA   *See* Government National Mortgage Association.

good repair   A borrower has an obligation to maintain the condition of mortgaged property.

Government National Mortgage Association   An arm of the federal government that purchases loans. Currently GNMA buys over 90 percent of all VA loans.

grant   A transfer of an interest in land.

guarantee   The VA guarantees repayment of a VA loan to the private lender who made it. Actually this guarantee amounts to an agreement by the VA to cover a loss up to a certain dollar figure on a loan of a given size that goes into default and foreclosure.

hearing   A proceeding before a court.

holder in due course   A legal doctrine that holds that a person or entity that obtains a note without notice of any borrower defenses to its enforcement may enforce payment of that note in a court despite any borrower defense or other reason for not paying.

homestead   Special legal protection that many states give to a person's principal residence.

Housing and Urban Development   A department of the federal government that administers housing programs. *See also* Federal Housing Authority.

HUD   *See* Housing and Urban Development.

instrument   A legal document.

intermediate theory   Some states hold that the borrower owns a mortgaged property, while other states hold that the lender owns a mortgaged property. Intermediate theory states give some ownership rights to each.

Internal Revenue Service   The arm of the U.S. government that collects taxes.

IOU   An obligation to pay money.

IRS   *See* Internal Revenue Service.

judgment   The final decision of a court. See also abstract of judgment.

judicial foreclosure   Court-ordered foreclosure. The lender obtains the right to foreclose by filing and winning a lawsuit.

junior lienholder   A holder of a right to force the sale of property that is inferior and subordinate to another lienholder's right to do the same. A junior lienholder who forces the sale of the real estate must either pay off the senior lien or make arrangements to make payments on it to prevent it from being foreclosed. The foreclosure of a first lien destroys the right of a junior lienholder to foreclose, but the foreclosure of a junior lien does not affect the right of a senior lien to foreclose. *See also* first lien.

key toss   The practice of mailing the house keys to a lender upon abandoning a home in advance of a foreclosure.

late payments   Payments that are made past their due dates according to the loan documents.

lease with option to buy   An arrangement in which the owner of a property rents it to a tenant, but gives the tenant the right to purchase the property on agreed terms.

lender approval A lender's agreement to allow an assumption after its review of a borrower's creditworthiness and income. Lender approval can also apply to an initial loan.

lender liability The legal doctrine that holds lenders legally responsible to pay damages for legal misdeeds committed against borrowers in the course of making loans.

liability The obligation to pay a debt.

lien The right to force the sale of property to pay a debt.

lienholder The person or institution that controls a lien.

lien theory A legal theory followed by some states that the borrower owns a property while repaying a loan on it.

liquidating plan A plan by which a borrower repays missed payments to the lender over time.

liquidation appraisal An estimate of the value of property when it is sold quickly in a forced sale. Usually this figure is lower than the fair market value for a regularly conducted sale.

lis pendens A recorded notice that tells the world that a lawsuit is in progress, the outcome of which could affect the title to a particular piece of land.

listing agreement The agreement by which a seller hires a real estate broker to sell a house, usually for a commission.

loan balance The amount a borrower owes on a loan.

loan default *See* default.

loan modification A procedure in which a loan's terms, such as the interest rate, monthly payment or term, are altered.

loan officer A person paid commissions to find and sign up borrowers for loans.

loan pool A group of mortgages in which investors own shares. *See also* collateralized mortgage obligations (CMOs).

loan processor The person who gathers and prepares the paperwork used by a lender to decide whether or not a loan should be made.

market value *See* fair market value.

MGIC *See* Mortgage Guaranty Insurance Corporation.

MI *See* mortgage insurance.

misrepresentation Making false statements in the course of a business transaction.

modification *See* loan modification.

mod squad The personnel in a lending institution who arrange loan modifications.

money damages *See* damages.

moot The legal doctrine that an issue has effectively been resolved or decided prior to being brought to court.

mortgage The French words *mort* and *gage* together mean "dead pledge." This is an arrangement in which a borrower agrees to give up title to a piece of property if he or she fails to repay a loan as agreed. The pledge of the property ceases, or dies, when the loan is paid off as agreed.

mortgage company A company that makes home loans to borrowers. Most mortgage companies sell the loans they make on the secondary market to loan buyers, but continue to service the loans under contracts, collecting payments from borrowers and handling trouble with the loan, such as default and foreclosure.

mortgagee The lender.

mortgagee's title policy A title insurance policy that will pay off the lender's loss if the title to the mortgaged property fails.

Mortgage Guaranty Insurance Corporation A major private insurer of mortgage loans in the United States.

mortgage instrument The legal paperwork to create a mortgage.

mortgage insurance Insurance that will compensate a lender for a loss if an insured loan is not repaid by the borrower.

mortgage lien The right of a mortgage lender to force the sale of the mortgaged property if the borrower fails to repay the loan as agreed.

mortgagor The borrower.

motion to lift stay A formal request to a bankruptcy court to dissolve an automatic stay that prevents a lender from foreclosing. Once the motion is granted, the lender may proceed to foreclose unless the borrower can keep up the payments.

negative equity A position in which a borrower owes more on a property than the property is worth.

no bid A situation in which VA will not take title to a house that a lender has acquired through foreclosure on a VA loan because the fair market value of the property is so low that VA could not resell it for a sum equal to the loan balance minus the amount of the guarantee. In this event VA will write the lender a check for the full amount of its guarantee and tell the lender to keep the house and resell it without VA assistance.

nonjudicial foreclosure Foreclosure on a mortgage without filing a lawsuit or obtaining a court order. Generally such sales occur because the borrower has signed a document, such as a deed of trust, giving a trustee preauthorization to sell the real estate to pay off the debt.

note The legal document that specifies the terms of the borrower's loan such as the length of time to repay it, the interest rate, the monthly payment amounts and provisions to deal with the borrower's failure to pay on a timely basis.

one action rule A rule of law, used heavily in California, that forces a lender to bring only one court action or proceeding against a borrower in a foreclosure. The one action rule makes it difficult for a lender to obtain a deficiency judgment against a borrower.

original petition   *See* plaintiff's original petition.

origination   Creation of a loan.

out-of-court foreclosure   *See* nonjudicial foreclosure.

owner-occupied   The borrower who owns the home lives in it.

partial payments   Payments that are less than the full payment the borrower owes on a loan.

plaintiff's original petition   The initial document filed by a person who starts a lawsuit.

PMI   *See* mortgage insurance.

PMI-assisted presale   An arrangement in which a private mortgage insurance company pays for part of the loss that occurs when a house with negative equity (one worth less than the balance on the existing mortgage loan) is sold by regular means prior to a foreclosure.

positive equity   The situation in which a house has a value in excess of what is due on the mortgage.

posting   The act of placing a legal notice, such as a notice specifying the date, time and place of a foreclosure sale, on public display in the proper place for such notices.

power of sale clause   The clause in a deed of trust or mortgage, by which the borrower preauthorizes the sale of a house to pay off the balance on a loan in the event of the borrower's default. Usually a trustee conducts the sale, although in some states the sheriff or constable does this.

prepaids   The costs of purchasing a house that the buyer must pay at the time of closing to a party other than the seller.

presale   *See* PMI-assisted presale.

primary lender   The lender that deals directly with the borrower.

promissory estoppel   A legal doctrine that holds that lenders and sellers must honor their promises and are legally prevented, or estopped, from denying the obligation to honor promises.

promissory note   *See* note.

property condition   The physical state of the property.

prorations   The division of the ongoing yearly costs of operating a property, such as property taxes, between the seller and the buyer at closing. Each party usually pays for the portion of the year in which he or she occupied the house.

publicly post   *See* posting.

qualifying   The process a lender undertakes prior to agreeing to make a loan, which consists of evaluating a buyer's income and credit and the property's physical condition, and comparing the figures with the lender's guidelines.

If the guidelines are met or exceeded, then the lender will approve a mortgage loan.

real estate lien note *See* note.

real estate owned When a financial institution forecloses on homes or other real estate, the properties so acquired are referred to as real estate owned, or REO for short.

recasting Restructuring a loan with a new interest rate and term. It may be the same loan from the same lender, but the terms change. FHA has a formal procedure to recast loans to assist homebuyers to stay in their houses.

receivership After a bank is taken over by FDIC, it may be placed in receivership to liquidate its assets. The employees are fired and the assets shipped off to be sold at auction. The real estate is turned over to the RTC or the FDIC's liquidation division. Existing contracts with the institution in receivership are voidable at the option of the FDIC.

recording The process of filing documents with an official state agency to be held as a permanent record. Deeds and other documents that affect title must be recorded.

redemption The right of a borrower to recover title to real estate lost in a foreclosure sale by paying up missing payments in some states, or the full unpaid loan balance in other states. State statutes normally define redemption rights, specifying longer or shorter periods. IRS and most property tax foreclosure sales also have rights of redemption.

refinance The process of replacing an old loan with a high interest rate with a new one, usually at a lower interest rate.

refunding A VA procedure in which it purchases a loan from a private lender. The VA will then service the loan. This procedure helps borrowers who are having trouble making payments and who need extra time under circumstances that appear to justify the added time.

release from liability The document that relieves a person who is obligated to pay a loan of any further obligation. It may be obtained when a buyer takes over the payments on the seller's old loan, provide the buyer meets the lender's standards for income and creditworthiness. If granted, the release of liability means the seller will not be responsible if the buyer fails to pay.

relief Various types of loans, depending on their insurers (FHA, PMI companies, etc.) or their owners (FNMA, FHLMC), will offer various types of special payment plans or other assistance for borrowers who have missed payments. If it appears that the borrower can bring the loan current, the lender can allow a period of reduced payments with the difference made up at a later time during the loan. The lender also could assist with an early sale.

removal The process of transferring a case from state court to federal court.

REO *See* real estate owned.

repayment plan A plan for repaying missed payments over time.

Resolution Trust Corporation A government chartered corporation whose primary function is to manage and liquidate the assets of S&Ls that have lost too much money and have been taken over and shut down by the FDIC. The Resolution Trust Corporation was created by FIRREA. It is probably the largest owner of real estate in the world.

retroactive release from liability A VA procedure in which a borrower who sold a house on a simple assumption to a buyer who defaulted may go back in time and show that the buyer made the first 12 monthly payments, agreed to be liable for the loan and was sufficiently creditworthy to merit lender approval. This allows the seller, who would have been liable for the default, to escape the obligation to pay the loan. However, the borrower who secures a retroactive release of liability may not obtain a new VA loan until the VA's loss on the old one is repaid.

right of redemption *See* redemption.

right of rescission The right to back out of a contract.

RTC *See* Resolution Trust Corporation.

rule against assignments The legal concept that a debtor may not give away the obligation to pay on a debt without the lender's permission. Even if a buyer assumes a loan, the seller remains liable to repay the loan unless the lender approves the buyer's income and creditworthiness and releases the seller from liability.

sales contract *See* earnest money contract.

savings and loan association A financial institution that makes loans. Savings and loans were originally set up to make home loans, but during the 1980s, deregulation allowed them to make commercial loans as well.

scire facias A court command to a borrower to show up at a hearing and show cause why a foreclosure should not be authorized.

secondary market The market in which investors buy loans from primary lenders, who deal directly with borrowers to originate loans.

second lien *See* junior lienholder.

second mortgage *See* junior lienholder.

servicing The process of administering a mortgage loan including collecting payments, maintaining insurance and undertaking special measures such as workouts and foreclosures when they prove necessary.

short payoff A workout procedure in which the lender accepts less than the full balance due on the loan as part of a deal in which the borrower cooperates with the lender to obtain a quick sale. The lender skips foreclosure, which would take time, cost money and expose the house to vandalism, further declines in market value and marketing costs for resale.

silent wrap An illegal assumption arrangement in which the seller moves out and the buyer moves in and makes payments in violation of a due on sale or due on encumbrance clause. This violation gives the lender a legal right to foreclose. However, the lender may not discover the arrangement for some time, if ever. In this case, the seller and buyer may get away with the deal.

simple assumption An assumption arrangement in which the seller conveys title to the property to the buyer and moves out while the buyer moves in and makes payment on the old loan. The lender does not approve the buyer's credit and income, so the deal may be called a *no approval loan*. However, the seller remains liable on the old loan under such circumstance. Only loans without strong due on sale clauses are assumable without approval. This includes VA loans made before March 1, 1988, FHA loans made before December 15, 1989, and conventional loans made before 1973.

S&L *See* savings and loan association.

special relief *See* relief.

special servicing *See* servicing.

statute of limitations The time limit during which a potential litigant must file a lawsuit before being barred by the passage of time. Most states have elaborate and complex statutes of limitations, many imposing short statutes of limitations for deficiency judgments or foreclosure-related claims.

stay *See* automatic stay.

strict foreclosure A legal premise followed by some states that the lender owns the property and may simply evict the borrower for nonpayment and gain full and complete title free of the borrower's claims by waiting a prescribed period of time until the borrower's right to redeem ends. The lender gains the value of the land above what is owed on the loan.

subject to clause A clause in a deed that transfers title from a seller to a buyer in an assumption transaction, or in other paperwork for the assumption transaction, in which the borrower refuses to accept legal liability to make payments, although the buyer expects to do so. The lender's remedy for nonpayment is limited to foreclosure, and neither the lender nor the seller can sue the defaulting buyer for missed payments on the loan balance.

subrogation for mortgage insurers The right of a mortgage insurance company to file a suit to recover from the borrower sums it must pay out to a lender as a result of the borrower's default on a loan.

Summary Judgment A legal procedure in which one side wins a lawsuit without a trial by showing that the case involves no material fact issues, but only legal issues that can be decided by the judge. If the judge agrees, then one side wins by Summary Judgment.

supplemental servicing Extra servicing VA will perform beyond that performed by the lender. *See also* servicing.

temporary injunction A court order that freezes the status quo for an extended time period, typically until a full court trial on the merits of a case can be held. It often requires posting a bond, although many states' laws waive the bond requirement in cases involving the foreclosure of a home.

temporary restraining order A court command that freezes the status quo for a short period of time until other legal relief is awarded or a settlement between the litigants can be reached.

title Ownership.

title insurance A specialized form of insurance that verifies that a borrower has obtained full ownership of real property, subject to a few exceptions stated in the policy.

title report A report issued by a title insurance company that shows current ownership and nonowners' claims to a piece of real estate and the terms on which a title company would be willing to insure title.

title theory A legal concept that holds that the lender owns real property while the borrower repays a loan used to buy it.

TRO *See* temporary restraining order.

trust deed A type of mortgage that gives a lender the power to foreclose and take title away from the borrower.

trustee A person who is named in a deed of trust or other mortgage to conduct any foreclosure proceedings and sell the property to pay off the mortgage loan balance.

trustee's deed A type of deed issued to the buyer at a foreclosure by the trustee.

Truth in Lending Act A federal law that requires lenders to make certain disclosures to borrowers concerning a loan, such as the interest, the annual percentage rate, the total cost of the loan, the total of all payments and the use of disclosure forms at the loan application and closing.

turnover order A court command to a debtor to give title to certain assets to a creditor.

underwriter The person who makes the final decision on whether a loan should be granted or not at most mortgage companies.

upside down home A house that is worth less than what is owed on the mortgage it secures.

VA *See* Department of Veterans Affairs.

VA guarantee The dollar figure the VA agrees to pay for a loss to a lender from foreclosing on a VA loan.

vendee loan A VA loan made to help VA resell a property acquired by VA after foreclosure. Can be made to a nonvet.

verification of deposit A form sent to a financial institution by a lender to verify that a borrower has a certain sum on deposit.

verification of employment A form sent to an employer by a lender to verify that a borrower is employed at a certain salary.

Veterans Administration *See* Department of Veterans Affairs.

VOD *See* verification of deposit.

VOE *See* verification of employment.

wage earner plan A nickname for Chapter 13 bankruptcy. *See also* Chapter 13.

walk the house The act of abandoning a house to the lender, which will foreclose on it.

warranty deed A deed in which the seller guarantees (warrants) that good title can be traced backward in time from true owner to true owner to the time when the land was owned by a country, such as the United States. *See also* deed.

workout The process by which a borrower comes to a mutually acceptable financial arrangement with a lender in order to avoid an impending foreclosure.

wraparound A type of mortgage in which the obligation to pay a second- or later-lien mortgage includes the obligation to pay an earlier-lien mortgage. The later mortgage wraps around the earlier mortgage. Default on the earlier-lien mortgage is automatically a default on the later-lien mortgage.

writ of entry Very similar to a writ of possession.

writ of execution A court order authorizing the holder to seize and sell a debtor's property to pay off a judgment.

writ of garnishment A court order commanding a person who holds assets for another person, such as a banker who holds funds on deposit, an employer who holds a paycheck or a stock broker who holds an account for an investor, to give those assets up to a creditor.

writ of possession A court document (writ) that authorizes a constable or other officer of the law to break down a tenant's door, drag the tenant from the premises and throw the tenant's belongings out of the house or apartment.

wrongful foreclosure A foreclosure that was legally improper and that caused a borrower to suffer damages.

RESOURCES

The resources listed below are the main sources of information about foreclosures that I have personally come across. There may be other services in your local area.

CLEARINGHOUSE SERVICES

The only national clearinghouse service I have run across is an online network called **The Federal Information Network** operated by Business Information Network, Inc., in Washington, D.C. This excellent resource contains almost all the approximately 50,000 properties owned by government agencies, banks and other mortgage makers. The network is very easy to use, is fast and takes out most of the drudgery involved in finding foreclosures that institutions have taken back. The main advantages to the network are its ability to give you current information at any time of day and its comprehensive coverage from thousands of sources (some of which you would never think to contact!), including RTC, FDIC, VA, HUD, Fannie Mae, Freddie Mac, Farm Credit, banks, savings and loans, insurance companies and mortgage companies. There are fees involved in accessing the service, but if you are serious about buying foreclosures for investment, the best thing you can do for yourself is to sign up for this service. Call 800-9000-REO for a brochure and demonstration disk.

GOVERNMENT AGENCIES

The **RTC** is remarkably well set up to respond to inquiries from the public about properties for sale. For listings by mail, call 800-RTC-3006; you can also ask for RTC publications on how to buy property. The RTC also sponsors an online network that allows you to get the listings quicker and carries all the RTC's publications; call 800-366-9246 for subscription information.

The **FDIC** handles information requests out of their regional and consolidated offices. There are regional offices in Chicago, Dallas, New York and San Francisco. Consolidated offices are peppered throughout the country. The FDIC's main number in Washington, D.C., is 202-393-8400.

HUD liquidates its foreclosures through regional and field offices. There are regional offices in Boston, New York, Philadelphia, Atlanta, Chicago, Fort Worth, Kansas City, Denver, San Francisco and Seattle. HUD's main number in Washington, D.C., is 202-708-1422. Most HUD offices advertise their properties in the local paper.

Like HUD, the **VA** liquidates its foreclosures through local offices. There is one in nearly every state. VA also advertises available properties in local papers. The VA's main number in Washington, D.C., is 202-737-5050.

FNMA (Fannie Mae) and **FHLMC (Freddie Mac)** are congressionally chartered companies that buy mortgages from banks and S&Ls. For information about their foreclosure holdings, contact the Fannie Mae or Freddie Mac office in your area. Fannie Mae's main number in Washington, D.C., is 202-752-7000. Freddie Mac's main number in McLean, Virginia, is 703-903-2000.

Other government agencies that have REO holdings are Farm Credit, the General Services Administration, the Department of Defense and the Department of Justice.

BANKS AND SAVINGS AND LOANS

It is obviously impossible to list the more than 10,000 banks and savings and loans that exist in this country. I suggest that you contact lending institutions in your area and ask to be put on their mailing list for REO holdings and upcoming auctions. Beware, however, that some institutions are more willing than others to divulge this information.

AUCTION COMPANIES

There are dozens of companies that specialize in selling loans and real estate for government agencies and lending institutions. Check the real estate section of your local paper or business journal for announcements about auctions in your area. Some of the biggest companies are: Fisher Auction Company, Hudson & Marshall, JP King Auctioneers, Kennedy-Wilson Company, Larry Latham Auctioneers, NRC Auctions, Ross Dove & Company and Sheldon Good & Company. Find out which companies operate in your area and get on their mailing lists.

INDEX